Charles Robert Patterson

# BLOW
# THE
# MAN
# DOWN!

# BLOW THE MAN DOWN!

A Yankee Seaman's Adventures Under Sail

*An Autobiographical Narrative*

BASED UPON THE WRITINGS OF

## James H. Williams

AS ARRANGED AND EDITED BY

## Warren F. Kuehl

NEW YORK, 1959
E. P. DUTTON & CO., INC.

Williams, James H, 1864-1927. Blow the
man down! A Yankee seaman's adven-
tures under sail; an autobiographical nar-
rative based upon the writings of James
H. Williams as arranged and edited by
Warren F. Kuehl. ₁1st ed.₁ New York,
Dutton, 1959. 255 p. illus. 22 cm.
1. Merchant seamen—U. S.    I. Kuehl,
Warren F., 1924-      ed.      II.    Title.
HD8039.S42U74      923.873      59-5821 ‡
Library of Congress

# CONTENTS

# ILLUSTRATIONS

# ACKNOWLEDGMENTS

In my search to confirm details and facts mentioned by James Williams and to identify men and vessels, I consulted numerous agencies and persons. I wish to express my particular gratitude to the efficient personnel of the General Register and Record Office of Shipping and Seamen at Cardiff, Wales, for diligent effort and prompt response to my many inquiries. I also owe a debt to the General Services Administration of the National Archives and Records Service in Washington, to the Trustees of Sailors' Snug Harbor for allowing me to examine their files, and to Mr. John L. Lochhead and the staff of the Mariners Museum at Newport News, Virginia. Of the many persons whom I consulted concerning the manuscript, I would like to especially thank Mr. Felix Reisenberg, Jr., and Dr. John Lyman. Finally, I wish to record my obligation to the officials of Rollins College for allowing me the use of the James H. Williams manuscript from the Hamilton Holt Papers.

W.F.K.

# EDITOR'S PREFACE

**S**ome years ago while gathering material for a biography of Hamilton Holt, the late president of Rollins College and former editor of *The Independent* magazine, I discovered among Holt's papers a weathered manuscript which attracted my immediate attention. In style and story, it held me spellbound. Here were daring adventures, heroic deeds, and colorful descriptive passages. And here was the lure of a romantic age now lost save in our imagination.

I soon learned more about the author. He called himself a common sailor, but he was a most uncommon man. With little formal education, he wrote in a style which would embarrass many polished scribes. Although a self-confessed murderer according to his own account, he possessed a high sense of moral virtue which like an unseen hand directed his actions. Although a practical man who survived innumerable storms and two major shipwrecks, he was a romantic soul who instinctively sought out the ships of masts and spars in an age in which the merchant marine was making its transition from sail to steam, from wood to steel. Within him, too, burned a reforming fever so intense that he became an uncompromising enemy of crimps, jackals, avaricious shipowners, heartless masters, and all who preyed upon the common seaman. And he labored with some success to achieve through unions and legislation the humane treatment and legal rights which he felt his comrades of the sea deserved.

This was James H. Williams, Negro seaman with reddish hair and light-brown skin. He was born in Fall River, Massachusetts, on May 21, 1864, the son of James C. and Margaret Crotty Williams and, as he narrates in describing his family background and childhood experiences, went to sea at an early age. It was in 1897 that he first began to write about life in the old merchant marine. He

9

was then thirty-three years old and had been a sailor for twenty-one years. Hamilton Holt, then the managing editor of *The Independent,* a prominent national magazine, opened the columns of his journal to Williams and subsequently printed over thirty articles and editorials from Williams' pen.

These writings, in the tradition in American seafaring literature of Richard Henry Dana's *Two Years Before the Mast* (1840) and Herman Melville's *White-Jacket* (1850), sought to awaken readers to the injustices and cruelties inherent in the life of the men before the mast. Although Williams' vivid and spirited writings appeared only in magazines and have not before been published in book form, they offered a graphic firsthand portrayal of conditions at sea, and they exerted a constructive influence in ameliorating the life of seamen and in gaining legislation which outlawed many abuses to which sailors were subjected.

Such reforms did not come easily, however. There has been a tendency among writers of the sea to romanticize their subject, to bestow upon the men and the life they led a quality of virtue and nobility, and to neglect the aspects of brutality so prevalent in the days of sailing ships. The general public, therefore, was not and may still not be aware of the inhuman, often fiendish, acts practiced. Moreover, there has been a traditional concept of the sailor as indigent and ignorant, devoid of character and unworthy of serious consideration—a viewpoint the origins of which lie far back in history. No wonder then that the American seaman's life and liberty until very recent years were seriously curtailed, that he labored under intolerable conditions harmful to health and life, that he was subject to brutal treatment, punishment, and even death at the hands of his superiors, that he lost control of his right to contract for his own employment because of ingenious arrangements between crimps, shipowners, and captains, that the law gave him little or no protection against unscrupulous vultures, and that he received a wage scarcely worthy of consideration.

A few crusaders had campaigned for years against the many evils which prevailed, yet by 1898 little had been done to correct the situation. In 1872, 1884, 1886, and 1895, Congress approved various measures designed to protect the seamen, but this legislation proved to be virtually unenforceable. Williams, in Chapter 15, describes most of these acts and reveals the flaws which still left the sailor at the mercy of his exploiters. Finally, in 1898 and 1915, as Williams points out, with the passage of the White Act and the La Follette Seamen's Act Congress managed to end the most flagrant abuses and to guarantee the sailor a degree of personal freedom and protection.

While it is difficult to assess the contribution of any one person in this crusade which awakened the American people to conditions and finally shocked Congress into action, Williams was undoubtedly of influence. Through his realistic articles in *The Independent*, he reached citizens of prominence and power who must have been impressed by his vivid descriptions of cruelty and injustice. In 1915, one of every seven subscribers to *The Independent* in New York City was listed in *Who's Who in America*, and the magazine often reprinted the remark of an unnamed senator who claimed that after pressing a measure three times on the floor of the Senate he obtained results only after writing an article on the subject in *The Independent*. This comment would indicate that Williams could not have asked for a more influential journal.

But Williams did not rely upon the pen alone. Working through organizations, he also awakened considerable interest in the plight of the common sailor. The Social Reform Club, whose list of members included the names of many of New York City's most prominent citizens, when aroused by Williams, exerted considerable pressure, as Williams describes in Chapter 15, upon legislators for reform laws.

Since Williams perceived that legislation alone could not solve all the American seaman's problems, he also joined ranks with those sailors struggling to create an effective maritime union on the Atlantic seaboard. Their work was exceedingly difficult, as Williams reveals in his writings. The abundance of harbors, the geographical distances involved, and the power of shipowners and crimps all acted to curtail their efforts. On the Pacific Coast where conditions were more suitable, the seamen were more successful, and the unions of that area eventually assumed command of the movement. It has been the tendency of scholars, therefore, to emphasize the role of the West Coast organizations in assessing achievements. While this interpretation is correct, it minimizes the work of the Atlantic seamen. An editorial preface to one of Williams' articles in *The Independent* in 1902 indicated that wages of seamen had been increased nearly 50 per cent in the previous four years. "Credit for the present improved condition of the American sailor," it added, "probably belongs to Mr. Williams more than to any other man." *

It would be an exaggeration to claim that the Atlantic Coast Seamen's Union, organized in 1888, or the National Seamen's Union, formed in 1892 and later called the International Seamen's Union, succeeded prior to 1915 in doing much more for sailors than raising their wages. Membership, especially on the East Coast, was always small, and the organization was continually plagued by internal problems. One of the most difficult issues was the racial question. Williams, interestingly, is silent upon this point. By 1910, however, it was virtually impossible for a Negro to be a union member except in the Marine Cooks and Stewards branch. This fact may explain why Williams returned to the sea and apparently abandoned the vigorous union activities he describes in Chapter 15.

In 1922, five years before his death, Williams assembled his writings, revised several of them, added a preface and introduction, and apparently hoped to present his manuscript for publication. In some way the material found its way into the Holt papers; there it lay neglected for nearly three decades.

In his last revision, Williams made no effort to arrange his writings chronologically to provide an autobiographical narrative. Per-

* Editorial preface probably written by Hamilton Holt to James H. Williams, "Autobiography of a Labor Leader," *The Independent,* LIV (November 6, 1902), 2634.

ceiving this possibility, I photostated all of his accounts in their printed form for comparison with the revised manuscript and for arrangement. This compiling was an easy task since nearly all of Williams' tales appeared in *The Independent,* the first in 1897, the last in 1921. Only two other articles included in this book had been printed elsewhere, both appearing in the *Seafarer and Marine Pictorial,* a short-lived publishing venture of the early 1920's.

In my capacity as editor, I adopted five basic rules: (1) to collate the revised manuscript and printed articles in order to select the best passages from each; (2) to arrange the accounts as an autobiographical narrative; (3) to inject whatever words or sentences were necessary for continuity and clarity and to delete extraneous material; (4) to replace as fully as possible the fictitious names of ships and persons which Williams had employed with the real names of vessels and men; and (5) to correct minor errors and provide consistency in punctuation, spelling, and grammatical form.

In the task of collation, the form of the revised manuscript generally prevailed. In only two chapters did this work entail more than a simple comparison of texts. Chapter 1 involved the integration of a preface Williams had written in 1922 with his article, "A Son of Ishmael," written in 1906. Chapter 15, the most composite section of the book, was compiled from four published articles, "Jack in the Doghole," written in 1912; "The Autobiography of a Labor Leader," originally dated 1902; "The Sailor and the Law," printed in 1900; and "The Crimping System," which appeared in 1897. It also included an introductory section from "Shanghaied," dated 1903, and an editorial from *The Independent* of April 25, 1912, "The Reform of Maritime Law," which internal evidence indicates was probably written by Williams.

This process of editing may account in part for some unevenness of style in the various chapters. Actually, however, Williams wrote these stories over a span of twenty-five years and that factor alone might easily explain any variation in quality. At times, too, Williams, with his own limited education, may have consciously sought to imitate other writers. Chapters 6 and 7, "The Passing of

Pengelley," and "Burial at Sea," written in 1921, are notable in this respect. In spite of cautious editing of excess verbiage in these chapters, they still fail to compare in quality with many of his other tales, leading one to suspect that Williams may have sought, at a time of low ebb in writing, to be imitative. In so striving, he was probably blissfully unaware that in his own natural style he was far superior to those writers whom he may have sought to emulate. Even in these chapters, however, in passages like those on pages 93-94 where Williams describes a storm and the resulting deck noises, there is ample evidence of his outstanding literary ability.

The arrangement of these articles chronologically proved to be a most intriguing piece of detective work, based as it was upon internal evidence. I am satisfied that the following organization is reasonably correct and, wherever it has been possible to substantiate facts, the order has been confirmed. There are gaps in time, but these are not important to the narrative generally. There is only one conscious departure from the rule of chronology, Chapter 9, entitled "Billy." The events described therein probably occurred prior to 1880 while Williams was a relatively young lad. It seemed wise at that particular point to insert a lighter note, hence the exception.

When these accounts were first printed, most of the persons described were still living and many of the ships mentioned were still afloat. Williams, therefore, for understandable reasons, changed the name of virtually every vessel and man mentioned. I have naturally sought to restore original names wherever possible and to verify Williams' stories.

By diligently combing the shipping columns of the New York *Herald* and the London *Times,* by utilizing *Lloyd's Register of Merchant Shipping,* by searching in the records of the National Archives in Washington, and by corresponding with the General Register and Record Office of Shipping and Seamen at Cardiff, Wales, it was possible to determine not only the correct names of several of the ships and men, but also to substantiate particular experiences which Williams describes. The files of Sailors' Snug Harbor, which contain data on Williams, and the correspondence between Williams and Hamilton Holt in the Holt Papers provided further evidence which aided in the process of verification.

In most instances, such checking showed Williams to be an unusually accurate chronicler. He kept no journal but remembered details with exactness. On pages 183 and 184, he reports that on a voyage from New York to Japan in 1890 he arrived on June 19 and that the return trip took 176 days. The records show both facts to be correct. The remarkable feat is that Williams, writing about them seventeen years later, recalled them so clearly.

In a few stories, Williams retained real names, and these, too, have been confirmed. Joseph O'Brien, described in Chapter 10, was, according to the General Register and Record Office of Shipping and Seamen, exactly as Williams depicts him. Thomas Swindell, appearing in the same story, is an authentic name which Williams retained, for he could probably not resist the play on words incorporated on page 143. Throughout all chapters I have used the dagger symbol (†) to indicate persons and ships which I have positively identified. Names so marked are known to be the actual ones. In addition, all names in the Author's Foreword have been verified and are real.

A diligent search in existing records leaves me convinced that Williams' claims as to his tales' authenticity are valid. He may, of course, as a literary artist, have embellished his accounts; that does not, however, detract from their basic truthfulness. Careful scrutiny of the manuscript discloses no internal conflicting evidence or anachronism in spite of the fact that it was written over a long span of years. Indeed, the errors which do exist merely confirm the fact that Williams was an honest writer with natural limitations. Had he been writing an imaginative tale, he would have been too concerned with accuracy to have made such mistakes. The best illustration of such a flaw appears on pages 177-178 where Williams, in expounding upon cyclonic winds in the Southern Hemisphere, presents an entirely incorrect description, the winds moving in exactly the opposite direction from what he describes. He correctly explains what he had apparently been told to do as helmsman in order to move the ship out of danger, but in so doing he reveals the limited knowledge which one would expect of a common sailor.

Further assurance that the tales are true can be derived from the editorial prefaces to Williams' articles in *The Independent,* a respected and reliable journal. An unusual bond existed between Hamilton Holt and Williams; hence Holt was in a position to testify concerning Williams' writings. A "true 'yarn,'" "Another True Story," "strictly true," "a true account," and similar phrases, probably written by Holt, offer additional evidence that Williams was a valid and truthful chronicler of life in the old merchant marine.

After innumerable voyages, Williams in the 1920's confined himself to odd jobs around the port of New York. His health had not been good and finally, ill, he reluctantly abandoned his independence in 1926 when he gained admission to that famous home for superannuated seamen on Staten Island, Sailors' Snug Harbor. There he suffered from dengue fever and other unknown ills. Finally, in tragic letters, he appealed to his old friend Hamilton Holt to arrange for analysis by medical specialists. Holt solicited the aid of his Yale classmate, Dr. John B. Solley, who had Williams removed to St. Luke's Hospital in New York City where his illness was pessimistically diagnosed as cancer of the throat. An operation failed to alleviate the condition and Williams died at 6:45 P.M. on August 24, 1927, at the age of sixty-three, leaving no issue or estate other than the manuscript which served as the partial basis for this volume.

He lies buried in Plot Twelve, Row Two, Grave Sixty-Six of the Sailors' Snug Harbor Cemetery. He was but an unusual spokesman for those toilers of the sea who rest beside him, for most of them undoubtedly endured privations and pain and experienced adventures as terrifying and noble as those described in this book. The age is gone, the extreme injustices are gone, but even today maritime seamen do not possess rights as extensive as those who labor ashore. What they do enjoy, however, in improved status and conditions is owing in some part to the efforts of James H. Williams.

This volume does not contain all of Williams' writings. He would not have wished it so. He would also, I suspect, have scoffed at the glossary of nautical terms which I have added for the easy enlightenment of landlubbers and modern-day sailors.

W.F.K.

Mississippi State University
October, 1958

# BLOW
# THE
# MAN
# DOWN!

*Come all you young fellows who follow the sea,*
*    (Chorus) To me way, hay, blow the man down,*
*Now, please pay attention and listen to me,*
*    (Chorus) Give me some time to blow the man down!*

*I'm a deep-water sailor just come from Hong Kong.*
*If you give me some whisky I'll sing you a song.*

*On a trim Black Ball liner I first served my time.*
*On a trim Black Ball liner I wasted my prime.*

*When a trim Black Ball liner's preparing for sea,*
*You'd split your sides laughin', such sights you would see.*

*There's tinkers and tailors, shoemakers and all,*
*They're all shipped for sailors on board the Black Ball.*

*When a big Black Ball liner's a-leaving her dock,*
*The boys and the girls on the pierhead do flock.*

*Now, when the big liner is clear of the land,*
*Our bosun he roars out the word of command.*

*"Come quickly lay aft to the break of the poop,*
*Or I'll help you along with the toe of my boot!"*

*"Pay attention to orders, now you one and all,*
*For see, right above you there flies the Black Ball!*

*" 'Tis larboard and starboard on deck you will sprawl,*
*For Kicking Jack Rogers commands the Black Ball!"*

—James H. Williams' version of the traditional
halyard chantey, from his manuscripts

# AUTHOR'S FOREWORD

In presenting this modest volume of wayward sea yarns to a highly cultured and discerning American public, the author feels it incumbent upon himself to offer some satisfactory explanation of their origin and source. The necessity for such an explanation has been rendered more and more urgent with the passing years by the incredulity of certain well-meaning and appreciative friends who have persistently refused to believe either that these accounts are true or that they could have been written by a "common" sailor.

In the course of my lifetime, especially after I began to contribute articles and sea yarns to *The Independent* magazine, the question has often been asked of me: "Where were you educated?"

To these well-meant inquiries, I have almost invariably answered: "In the forecastle; in the forecastles of a hundred ships." But now that I have arrived at the age of portliness and wisdom, and have wisely retired from the sea, I feel that I have been guilty of ingratitude toward many loyal and helpful friends in my younger days, and that this careless boast was invariably prompted by personal vanity and class pride rather than by true humility or a desire to be conscientious.

Sea-sense is a talent in itself that can only be developed by long practical experience and intensive training; but literary talent is a divine gift to be developed by hard study and close observation. The same individual may be originally endowed with both, but in that case he will usually sacrifice one in the development of the other.

In this respect, I have been a little more fortunate than the great majority of sailors, that is all. For I am a "common" sailor, to the manner born and bred, and so trained from early childhood,

21

thanks to the will of Providence that created me a man instead of a jackal. I am proud of my hard-earned distinction as a maritime A.B. and of my lifetime of intimate and fraternal association with the "common" sailors of the old merchant marine. No nobler or braver or more loyal, devoted and self-sacrificing martyrs than the merchant seamen ever lived.

All of these stories are authentic records of actual happenings at sea or in the merchant service. They are dried leaves from the life experience of an American sailor. It will be quickly noted that with one exception all the following stories relate to separate and distinct voyages made by the author, or to events experienced during his career at sea. The old-time windjammer was a true citizen of the world and he entertained a fixed aversion against serving on two consecutive voyages in the same ship. Any sailor who did so was stigmatized as a "ship's cousin," and shunned with suspicion by his mates.

The observant reader will also notice that most of the voyages were on British ships. This regrettable fact is entirely the result of chance and not of choice on the sailor's part. During the commercial period through which I lived, the deplorable decline of the American merchant marine reached its lowest ebb. Indeed, it practically ceased to be a potential factor in world commerce. Subsequent to 1872, the construction of deepwater ships in the United States virtually ceased. The attention of American shipowners and builders became almost entirely centered in the development of our enormous coastwise trade; and the old square-rigged fortune hunters went completely out of fashion as well as out of commission.

I was indentured to the sea service in February, 1876, and subsequently served exclusively in American ships during the first ten years of my sea career. But all the big new square-riggers that left American dockyards after that can be counted on my fingers. In the decade from 1885 to 1895, I recall but six superior ships that were launched and owned under American registry. They were the *Frederick Billings*, the *Rappahannock*, the *Roanoke*, the *Shenan-*

*doah,* the *Aryan,* and the ill-starred, ill-found, ill-fated, and infamous *T. F. Oakes* of evil memory and disastrous career.\* Within the next five or six years, the first-class sailing ships *Erskine M. Phelps,* and *Acme* were launched at Bath, Maine.

None of these ships should be confounded with the experimental ships *Clarence S. Bement, Kenilworth,* and *May Flint.* The frames of the *Bement* were imported from England and assembled in the United States. The *Kenilworth* was a converted British steamer; and the *Flint* was likewise a converted steamer of some kind, so that none of them were originally designed as true American sailing ships. None of these latter vessels ever became commercially successful or internationally famous, except, perhaps, as magnificent maritime failures. Meanwhile, the once proud and invincible fleets of American merchant ships were constantly and rapidly disappearing before our very eyes.

Many of these vessels were sold to foreign owners. Some were condemned for coal hulks and laid up at their moorings in foreign coal pockets to supply bunkers to passing steamers. Many others were wantonly dismantled and converted into tow barges to compete with the big schooners in the coastwise trade of the United States. And many others were either sent to Rotten Row, or else went to the "Port of Missing Ships."

This lamentable decline in American tonnage finally became so absolute and complete that, during the last decade of the nineteenth century, only one hundred fifty square-rigged vessels of all classes remained afloat beneath the United States flag—the sole and scattered survivors of our world-renowned sea power. By this time, the American fleets had been almost entirely displaced by cheaper foreign bottoms. Of these ships, about 75 per cent were British and the balance of our enormous commerce was distributed among the ships of other foreign nations—mainly Scandinavian.

---

\* The *T. F. Oakes* arrived in port in March, 1897, with one-third of her crew dead and the remainder rotten with scurvy. See pp. 228-229. Williams, in 1922, recalled the names of the above ships with accuracy. Actually, he might have included the *Susquehanna,* which was built at Bath, Maine, in 1891. (Ed.)

Under such deplorable conditions, the American youth with an inclination for sea service had no alternative but to sail under foreign flags or remain ashore. Under the circumstances, most of us adopted the lesser evil and became foreigners. Many stalwart American seamen became confirmed Limejuicers and ended their careers by marrying and settling in the British Isles, Australia, or other British colonies. I served about twelve years in British vessels. At various times, I shipped in Norwegian, Swedish, Danish, Dutch, and Portuguese ships, and in one memorable instance served as supercargo in a prehistoric Chinese junk for four notable months. But in nearly all cases the ships described were engaged exclusively, for the time at least, in American trade. This explains the Limey character of some of these wayfaring yarns.

Frankly speaking, most of these stories were written for the amusement or entertainment of my many shipmates and seafaring friends. In their original text, many of them were hastily scribbled with a lead pencil on wastepaper, and so submitted to the editors without revision or improvement. In those days, I used to go to my room at odd moments and scribble vagrant yarns, then bring them down into a barroom or any other place wherein sailors were wont to foregather and read them aloud as a sort of light diversion. Because my mates always enjoyed and approved my scribblings, I realized that they rang true and were, therefore, likely to prove acceptable to discerning editors.

My major purpose in writing these yarns, however, was always to draw public attention to the injustices and unnecessary hazards to which seamen have always been exposed. I have become, I believe, instrumental in some slight degree in ameliorating the hardships of their lives by telling the truth about their miseries and lamentable conditions.

I was aided in my task by my participation for seven and one-half years in the Atlantic Coast Seamen's Union, where I served as business agent. At the time of my election to this position, I was just thirty years old and had been eighteen years at sea. I was, therefore, well qualified by experience for my job, but my lack of education appalled me.

Fortunately, I was nominated as a member of the Social Reform Club of New York, that remarkable civic and social organization devoted to the improvement of all mankind by the elevation of the laboring class. Through this organization, I met many distinguished people and participated in and listened to many discussions on a wide range of subjects. The various fields of activity and thought that were covered and elucidated by the most eloquent and gifted authorities in each field of human effort furnished exactly the kind of instruction I earnestly needed, while my constant association on equal terms with that splendid band of cultured and refined ladies and gentlemen amounted to a liberal education to an obscure but earnest sailor like me.

It was also to the Social Reform Club, as I shall later relate, that I revealed the conditions and needs of maritime workers; and that organization at last devoted its power and influence almost entirely to the abolition of the old, established crimping system and to the protection of American seamen ashore and afloat.

It was at one of the meetings of the Club, when I happened to be the speaker of the evening, that I first met Mr. Hamilton Holt, then managing editor of *The Independent*. Mr. Holt had attended the meeting to hear my subject, which was new to him as it had formerly been to everybody else, for everyone was loath to believe that such atrocities as I had described could have been possible under the American flag.

At the close of the meeting, Mr. Holt and I were introduced to each other by Mr. Charles B. Spahr, who was then president of the Club. Mr. Holt could not have been much over twenty-two years of age at that time, and I surmise it must have been shortly after his graduation from college. I could not help liking this kind, courtly, unassuming young gentleman, and from that hour a mutual bond of common fellowship existed between us which neither time nor distance nor changing circumstances has undone.

The very morning after that meeting, I received a letter from

Mr. Holt requesting me to write an article for his magazine on the subject of my discourse of the evening previous. "I think this subject is new to most of our readers," wrote Mr. Holt, and he added: "Of course, you understand we intend to pay for it."

In compliance with Mr. Holt's request, I wrote the article which was published in *The Independent* for February 11, 1897. That was the first literary production for which I was ever paid. For a number of years thereafter, I contributed articles at long intervals to Mr. Holt's paper. They met with a cordial reception from readers of the magazine, more, no doubt, because of the unusual character of the subject than for their literary merit. But, nevertheless, the editors of *The Independent* constantly encouraged me to contribute to their pages in the hope of obtaining as much actual knowledge of sea life as possible. For wise men learn wisdom from fools, and none but fools and pure-blind sailors ever followed the sea without learning the truth and striving to dispel the charming illusions regarding sea life engendered in credulous minds by designing crimps and professional writers of the sea.

In conclusion, I hope that the foregoing sketch will help to explain why a "common" sailor could learn to write intelligently of his own experiences and why he has felt compelled to do so.

And now in the afternoon of life when I can sit quietly in the pleasant sunshine of youthful faces and spin ancient yarns of wonderful voyages and wild adventures amid the remotest solitudes of the seven seas, I feel that it is becoming to render thanks to Divine Providence that has brought me safe and sound through all the tribulations of a long and vagrant life and rescued me many times from the perils of the mighty deep so that I might tell the marvels of my wanderings to a complacent and incredulous world.

I wish also to thank my many friends throughout the world—for I have never been anywhere but that God always raised me up a friend—for their multitude acts of personal kindness and charitable service when I was astray and knew not whither I was bound.

Finally, I want to thank my thousands of loyal shipmates, seafaring friends, and lifelong associates, living or dead, for their loving fellowship and generous support and for making it possible for me to remain ashore for seven beautiful years and improve my mind that I might learn to speak and write and tell the story of their lives as never mortal told it before. To them, and to them alone my life and labors belong; and to them alone, in whose name it has been written, I humbly dedicate this book.

New York.
October 18, 1922.

# 1 · A SON OF ISHMAEL

**B**ehold: I am an Ishmaelite, a lineal descendant of the despised House of Bondage. I was born under protest but have continued to "dwell in the presence of my brethren. Many hands have been turned against me," but most of them have been turned back. "And none can remove me from my place."

My paternal grandmother's name *was* Hagar; and for aught I know that may have been the only lawful name she ever had. She was born in slavery in North Carolina and lived, by actual record, one hundred and four years. In her youth, she was bought for nine hundred dollars and brought to New York State.

My father was her eldest son. Her daughter, Elizabeth, married a sea captain and lived in New Jersey; her remaining son, good, generous, jovial Uncle John, died in the old Tombs prison while awaiting trial for killing a man on board a steamboat in valiant self-defense.

The white branch of my family belonged in Massachusetts, my mother being the oldest of a family of twenty-one children. She was a woman of no education and was more remarkable for her native intelligence and physical strength than for her beauty. There was not a merchant in our town who would dare to offer her a barrel of flour for taking it home.

She was a splendid mother and a good woman who wrought unceasingly with her hands and nursed her own children from her ample breasts while the puny brats of her more wealthy but effete neighbors fared sumptuously at the same generous font.

In the course of chronological events, I arrived on the morning of May 21, 1864, in a little brown-painted frame house locally known as the "bandbox" at 17 Washington Street in Fall River, Massachusetts. I have it on the indubitable authority of my mother and "Mother" Murray, the midwife, that I was a healthy, husky youngster, born without blemish and above average weight.

My father was a sailor. He was born in the State of New York in 1809, and was, therefore, a contemporary of Abraham Lincoln. When Father was fifteen years old, he ran away from home and went to sea. Thereafter, he followed the sea as boy and man to within one year of his death, which occurred in Newport, Rhode Island, on the first Monday in November, 1870.

At the time of my birth, Father was a pilot on Long Island Sound. He was fifty-five years of age when I arrived, my mother being his second wife. His first wife was a Negress and by her he had no issue. He was a large, stern, powerful man, with a light brown skin, good features, and a rather reserved though kindly manner. He was familiarly and affectionately known the coast around as "Uncle Jim," and highly respected by all who knew him.

I was, obviously, the son of his old age and the apple of his eye. His greatest ambition in life was to send me to college, but he did not live to carry out this cherished plan. When I was four years old, he taught me to read and write and instructed me in the fundamentals of arithmetic. Every day of his life, when he was at home, he continued to give me systematic instruction. I was a precocious child with a very receptive mind and a tenacious memory, and Father took uncommon interest and paternal delight in teaching me. The last act of his life on the morning of his death was to send me to school; when I returned at noon my father was dead, and whatever prospects I may have entertained of a college education, a scholastic degree, or a professional career was interred with his bones.

I was six years and five months old at the time of Father's death, and hence my fortunes were left entirely to chance and the protecting influence of a devoted but illiterate mother. Realizing her own inability to carry on the instruction which my father had so earnestly begun, my mother sent me to live in the country for some time. There I dwelt very happily with an elderly lady of comfortable means who was very fond of me, and being herself childless, she took me entirely to her heart. But because I was a colored child, she could not adopt me. At this home, my education progressed very favorably. There was an abundance of good literature at hand as well as wise and discerning instructors, and I was given free rein and practically unlimited range to gratify my inborn love of reading.

But when I was eight years old, I became stone blind from a severe attack of measles, and for the ensuing two years I could neither read nor go to school. Even then, my education was not entirely neglected, for many kind neighbors and sympathetic friends took my case in hand and I was sent to a famous eye and ear infirmary where I was placed under the care and treatment of the most eminent specialists of the period.

During this season of darkness, my time was divided between the distant hospital and my mother's home. I spent the winters at the infirmary and the summers with my mother. It was during one of the long, lonely, home seasons, when I had to sit in solitary darkness with no one to talk to and no pastime or occupation to gladden the tedious hours or elevate my thoughts, that God sent me a new preceptress. She was a schoolteacher from Missouri; her name was Miss Alden, and she had come east to spend her long vacation with relatives in Massachusetts. This kind-hearted lady learned of my pitiful condition almost as soon as she arrived, and at once made my mother's acquaintance and offered her sympathy and services.

For three long, beautiful, interesting months, this devoted, self-sacrificing young lady spent her entire time and attention on my instruction and amusement. She gave me object lessons and instructive exercises every day, and she would read aloud to me for hours at a time. She ruined her entire vacation and afterward secured a month's extension from her work for my benefit; and the inspiring influence of her devoted personality and patient painstaking instruction have remained with me all my life.

By slow and lingering degrees my eyes gradually yielded to optical treatment and eventually my sight was restored; but, sad to say, it has always remained defective, and the marks left by the measles have never disappeared. And this explains, largely, why I have been forced to remain throughout my life a "common" sailor, a man before the mast. For, while my eyesight has always been keen enough for ordinary purposes, even for keeping a lookout at sea, it was so much reduced that I could never pass the examining tests required for promotion, for regular naval service, or for enrollment with exploring expeditions. I could not secure either a master mariner's, mate's, or pilot's license because of defective vision, particularly regarding the sight of my right eye, which since my childhood affliction has always remained partially blind. This unfortunate handicap has always been a great bane and sorrow to me, for in all other respects I was remarkably well adapted to a maritime career. And it has always been a constant and hopeless source of secret bitterness that through this early misfortune I should be forever disqualified from serving with distinction and success in the only profession I could ever reconcile my mind to adopt as a lifelong career.

It was as natural that I should become a sailor as that an unmanned boat should drift with the tide. Descended from maritime stock and born in a maritime district as I was, all my earliest impressions were of the sea. All my earliest acquaintances and associates were seafaring people, and my playground was among the shipping.

I can never forget the exquisite sensation which thrilled me when I first saw a small boat. I had toddled down to the wharf unattended, and there I discovered a white boat bobbing about jauntily

Fall River, Massachusetts, around the time of Williams' birth in 1864. (*Mariners Museum*)

ABOVE: The whaling ship *Niger,* of New Bedford, possibly the vessel Williams describes as the *Ramirez.* (*Mariners Museum*) BE-LOW: Whaling in the South Seas. From a lithograph by Lebreton. (*Mariners Museum*)

on the choppy water by the pier. The feeling that went through me was simply indescribable. It was like the first thrill of a lover's kiss, only more delightful. I climbed unobserved into the little shell and rocked and played in infantile bliss until I fell asleep. Finally, I was rescued by a fisherman and carried home, kicking and squalling a lusty protest all the way.

When I was twelve years old, after having attended the public schools for about three years, I was bound out to a shipmaster. My guardian died two years later at Barbados, and thus I found myself adrift in a foreign port when scarcely fourteen. So I was engaged as a cabin boy on a fine American clipper and began my career in a voluntary—or is it involuntary?—slavery.

I shall not attempt a bald recital of all I saw and endured during the next few years. I can only say that in my opinion a Yankee ship was a floating synonym for Purgatory, if there is such a place, and that some of my officers must have graduated with diabolical honors at a place still further down the road. In spite of all our national mourning at certain periods of the past over the departed glory of the seas, I cannot help regarding the astounding decline and practical annihilation of our once proud merchant marine as divine judgment visited against an institution whose enormities were past forgiveness.

So I grew up to manhood. I started out so young that I never found time to grow very tall. But what I lacked in stature I made up in sturdiness, like "Jerry the Miller." I became thoroughly seasoned and inured to the sea and was a veritable glutton for hardtack. Many of my hardened shipmates marveled at my strength and endurance. For my own part I gloried in my own powers, for I had acquired nothing else in the course of my strenuous career to be proud of.

As a fortune hunter, I have been anything but a success. The "common" sailor usually got "more kicks than coppers." His wages were, as a rule, sifted through a ladder. The crimps and shipowner took what fell through, while Jack's portion was what stuck to the rungs. And the rungs were set devilishly wide apart.

But after all, my cross of life, bitter and tragic though it has been, has not been without its compensating blessings. Compelled to remain in the fellowship of the unfortunate because I myself was unfortunate, I have learned to know and admire and love the real seamen as none but brothers can ever love each other.

## 2 · THAR SHE BLOWS

In 1880, I was sixteen years old and had completed four years' tall-water sea service. I had traded two years in the Western Ocean, sailed to the East as well as the West Indies, crossed the equator four times, doubled both Cape Horn and the Cape of Good Hope, and circumnavigated the globe. Therefore, I justly considered myself some sailorman and forthwith concluded that a four-year whaling voyage was all that I needed to round out my career and establish my prestige as the most famous youngster who had ever sailed from the shores of Narragansett Bay.

As a boy, I had always harbored a secret desire to make a whaling voyage. This laudable but dangerous ambition was shared by a good many other healthy but humble youngsters in our locality, for we lived but fourteen miles from New Bedford, the great "Sperm City," and the reek of blubber was in the atmosphere.

Whaling was, then, a game of chance, a mere gamble against long odds, and a losing venture. But nearly every boy in town knew some older lad who had made a lucky voyage in a Bedford blubber hunter, won a few thousand dollars in the common hazard of a fortunate cruise, married the girl of his choice, bought a farm or otherwise established himself, and settled down to a life of contented respectability.

Personally, I cannot say that I shared in the prevailing ambition so common among my youthful companions to make a whaling voyage merely as a stepping stone to a peaceful stay at home. I was born with a roving commission. There never was a man in our home town for whom I was willing to work or a girl to whom I dared pay court, for my real love was the roaring sea. It is better to leave a maiden unkissed than a widow to mourn.

My first attempt, in 1880, to sign on a whaler, I must confess, proved unsuccessful. The local crimps of New Bedford, unscrupulous as they were, dared not ship me in spite of my previous sea experience and evident fitness because of my extreme youth. The law imposed a barrier which even they dared not overstep. They, therefore, advised me to go home and return when I was older. So I was reluctantly obliged, for the time, to resume my course in the ordinary service of the merchant marine.

I did not, however, forget my original determination to make a whaling voyage, and two years later I again presented myself to the local crimps in the port of New Bedford, lied my way through, and gained my long-coveted position among a blubber hunter's crew.

It was early in March, 1882, that I was mustered into whale fishery through the agency of old Tom Codd, the famous, but still more infamous shanghai prince of the place and period. He sent me to sea in the good ship *Ramirez*, 350 tons, Captain Dodge, for a four years' cruise. My ambition was to be gratified at last, but my trials had just begun. Many times during that memorable voyage, I cursed the day I met old Tom Codd and vowed that if ever I got my grapplings on him again I would make short work of him.

It was a bitter cold morning when we lined up in front of the shipping office on Water Street for first inspection and final selection by sturdy old Cap'n Dodge. We were a motley, unkempt assortment of various nations and races of men, most of us victims of dire adversity.

There were but few sailors and only three Americans in the crowd. The rest were human derelicts attracted together from far and near by decoy advertisements circulated broadcast by the wily crimps who realized a one-hundred-dollar bonus on every man secured through their insidious methods, regardless of whether he was a sailor, soldier, peddler, or farmer. Among the crowd, I noticed but one acquaintance, Tom Dennis of Dartmouth. Tom and I had been playmates in early childhood and I was delighted to see him among the crowd of possibilities, not only because I knew him but also because, being somewhat older than myself, he had already one "plum pudding" voyage of seven or eight months to his credit. I felt that he would be a helpful shipmate and valuable instructor to a person in my state of inexperienced enthusiasm.

By far the most noticeable personality among the motley crowd of tousled stragglers was a big, rawboned, verdant giant from East Down East. As fresh and unsophisticated as his native hills are green, he answered to the name of Hiram, and said that he hailed from "Vermount."

Old Tom Codd and big Joe "Beef," Codd's overfed and corpulent side partner in legalized iniquity, were strutting pompously around among the roundup of unfortunate send-offs appraising the individual merits of their promiscuous herd with all the critical shrewdness of a pair of drovers exhibiting a herd of steers.

"Thar ye ar', Cap'n," grinned old Tom Codd with an appreciative leer as he approached the big Yankee and proceeded to paw him over to emphasize his good points. "Thar's suthin' fer ye; jes lookud 'im; han's on 'im like a whale's fluke; heave a harpoon in clean out o' sight every time."

"Hey, yew ol' vagabon', I ain't no beef critter, consarn ye," grunted the big greenhorn resentfully, and with a disdainful shove he sent Tom Codd sprawling into the frozen gutter six feet away. A general laugh greeted the fallen crimp's discomfiture in which the whaling skipper joined, the heartiest of all.

"All right, Tom," he bellowed mirthfully as the old beach pirate scrambled wrathfully to his feet. "I'll take that feller on your recommendashun, but you oughtta come along too, jest to exercise him; he seems kinder fracshus."

Amid the titter of unsuppressed merriment that went around, Tom sneaked away crestfallen and furious. He left the skipper to choose his crew according to his own judgment, and the next day the selected members of the *Ramirez'* crew assembled at the shipping commissioner's office to sign articles.

The shipping agreement for whalers differed in some essential particulars from the ordinary shipping articles prescribed for seamen entering for service in the general merchant marine. This was considered necessary because of the unusual length of the voyages, from three to five years, because of the greater hazards and unusual labors, and also because the requirements of the trade necessitated large crews and small ships, which meant that the men had to accept closer and more crowded quarters than those provided in cargo ships.

But the principal distinction was in regard to compensation. Whaling and fishing crews were engaged on a no-catch no-pay basis. All hands, masters, mates, and men, were hired on shares, usually referred to in the trade as a "lay." The entire profits of the cruise were, therefore, divided in very unequal ratio among the owners, masters, mates, and crews and were presumed, of course, to be based upon the prevailing price of oil and other substances gathered during the voyage at the time of delivery.

In the *Ramirez*, the sailor portion of the crew was signed for the eightieth lay. One portion in eighty, whether of oil, baleen, ambergris, or any other product was to be our share. It was a pretty long lay, but we took it.

Big Hiram found the official proceedings of signing on entirely new to him, but he got through fairly well. He gave his name as Hiram Stebbins, his age as twenty-four, his native state as "Vermount." His father, Abner, it appeared, owned a farm "jest a short piece outside o' Rutland." When questioned as to his stature, he replied: "Wal, I'm either six foot an' two inches or two foot 'n' six inches, I fergit which." But green and unsophisticated though he was, Hiram proved a good shipmate and a firm and faithful friend. In time, he developed into a good whaler and fully verified Tom

Codd's reckless prediction about heaving a whale iron home in a cachalot's flank.

Hiram was, without exception, the most inexperienced of all the greenhorns I have ever seen aboard ship. He had no idea the sea was salt; it was "a mighty big river." According to his ideas, the forepeak, where the crew lived, was "down cellar," the tops were "upstairs," and the crow's-nest was "up in the garret." It required a month of instruction from all hands to impress upon his mind the value of sea etiquette and break him of calling the Old Man "boss" and the mates "fellers."

The rest of the crowd dubbed him "Country," though most of them were just as green as himself in all matters pertaining to practical seamanship. But after "Country" had got over his first fright, recovered from a severe attack of seasickness, and become somewhat reconciled to the scanty rations and night watches, he really became a prize member of our crew.

At the beginning of our cruise, we slanted leisurely along the American coast and sighted our first school of whales off Cape Hatteras. We lowered our boats and managed to kill three specimens before the school took fright and sounded. By the time the three whales had "finned out," the ship had been left far behind and darkness was approaching. So we made fast to our prizes and lay all night in a slick formed by the oil exuding from the dead carcasses of our catch.

At dawn, we munched a little hardtack and pemmican, made fast to the three great carcasses, and began the slow, tedious operation of towing down the wind to meet the ship which we knew was beating up to windward to pick us up. About an hour after sunrise, we sighted the *Ramirez* working toward us with her royals furled, as the wind was freshing from the eastward and the weather looked threatening. In an hour or so we lay alongside, secured our whales to the ship by fluke chains, and then got the ship under easy sail as a storm was imminent. The sea was too rough to begin cutting in our whales, so we hove to and prepared to ride it out.

That night the wind blew hard from the Northeast and kicked

up a tumultuous sea. In the middle watch, the fluke chains parted and we lost the two largest of our valuable prizes. It was a bad beginning, and old Captain Dodge cried like a child over his loss.

After leaving the coast, we cruised for some time among the Azores and Cape de Verde Islands; then we meandered leisurely down the African coast, doubled the Cape of Good Hope, made an extended tour of the Indian Ocean with fair success and little excitement, and on May 24, 1883, entered the harbor of Singapore with a full cargo of oil.

After unloading, we cruised southward through Oceanica to Desolation Island, where we remained six weeks. We then doubled back across the South Atlantic to Tierra del Fuego, Patagonia, and the Falklands, where we encountered fairly good results for three months.

Early the following spring, we traversed the North Pacific and continued northward into the Bering Sea where we spent quite a profitable season. We cruised among the Aleutians and the Alaskan bays until early September and then bore southward just fast enough to avoid being nipped in the great ice pack which was continually working south. Eventually we were forced back into the clear, deep waters of the Pacific and shaped our course for the Sandwich (now the Hawaiian) Islands.

By this time, after two and a half years of training and experience, "Country" had developed into a very capable whaler as well as a good average sailor, and was easily the most popular man among the *Ramirez'* crew. The finer arts of sailoring he never mastered, but he was a strong fearless hand, alow or aloft, and a whole team at shortening sail. He could beat some of our oldest harpooners driving a whale iron, but he had never been rated a boat-steerer or official harpooner. He lacked the practical skill in whaleboat handling which is a most important part of every boat-steerer's trade. But he really became an expert with the harpoon, and because of the great leverage his extra height and weight gave him, his unerring aim, and the amazing force and speed of his throw, "Country" was often given the honor by common consent of taking

the regular harpooner's place in the bows when we raised an unusually lively or pugnacious whale.

One day off the coast of Lower California, we sighted a lone
grayling cow swimming leisurely along with a calf under her fin.
These graylings, or California grays, as they are called, are of
medium size, smaller by far than either the bowheads, the cacha-
lots, or the humpbacks, but they are considered good prizes as they
are true whales and when full grown will yield from sixty-five to
eighty barrels of oil. They are much lighter in color than any of the
other species of whales, whence the appellation of "grays" usually
applied to them. But they bear a very bad reputation as fighters,
especially in defending their young. If you kill a grayling calf before you do the cow, she will chase you ashore and up a tree. That
is exactly what our fool of a mate did, and that was how we lost
poor "Country."

"Country" and I both belonged to the first mate's boat crew, and
when we lowered away to attack the grayling the mate had smug-
gled a new-fangled bomb gun into the boat which he had always
wanted to try but which the skipper had as persistently prohibited.
The old-time whaling captains were ultraconservative, as well as
good sports, and did not believe in any new whaling contrivances,
especially of the explosive type, which they stoutly protested did
not give the whale a chance. But the mate had sneaked the cumber-
some and dangerous device into the rack without the Old Man's
knowledge and we had no option in the matter.

We sailed our boat to the flank of the unsuspicious grayling quite
unobserved. She was too deeply solicitous of her nursing baby to
notice our approach. Indian Joe, a Gay Head Indian, was our boat-
steerer that day, and he stood up in the bows and let fly two har-
poons in quick succession and with remarkable skill, and both irons
sank to the shafts in the whale's naked flank almost before she
became conscious of our presence.

But beyond a convulsive quiver of her massive bulk, an involuntary twitching of her spreading flukes, and a quickening of her pace
through the water, she exhibited no sign of the intense agony she

must have felt. The poor creature could not turn and fight us without injuring her calf, and she could not sound without drowning it, for baby whales cannot swim. Therefore, the stricken mother sought to escape by flight, towing our big whaleboat with her.

It was at this point our smart mate attempted to show off his skill with the newly invented bomb lance. Ordering us to belay the whale lines short, he exchanged places with Indian Joe and then raising the weighty instrument of destruction and resting it carefully on the gunwale, he took a long deliberate aim and let fly. The recoil of the gun kicked him into the bottom of the boat, and the charge exploding blew the calf to pieces but never injured the cow.

The situation changed in a flash. The bereaved and maddened whale leaped entirely out of the sea as lively as a sprat. She lashed about with her ponderous flukes until the whole Pacific Ocean as far as we could see was in a smother of foam. Then she turned like a flash and charged and recharged in a series of wild rushes directly for the boat. By quick work and good oarsmanship, aided by the blind fury of the wounded whale herself, we managed to elude her repeated rushes until she suddenly changed her tactics and sounded, or pretended to.

But the next instant she rose directly beneath our keel. The boat, crew, gear, and all, were hurled high into the air, and I suddenly felt myself skidding swiftly down that whale's back into the sea with the celerity of a toboggan slide. I was too busy for the next few minutes taking care of myself to realize what was happening. Fortunately, two more boats from the ship had reached the scene by this time and we were rescued—all except poor "Country." He had been caught on an upward sweep of the whale's fluke and tossed twenty-five feet in the air. He was dead before his body struck the water. The whale's blow had killed him.

By quick work, we recovered Hiram's body and took it aboard the *Ramirez* where we placed it on the hatch, just forward of the tryworks. Tom Dennis and I, being the only two Americans left in the forecastle, were appointed a guard of honor to prepare the body for burial. I was busy at the dead man's feet trying to remove his boots when a low exclamation from Tom, who was working at the head of the corpse, brought me to his side. Tom had unfastened the dead man's shirt collar, and when I reached him I found him holding a large silver locket and gazing in sad-eyed wonder at a miniature photograph.

It was a picture of a comely and purposeful young woman. It was not one of those dazzling types of unearthly beauty such as artists love to portray and connoisseurs rave over, nor was it a composite type of symbolic American beauty as exemplified in the remarkable delineation of the Gibson Girl. It was the face of one of those real American women that good men adore and bad men respect. It embodied grace and dignity of character and conscious reserve of mind. It revealed gentleness of soul, austerity of conduct, and charming manner. Tom and I were from the same part of the country and well knew the type of maiden depicted in that sacred locket.

On the reverse side of the picture, written in neat female hand, was the inscription: "To Hiram from Deborah. Christmas, 1881." At length, Tom turned wet eyes to mine. "What'll we do with it, Jim?" he asked in sorrowful tone.

I pondered a moment before answering. "Let's leave it where we found it, Tom, and say nothing about it," I finally replied. "I think that is what Hiram would want us to do."

That same day, we buried "Country" ashore in a beautiful bay called Altata on the coast of Lower California.

We killed that whale for revenge, but it took three boats' crews a whole day at the risk of all our lives to do it. She certainly died hard. We towed the carcass to Altata Bay and cut it in in smooth water. It netted us seventy-five barrels.

That grayling was the last whale ever caught by the *Ramirez*. The ship was sixty years old, and being too decrepit for further service she was condemned and broken up at Honolulu.

### 3 · THE "INQUISITION"

**I**n the latter part of the year 1884, I was paid off and legally discharged from the *Ramirez* in Honolulu. My share of the eightieth lay had netted me $180 in gold. Of course, I was entitled to considerably more, but why complain? A sailor's wages are always what he gets, not what he earns. According to maritime usage under the circumstances, I was also entitled to a passage to the nearest American port where we could be reshipped. But what's the use of going home when you can go anywhere else? I was only a little over twenty years old and the world is wide.

So I carefully sewed up my money in a canvas belt, strapped it securely around my waist next to my skin, and went off in search of another ship. I finally secured a berth in a Nova Scotia bark, the *Redwood,* which was "cleared for Guam," that is to say, she was free to go to any part of the world in ballast where she might secure a charter.

After a rather tiresome and aimless quest, we brought up in Kobe, Japan, where I promptly paid myself off with the jib downhaul * and went to lodge with Madame Otome in Kita Nagasa Dori Chicome, No. 18. A day or two later, my old frigate sailed, and

* Williams deserted. (Ed.)

I was left a free agent again. So I crawled out of my erstwhile place of concealment and boldly surveyed the town.

There were a number of fine sailing ships lying in Kobe Bay at the time and I elected to ship in one of them, the *Inquisition*. I preferred her to any of the other ships because she had just been chartered to trade on the Asiatic coast for three years and I thought it would afford me a fine opportunity to visit a wide variety of ports and broaden my sphere of experience. So it did, greatly to my ultimate sorrow and regret.

From Kobe, we went to Nagasaki and loaded coal for Iloilo in the Philippine Islands; from thence we went to Hong Kong in ballast for orders. That short voyage was a drill to be remembered. I had already been to sea about eight years but was now to have my eyes opened to the real character of tyrannical skippers and "bucko" mates and Yankee "hell ships," of which I had heard so often and so much. No language is severe enough to depict adequately the outrages I witnessed on that short coasting trip. We were continually hazed and hounded like wild beasts, driven like dumb cattle, beaten like mules, and worked like galley slaves. We were never allowed even to speak, to pass even the most casual remarks to each other while at work. We were deprived of our watches below, kept on our bare whack of food on a coast where fresh food was both abundant and cheap, reviled and cursed from morning to night, and constantly watched over by half a dozen burly, brutal, irresponsible lynx-eyed monsters who called themselves *officers.*

The slightest inadvertance on the part of any member of crew—to drop a spot of tar or paint on deck or even to ask a shipmate for a chew of tobacco—was always considered an infraction of the rules, and the unfortunate offender would be promptly attacked with a perfect hail of blows delivered with any article of hardware that might come to hand, accompanied by the vilest of epithets and the most frightful of curses.

Why did we meekly submit to such inhuman abuse? Because even the least word of protest or sign of resistance was insubordi-

## SHIP HENRY B. HYDE

Launched at the Bath, Maine, shipyard of Chapman & Flint in 1884. One of the finest wooden vessels of her rig ever produced by American builders. Length, 268 feet; beam, 45 feet; depth, 29 feet; 2,463 tons register.

1 Jib boom
2 Bowsprit
3 Dolphin striker
4 Bobstays
5 Bow
6 Hawsepipe
7 Cathead
8 Anchor on deck
9 Capstan
10 Running light
11 Forecastle head
12 Channels
13 Chain plate
14 Deadeye
15 Forward deckhouse
16 "Charlie Noble" (galley stack)

17 Ship's boats or longboats
18 Pump (on deck)
19 Yawl boats
20 Companionway
21 Poop deck
22 After companionway
23 Wheelhouse
24 Stern
25 Transom
26 Rudder

27 Fore-sky stay
28 Foreroyal stay
29 Fore-topgallant stay
30 Outer-jib stay
31 Inner-jib stay
32 Fore-topmast stay
33 Forestay
34 Jib sheets
35 Foretack
36 Reef points

37 Footropes
38 Foremast
39 Fore-topmast
40 Fore-topgallant mast
41 Foreroyal mast
42 Fore-skysail mast
43 Main-topgallant staysail shee
44 Main-royal staysail sheet
45 Fore-skysail braces
46 Foreroyal braces

*Drawing by John O'Hara Cosgrave II from* Shantymen and Shantyboys, *by William M. Doerflinger. By permission of The Macmillan Company. (©, 1951)*

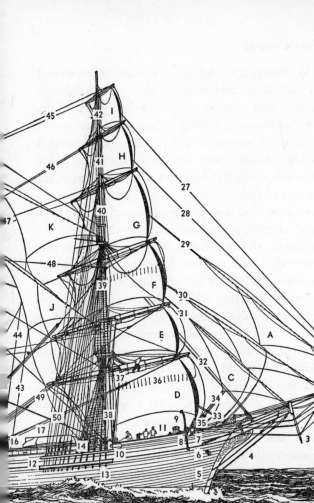

A Flying jib
B Outer jib
C Inner jib
D Forecourse
E Fore-lower topsail
F Fore-upper topsail
G Fore-topgallant
H Foreroyal
I Fore-skysail
J Main-topgallant staysail
K Main-royal staysail
L Main course
M Main lower topsail
N Main-upper topsail
O Main-topgallant
P Main-royal
Q Main-skysail
R Mizzen-topgallant staysail
S Mizzen-royal staysail
T Crossjack
U Mizzen-lower topsail
V Mizzen-upper topsail
W Mizzen-topgallant
X Mizzen-royal
Y Mizzen-skysail
Z Spanker

J. O. H. COSGRAVE II

47 Fore-topgallant braces
48 Upper-topsail brace
49 Starboard lower-topsail brace
50 Starboard forebrace
51 Mainmast
52 Main yard
53 Main lower-topsail yard
54 Main upper-topsail yard
55 Main-topgallant yard

56 Main-royal yard
57 Main-skysail yard
58 Main shrouds
59 Main-topmast shrouds
60 Main-topgallant-mast shrouds
61 Main-topmast backstays
62 Main-topgallant-mast backstays
63 Starboard main lift
64 Maintop

65 Main-topmast crosstrees
66 Main brace
67 Mizzenmast
68 Spanker boom
69 Spanker gaff
70 Spanker sheet
71 Vang
72 Monkey gaff
73 Mizzen-skysail braces

AN AMERICAN FULL-RIGGED SHIP OF JAMES H. WILLIAMS' PERIOD

nation punishable by "tricing up," chaining down, or imprisonment in the lazarette on hard bread and water as the master might direct. Open self-defense was mutiny, punishable by years of imprisonment in the penitentiary. United action was piracy and carried a death penalty. To beat or wound or starve or overwork a seaman was not even a crime under the then existing medieval maritime law—it was only discipline. Such was the substance of the law; resistance was out of the question.

The *Inquisition* was a large, stately clipper: a perfect specimen of that most graceful, elegant, and beautiful of all sailing craft, the American East Indiaman. In every detail of her construction and equipment she showed, in its highest development, the subtle cunning and wondrous skill of the shipbuilder's art—light, lofty, tapering masts and spars towering majestically on high above her snow-white decks; erect in stays, symmetrical in design, correct in rake and alignment, perfect in general proportions and complete in artistic finish, with sheer, high, graceful bows and gilded scroll-work on her classically carved "fiddlehead"; broad and ornate over-hanging stern and neatly molded run to emphasize the even contour of her exquisitely rounded ends. What a pity that such an inspiring marvel of elegant perfection, delicate grace, usefulness, and majestic power should be made a floating torture-house, a "blood packet," a beautifully sculptured shelter for human misery, grief, and despair, inhuman, fiendish cruelty, and wanton, unrestricted barbarities.

Our skipper's name was Gammon, and no man in the American merchant marine was ever more widely known, more sincerely hated, or more thoroughly detested by honest seamen the world over than he. He was a spare-built, wiry man about fifty years of age with thin, iron-gray hair, cold, cunning, heartless, ferret-like eyes, a flaming brandy knob on the end of his nose, and a face so sharp you could have split kindling wood with it. He had a shrill, squeaking, querulous voice entirely in keeping with his features. An irascible, peevish temper and a strong weakness for Three Star brandy rounded out his personality. The word honor was not in his vocabulary. He proudly and frequently boasted that he had "never paid off a son of a ———— of a sailor yet," and he'd be damned if he ever would.

The chief mate, Mister Roarer, was a big, raw-boned, iron-faced giant with a roar like a lion, arms like capstan bars, and fingers like belaying pins. He was a Canadian, quite as unprincipled as the captain in his way, and he could always be depended upon to do the latter's dirty work without question. His chief claim to distinction was that he had "never seen a ———— ———— sailor yet" that he couldn't lick.

The second mate, whose name was Prettyman, was a tall, lanky, loose-jointed, squint-eyed "Bluenoser" from the wilds of Nova Scotia. His features were not in his favor, for he had a low beetling forehead surmounted by a mop of bristling, fiery red hair, a broken nose, and a deeply scarred face. His claim to fame lay in his truculent, overbearing disposition, his incessant flow of naval profanity, the amazing dexterity and accuracy with which he could hurl belaying pins about, and his wonderful ability to kick with both feet. All these useful and highly professional accomplishments greatly endeared him to the heart of the hatchet-faced little skipper, so that he really was considered somebody on board in spite of his repulsive features and ungainly appearance.

There were also a third mate, a bos'n, a carpenter, and some other inferior supernumeraries, but they are not worth mentioning. All were domineering bullies, bull-drivers, and brutes selected by the Old Man for their detestable characters rather than for their ability to work.

Our crew was composed of the usual mixed and motley crowd of vagrant unfortunates commonly assembled to fill out the complement of a deepwater ship. Nearly every nationality and tribe among the human race was represented. Only two were native Americans, myself and a young Gloucester fisherman named Al Staples who had been enticed into a crimping den while on a spree in Boston. He had been fleeced and robbed and subsequently shanghaied for one year's service in the *Inquisition*. Staples was the only member of the original crew which had sailed from Boston. All the rest had deserted to a man, and the present crew had been recruited, just as I had been, among the different ports touched at since.

From Hong Kong, the *Inquisition* was ordered to Saigon in French Cochin China to load teakwood timber for export. While there, we were never allowed a moment's respite from hard, bone-racking labor. It was midsummer, with long twilights at each end of the day, and the weather was terribly hot as well as very unhealthy. Yet we were turned to with lamps in the hold every morning and knocked off by lamplight every night. On the Sabbath, we were given special consideration. We did not begin work in the morning until daylight and we were permitted to quit at dusk. We were usually allowed half an hour for meals and ten minutes for our early coffee at four in the morning.

After the coal dirt from the previous cargo had been removed, we had to wash out the hold as clean as a housewife's kitchen floor. Then came the painful, excruciating job of dry holystoning the 'tween decks, a performance as unnecessary and useless as it was difficult and laborious. For two long, tedious weeks we were kept constantly at work on our knees with those damnable holystones and infernal "prayerbooks" until we were all practically cripples. It was the refinement of inquisitorial torture.

Then came the timber—great, massive, square-cut monoliths of solid teak. Thereafter, four men were told off every day to stow cargo below decks, and the remainder of the crew was kept at work aloft or anywhere else about the ship. The hold gang was changed every morning, so that, by turns, we all worked at the delicate operation of stowing timber under the gentle objurgations and persuasive caresses of Mister Prettyman and a big stick.

We lay off shore and, of course, the timber had to be lightered off to us. When the lower hold began to fill up so as to make it necessary to jam the top courses under the deck beams, we found it impossible for four men to stow the timber as fast as a horde of howling coolies could heave it through the side ports. Therefore, it was decided one morning at breakfast time to ask for more help

below. The hold gang for that day consisted of an old Irish sailor
named Paddy, the oldest man in the ship; a young Swede named
Lars; a Dane whom we had nicknamed "Dutchy"; and my special
chum, Edward Murray (†).*

No sooner had we bolted our frugal breakfast of lobscouse and
hardtack, washed it down with "patent marine coffee" sweetened
with "long lick," and got a hasty five minutes' session with our pipes,
than we heard our ever alert and energetic bos'n, Jack Bender,
roaring at the top of his stentorian voice: "Turn to, there, for'ard;
look alive there, now, you d—d loafers!"

Then, before the echo of the bos'n's summons had ceased to
reverberate among the spars, the second mate thrust his hideous
features through the forecastle and bellowed out: "Come on here,
now, you _____ _____ _____ _____s! Comin' out like men,
er yer want ter be dragged out like lazy dogs? Come, shake er up
now, er I'll come in there an' help some o' you lazy _____s over
ther stopwater!"

In response to these gentle admonitions, we all scrambled hastily
on deck to resume our appointed tasks. Mister Prettyman went
down the hatch, as usual, to bully the hold gang. It had been previously arranged among the timber Jacks and acceded to by Paddy
himself that he, being the oldest man in the group, should act as
spokesman for the rest in asking for extra help. Accordingly, as
soon as the second mate got below, Paddy, addressing him with all
possible civility, said: "Mister Purttyman, she's gittin' that full agin
th' bames now we can't shtow th' logs as fasht as the' divils o'
nagurs do be stevin' thim in, an' we nades a few more min down
here ter kape up wid 'em."

"More help ye want, is it, yer _____ _____ lazy old stiff; I'll
gie yer more help, plenty uv it!" And with these words, he struck
old Paddy a terrific blow between the eyes, knocking him prostrate.

---

* The dagger symbol (†), throughout the chapters, indicates that the persons
or ships whose names are so marked on their first occurrence have been positively identified by the editor and that the names are the actual ones. (*See also*
Editor's Preface, p. 15.) (Ed.)

But the old man, though hurt and dazed, was still game and as soon as he could regain his feet he bravely attempted to retaliate on his tormentor. It was then the real cowardly nature of the unprincipled brute became manifest; for, instead of trying to repel the old man's feeble attack in the natural way, which he could easily have done, he whipped out a murderous-looking dirk from his belt.

But the instant the second mate attempted to use the knife on old Paddy, Edward Murray, who stood directly behind him, struck him a powerful blow on the head with a slice bar and knocked him senseless. Then the four men, maddened beyond endurance by months of constant hazing and unmerited abuse, all leaped upon the prostrate form of the fallen bucko and beat him unmercifully. They only desisted when they believed him dead, and Murray told me afterward it was their united determination at the time to kill him. Had they suspected that there still remained a single vestige of the spark of life in his detestable carcass, they would never have left him until it had been stamped out.

The noise of the fracas, however, had attracted the ever vigilant attention of the fallen bully's buckos up on deck and they soon came swarming below, all armed to the teeth with shooting irons and various kinds of cutlery. The four men were soon secured and brought on deck. There they were quickly triced up to the forward boat skids by stout loops of tarred spun yarn tightly seized around their thumbs.

We had a Chinese cook named Me-Chow, one of the "whitest" men I ever knew. Shortly after the men had been strung up, Me-Chow, unable to bear their agonizing screams, ran out of the galley with a carving knife with the humane intention of cutting them down. But he was quickly frustrated in his Christian intentions by the alert third mate and bos'n who were mounting guard for the express purpose of preventing just such a plot on the part of any members of the crew. Divining his charitable purpose, the two ruffians quickly pounced upon the poor Chinaman, and in a jiffy the unfortunate Mongolian was strung up by his pigtail beside the four seamen he had tried to rescue.

And so the five unfortunate men were left hanging in the broiling sun with the tips of their toes barely touching the planks beneath them from nine in the forenoon until two in the afternoon. Their shrieks could be heard all over the harbor, but there was none to succor them. At frequent intervals, they became unconscious; then, they would be lowered until they revived, probably on the principle that an unconscious man is cheating his persecutors because he is insensible to pain; then, the moment they revived they would be promptly strung up to the gallows once more. Their prayers for mercy were as unavailing as their supplications for water.

While in a paroxysm of delirious anguish, Edward Murray began to call down all manner of insane curses upon Captain Gammon and his fiendish mates. Whereupon, the bos'n seized an oaken heaver from a gypsy winch and struck the poor, writhing wretch a terrible blow in the mouth, knocking out all his front teeth. Such was one phase of disciplinary punishment as practiced on some of our stately, ornate clippers in the palmy days of our glorious and incomparable merchant marine.

After this frightful spectacle had been enacted in the presence of all beholders in the harbor of Saigon, every precaution was taken to prevent any authentic tidings of it from getting ashore. No one was allowed to leave the ship under any pretext whatsoever. No sampans were allowed alongside except the official bumboat. Every evening Captain Gammon and his group of official ruffians would sit together for hours on the poop deck shooting at the "jolly-boat" sampans to keep them at a respectful distance from the vessel; and every night as soon as the crew had quit work we were all locked in the stifling superheated forecastle for the night lest any of us should try to escape.

It was the most terrible experience mortal men ever endured and survived. When we returned to Hong Kong a few weeks later, the tortured were still unable to resume work. Their hands and arms were still terribly swollen and discolored from the long-sustained compression of their thumbs while triced up, and the cook's scalp had been nearly torn from his pate by the long spell of suspension he had endured.

Yet none of them had received any medical relief or other attention from aft. At Hong Kong, as at Saigon, no one was allowed ashore. The only change in the previous regime was that we were no longer locked in the forecastle at night, for Hong Kong, as a British port, had laws governing maritime practices and protecting seamen which were more strictly observed there than in other parts of China.

While the ship lay in Hong Kong, young Staple's term of service expired and he demanded his money and discharge. But this request the weasel-faced skipper wrathfully refused to consider and told Staples that he might get paid off when the ship returned to the United States, if he ever lived to see it.

That night, Staples slacked himself quietly over the side and swam ashore. He hung around the waterfront until morning and then went to the American consul's office, reported his own situation, pressed his demand for wages and discharge, and told of the crucifixion at Saigon. The American consul at Hong Kong at that time was a Southerner, an ex-Confederate army officer notoriously unfavorable toward seamen, however meritorious their cause, but doubly so if they happened to be Northerners. He could not very well overlook Staples' claim to wages, but he could shirk his duty toward the injured seamen on the technical ground of lack of jurisdiction, and that is precisely what he did.

Later in the day, the skipper, after receiving a summons, arrived and talked with the consul for some time. When they came out they persuaded young Staples to take a sampan and go off to the ship for his pay, as, it was explained to him, this arrangement would be more convenient since the captain had all his money and papers locked up in his cabin on board.

In youthful innocence, Staples foolishly agreed to this plan, went off to the ship, packed up his bag, and waited for the captain's return. As soon as the Old Man came on board, he ordered Staples aft to receive his pay. Staples found the captain seated at the cabin table with a bag of money and the ship's papers before him.

The young fellow had ninety dollars in gold due him, and this the Old Man counted out in shining gold pieces with rare good will, as Staples thought. He then turned the shipping articles and a prepared receipt for ninety dollars toward the seaman and pointed out to him where to sign "clear" and sign "off." The moment Staples affixed his signature to both papers, Captain Gammon sprang up, covered the little pile of shiners with one hand, pressed a loaded revolver against the boy's head with the other, and yelled: "Now, you ———— ———— ———— ————, git out of my cabin an' jump over the side quicker'n greased lightnin'! I'll teach you, you ———— skunk, to sneak up to the consulate an' make complaints ag'in me and my ship." So the lad was chased up the companion way at the point of the captain's gun and driven ashore bareheaded and penniless.

"There ye are," sneered the skipper derisively, leaning over the taffrail and waving the articles exultantly at the poor hoodwinked sailor as the sampan shoved off for the beach, "there ye are; you've got yer pay fer makin' complaints, an' I've got yer receipt fer ther money. Now ye kin go ashore an' complain an' be damned. That's how I pay all my men. Me, ol' Cap'n Gammon. T'ell wi' yer."

The next day, the crucified men were taken ashore and given a mock hearing at the consulate. But, as already intimated, the case was officially set aside on the convenient point of maritime jurisdiction. All the afterguard, excluding the third mate who was left in charge of the ship, went as witnesses for the master, but not one of the crew was taken to testify for the aggrieved seamen.

As soon as the captain had made his statement to the effect that these four men had mutinied, made an unprovoked attack on the second mate with intent to murder him, and had afterward run amuck in an effort to induce the entire crew to mutiny and take charge of the ship, the consul formally and finally dismissed the complaint against the captain and officers and ordered the four injured seamen back to the ship without even hearing a word of their testimony in rebuttal. When the poor fellows revealed their still helpless and distorted hands, and when Edward Murray pointed to his battered mouth and broken teeth and mumbled an almost unintelligible plea for justice, the only reply he received from the "dignified" United States representative was: "Tut! Tut! Say another word and I'll give you six months' shot drill! Go back to your ship and do your duty like men, and the captain may feel disposed to forgive you. I've no jurisdiction in this matter. If I had I'd send you all up for mutiny and attempted piracy."

As a matter of fact and of justice, and in accordance with the established and accepted principles of admiralty law the world over, he did have jurisdiction, for the men had been arbitrarily denied the right of recourse or appeal either to the local consul or to port authorities at Saigon. This was a fair sample of consular justice as meted out to American seamen in the early 1880's.

## 4 · BETRAYED!

I had been on the *Inquisition* for nearly four months, and I had long been heartsick, sore, and sorry for my foolish venture at Kobe. I heartily wished myself back in the old *Redwood* or even in that round-bellied, slab-sided, old blubber hunter which I had left at Honolulu. I was, therefore, secretly determined to seize the first opportunity to desert at whatever cost, hazard, or even loss.

I still had my cherished money belt securely strapped around my waist, a fact which no one on board ever suspected because I had prudently kept its existence a profound secret, so I was not concerned about "signing off" without my pay.

After the affair at the consul's office, we were granted a little more freedom and treated with a little more leniency by the afterguard. This was simply a matter of policy, of course, on the skipper's part, but we accepted it for what it was worth and made the most of it.

One fine morning, just after breakfast, we were all astounded by the sudden announcement that the port watch was ordered aft to receive liberty money and go ashore for the day. We naturally thought that such welcome news was a hoax, but started aft with palpitating hearts to investigate.

But sure enough, there stood the Old Man at the coach-house

door where he doled out five Mexican dollars to each of us, telling us to go ashore and be good and be sure to return on board before turn-to time next morning. He also added that we should have free sampan fare both ways if we were on time.

Then, with the generous, forgiving dispositions of deepwater sailors, we promptly forgot all our recent sufferings and sorrows and tribulations in our exuberant, overwhelming gratitude for one day's respite from our hardship and toil. So, we left the ship's side as lighthearted and jubilant as schoolboys released for recess, with three ringing cheers for the *Inquisition* as though she had been a prince consort to the famous missionary ship *Morning Star*.

The little diversions we enjoyed that day are not a part of this story, but one incident of my own experience is significant in view of what followed after. In Typhooshang, in Hong Kong, I met a quartermaster from an English steamer lying at one of the docks in front of the city. During our conversation, I told him of what had occurred on board the *Inquisition* and of my present anxiety to leave her.

There is a feeling of tacit freemasonry among deepwater sailors which always bids them help each other in distress and which does not take race, nationality, or color into account. The young Englishman fully understood my plight and volunteered to assist me or any of my shipmates who could reach his steamer after midnight or any time during her stay in port. As he always went on watch at midnight, he said he would try to find means of stowing us away until sailing time; after that there would be nothing to fear. On that particular night, he explained, he would not be on duty as he was ashore on twenty-four hours' leave. The steamer's name, he told me, was the *Sandon,* of Sunderland; like our own ship, she was chartered for a term of years on the coast, and she was scheduled to lay at Hong Kong three days longer. We parted late that evening with many expressions of friendship, and I went directly on board my own ship and turned in.

Next morning, all our boys showed up punctually at turn-to time with the exception of one or two laggards who were brought out later in the police boat and charged three dollars apiece for their ride. That day, the starboard watch went ashore and all went smoothly.

The idea of deserting grew upon me with the passing hours, and the more I thought about it the more determined I became to chance it. Of course, I could slip over the side unobserved in the darkness and swim ashore, but where would I hide? The captain would undoubtedly offer a reward for my apprehension and return. For this reason, I also considered it unwise to swim to the *Sandon* and take my friendly quartermaster at his word to stow me away, for once the hue and cry was raised every policeman and coolie in Hong Kong would be alert for my recapture and every ship in port would be thoroughly searched.

Moreover, I had a splendid outfit of clothes, the result of eight years of hard gathering and worth at least one hundred American dollars, which I hated to leave behind. A sailor without dunnage in a foreign port is in a hopeless position.

But I had long since decided that the *Inquisition* was no place for me. I felt sure that the sudden show of kindness exhibited toward us by Captain Gammon was only the merest pretense, a temporary truce which would be ended as soon as we left Hong Kong and got out of earshot of the port authorities.

The more I became possessed with the idea of desertion, the more determined I was to act. According to the universal custom in Far Eastern ports, Captain Gammon assigned a bumboat to the ship to supply us with such articles as we needed or wanted, such as clothes, small stores, tobacco, and food, rather than give us the opportunity to buy where we pleased. The bumboat man, of course, took full advantage of his situation and charged the sailors three prices for his third-rate wares. He then paid the captain 50 per cent commission for the privilege of robbing the crew.

Our bumboat man was an oily-mouthed, smooth-eyed, two-faced Mongolian whom everybody detested but with whom we were obliged to deal. He was known among the sailors frequenting the port by the somewhat opprobrious cognomen of "Cumshaw," which is pidgin English for "commission." Like all of his type, he was artful and cunning, utterly unscrupulous, cruel, treacherous, and as avaricious as old Shylock himself.

When Cumshaw came on board that particular morning, I invested much more liberally in his wares than usual and craftily induced some of my unsuspecting shipmates to do the same. Cumshaw was so highly pleased with my unwonted interest in his behalf that he gave me a fine camphorwood box and a couple of small curios by way of "baksheesh."

Having thus gotten into the good graces of the crafty Cumshaw, I coaxed him aside and offered him ten Mexican dollars to scull me ashore with my belongings after midnight that night. I took pains to exhibit the money as an evidence of good faith, and I could tell by the greedy twinkle of his wicked little almond eyes that it was a bargain. He simply could not resist the sight of money; it really was his god and high joss.

So it was agreed between us that he should come after me that night at two o'clock and take me ashore. With this understanding, we parted. Cumshaw sculled ashore, and I went about my day's work as usual with a head and a heart full of plans for the impending adventure.

Punctual to the minute, Cumshaw sculled his sampan silently beneath our bows while I sat on the knightheads with my bag ready packed and slung to the end of the jib downhaul ready for immediate departure. I was soon in the boat, dun and dunnage, and we sculled away into the darkness propelled by the long, half-rotary sweeps of the Chinaman's powerful oar.

Cumshaw sculled directly up to a deserted jetty fronting the native settlement on the extreme outskirts of the coolie quarter. Making his sampan fast, he shouldered my heavy bag and piloted me through a mystic maze of narrow, crooked, dark, and filthy streets until he came to a small but neat native house with two quaint but hideous-looking wooden images standing guard in the doorway. The diabolical grimaces which distorted their graven features were accentuated and rendered more intensely repulsive by a shaft of subdued light which fell athwart them through the glazed paper window.

Here Cumshaw dropped my bag and gave a low call. The door was promptly opened by an aged Chinese woman, and we walked in. We were evidently expected, for the woman seemed in nowise surprised by our sudden intrusion at such an unearthly hour. The ground floor of the house appeared to be divided into two rooms separated by sliding partitions. Overhead was a loft which was reached by a ladder extending from the floor below to a scuttle in the floor of the tiny attic above.

The interior of the house was perfectly neat and clean. It showed consistent attention, thrift, and simple good taste. The furniture was a sort of compromise between European and Chinese designs evidently intended to suit all comers. For instance, there were European tables and chairs for the accommodation of white, and low tables and squat mats for the convenience of native guests. There were, likewise, common plates and cups and saucers and knives and forks for the use of white people, and chopsticks and chow bowls for native service. A Yankee clock, made in Connecticut, ornamented a small shelf in one corner of the room, and a large American lamp with an enameled bowl stood upon an ordinary drop-leaf table and shed a brilliant light over the whole scene by the illuminating properties of Standard Oil. The walls were decorated in the usual Chinese fashion with painted paper flowers, fans, birds, and dragons, and further ornamented with hand-painted pictures of the familiar Chinese conception.

On the whole, the house was quite comfortable and attractive, and to my way-weary, homesick eyes it appeared like a haven of refuge and heavenly relief from the abominable surroundings on board the *Inquisition*.

After a brief conversation with the old woman who had admitted us, the exact import of which I could not, of course, understand, Cumshaw turned to me and said, pointing to the old crone by way of introduction, "Dis my ol' mama; him velly good ooman; muchee likee sailorman; s'pose you pay two dollar, t'ree dollar, you stop two day, t'ree day; plenty eatee, plenty sleepee, mama givee plentee chow—velly good chow. By'm'by, mornin' time, my sister comee; my sister velly smart gallee, go Clistian skulee, speakee plentee Inglese, you by'm'by makee plenty chin-chin. By'm'by you s'ip go 'way, me come tellee you, you takee 'nother s'ip homeside. Savvy?"

I savvied and paid Cumshaw the promised ten dollars and gave "old mama" three dollars more for chow; then Cumshaw departed and I retired to rest on a comfortable bamboo couch in the cock-loft.

Next morning, "old mama" called me to breakfast, and when I descended to the ground floor I met a young Chinese girl who might have been anywhere from ten to thirteen years old. She was seated demurely on a bamboo settee, but rose timidly to greet me as I came down the ladder. This was the alleged sister Cumshaw had referred to the night before. "Old mama" brought me clean water in an earthen basin, a ball of soap, and a large towel. After a refreshing splurge in the basin and a brisk session with the towel, I sat down to breakfast, an enjoyable repast at which "old mama" and the girl modestly declined to join me. It consisted of rice, prepared as only an Oriental can boil it, with every grain an individual tempting factor of the meal; small fishes deliciously cooked in oil, fresh duck eggs, water cress, vegetables, fresh wheat bread, and fragrant tea. After breakfast, "old mama" presented me with a package of cigarros and I proceeded to smoke and while away the time in an effort to draw the little girl out and induce her to talk about herself. She was very timid and shy at first, but by degrees her reserve melted, so that at the end of an hour or so we were on the most familiar and sociable terms.

She spoke excellent English with a very pretty accent and seemed to be in all respects entirely natural and childish. She said she had attended one of the mission schools almost from infancy, and that she was anxious to learn to teach. She also told me that she was not Cumshaw's sister (I had suspected as much), but his cousin, and that "old mama" was her grandmother and Cumshaw's aunt, not his mother as he had intimated.

It was rather irksome sitting in the house all day with nothing to do, and I was hopeful that Cumshaw would drop in in the evening and bring me some tidings of the ship. I dared not go out for fear of being observed, for information travels fast among the Mongolians, especially when you don't want it to.

After dinner, the little girl returned to her school duties and left me more lonesome than ever, for "old mama" could neither utter nor understand a syllable of English. After a hearty supper, I got a book out of my bag and sat down to read until ten o'clock. Then I went aloft and turned in and was soon fast asleep.

I had not slept long, however, when I was suddenly awakened by the bright glare of a bull's-eye lantern shining full in my face, a rough hand shaking me by the shoulder, and a loud voice commanding me in good, vigorous Anglo-Saxon to "get up and dress."

I started up in bed and my astonished gaze fell upon two uniformed British police and Cumshaw's cunning snakelike eyes peering at me sardonically from the background. Then the whole situation dawned upon me like a flash. Cumshaw had betrayed me! I was under arrest and would be sentenced without trial to three years in purgatory on board the *Inquisition!* I got out of bed mechanically and began slowly and absentmindedly to dress.

"What is the meaning of this, officer?" I asked as though I didn't know.

"Hit means that you are under arrest," replied one of them, drawing a Queen's warrant about a fathom long from his breast pocket, "on a charge of desertion from the American ship *Inquisition,* and we are under orders to deliver you back to that ship and its master. Do you want to hear the warrant read?"

"Yes," I replied, "you might as well do everything in regular order." I was not at all anxious to hear the warrant, but I wanted to gain time to collect my thoughts. So I let him wade through the long rigmarole of legalistic terms while in the meantime I fumbled nervously into my clothes. As soon as the officer had concluded the perusal of the warrant, I announced myself ready to go. While he was replacing the document in his breast pocket and buttoning up his coat, I asked how they came to know where I was.

"Why," said the officer, "as soon as you were missed the captain posted a reward of twenty dollars in gold with the Hamerican consul for your happrehension, and this Chink 'ere," indicating Cumshaw, "went up and hinformed on you to claim the reward; not hoften these beggars see twenty dollars in gold, you know."

"Ow came you to leave the ship?" asked the other officer, who until now had remained silent.

"Because she was a floating hell," I answered, "like too many of our American and Nova Scotia blood packets." Then I mentioned briefly some of the horrors which had occurred on board and how poor Staples had been paid off at Hong Kong.

"Hits a bloody houtrage," said the first officer feelingly, "an' h'I don't min' tellin' you, pore chap, as we don't 'arf like this yere job; but duty is duty, you know, an' we must hobey horders."

"I understand your position in the matter perfectly," I said, "and I sincerely thank you for your sympathy; so I'll go aboard with you without protest and face whatever is coming to me. I suppose you want to shackle me," I added, extending my hands toward them in token of humility.

"Naw!" exclaimed one officer disdainfully. "We ain't got no darbies with us and h'I wouldn't put 'em on you if we 'ad. You don't look like a troublesome chap an' you're a good lad, any'ow."

We descended the ladder and went out into the night. A drizzling rain was falling, a sort of "Scotch mist"; there was not a breath of wind. I walked silently along between the two policemen, Cumshaw preceding us with my bag on his shoulder through the maze of narrow streets leading by devious routes toward the quay.

Cumshaw's sampan was moored to the same little jetty where I had landed the previous night. The surface of the water was as placid as a millpond and the night was as dark as night ever was.

Without a word of ceremony, we entered the sampan and cast off. My bag was placed in the bows, the two officers seated themselves together in the stern sheets, while I took my place on a

Hong Kong, China, as it looked in the 1880's, when Williams visited that port. From a contemporary painting apparently by a Chinese artist. (*Official U.S. Navy Photo from Naval Historical Division*)

The schooner *Augustus Hunt*, in which Williams sailed on a brief coastal trip from November, 1888, to January, 1889, just before signing on the *Main*. (*Society for the Preservation of New England Antiquities*)

thwart just in front of them. Cumshaw took his position just forward of me, shipped his long, curved, and jointed sculling oar on the little knob which held it to the gunwale and gave way with long, regular sweeps back and forth in the ancient but efficient Chinese style.

So we started upstream against a swift ebb tide, our way illumined only by the faint glow from the little colza oil lamp burning dimly on our stem. Such a tumult of passionate thoughts as assailed my mind as I sat in that swaying sampan I have never experienced before or since. I knew that to return to the ship meant three years of brutal slavery under the most barbarous taskmasters that ever wielded a lash. I would be constantly subjected to every degree of humiliating drudgery, torture, abuse, and inquisitive punishment that devilish ingenuity could devise. There would be no chance of redress and no prospect of pay at the end. I well knew the character of the men with whom I should have to deal and that for three years to come I would be entirely at their fiendish mercy without hope of succor, escape, or relief. I would be triced up, shackled down, kicked, cuffed, beaten, maimed, starved, or killed according to the whim of Captain Gammon and his horde of "buckos." At every port we touched, I would be chained to a ring-bolt or locked down in the lazarette to prevent me from escaping.

This was my future if I returned on board. From what I knew of American ships in general and the *Inquisition* in particular, I felt that my mental picture did not exaggerate my probable fate. These thoughts in conjunction with my helpless, hopeless position in the sampan almost maddened me, and I began to cast about wildly for some means of escape. To leap overboard and try to get away by swimming would be useless; to attack the two big, well-armed policemen would be equally futile and even more foolhardy.

At length, as we wended our way through the assembled merchant fleet riding lazily at anchor, I could discern the outlines of the *Inquisition* swinging idly at her cables. I could tell her even in the almost impenetrable darkness, partly by her position, but mainly by long familiarity with her long, low, sneaking hull, the

graceful outline of her bows, and the exact rake and slender, tapering symmetry of her lofty spars, so different from those of other
ships in the harbor.

Yes, I saw her, a black, infernal specter silhouetted against the
night, and the sight aroused me to desperation and awakened
within me the determination of despair.

Then my gaze rested for a moment on the dim figure of the Chinese traitor laboring strongly at his oar, as unconcerned about my
future as though I had been a mad dog.

And then my blood boiled with ungovernable rage and consuming hatred toward this man who had betrayed me, who would sell
me into slavery for money earned with the wringing of my own
heart's blood. Then as I surveyed the swaying figure at the oar, a
desperate resolve entered my brain and took possession of my whole
being. "If I could get rid of him and that infernal oar," I thought,
"I might have one chance."

Lying across the thwarts in the sampan was a short length of a
small English oar with the blade sawed off. It was five feet of
oaken shaft, a most convenient and effective bludgeon. I had noticed it several times in the sampan before I left the ship but had
never been interested enough then to ask Cumshaw where he got
it. I presume, however, that he had salvaged it from the flotsam
and jetsam adrift in the bay.

This oar shaft was now within easy reach, and I clutched one
end of it firmly with my left hand. Then, for a brief interval, having
made sure of my weapon, I watched the dim figure swaying back
and forth in the murky darkness with his long queue moving with
pendulum-like regularity with each stroke.

Behind me, I could hear the two officers conversing in low tones,
apparently satisfied that their task was to be an easy one and that
it was about over. I realized that any chance of possible success
must be dependent upon my own quickness of action and sureness
of aim, but I was young, strong, and nimble, as well as desperate,
and, therefore, ready to take a chance.

So, watching my opportunity, just as Cumshaw started on an outward stroke, I suddenly arose and struck him with crushing force on the back of the head with that oar shaft. He fairly flew over the edge of the sampan, taking the sculling oar with him in a blind, deathlike clutch.* Then, before the astonished officers could interfere, I jumped quickly over the other side and swam down.

The sampan, caught in the surge of a powerful current, was swept rapidly downstream, and since the officers had nothing with which to propel or control their clumsy craft they were entirely at the mercy of the elements. As for me, I swam under water as long as possible to make a good offing from the sampan. When I came up to blow, I could hear the officers shouting and shooting blindly into the darkness.

As soon as I arose to the surface, I made a tangent for the shore. I could tell the direction by the thousands of lights gleaming thickly along the waterfront and more thinly scattered up the slopes of the great hills overlooking the city.

As I swam toward the shore, I could hear the shouting and the shooting of the forsaken officers growing fainter and fainter as they drifted rapidly downstream. My only fear now was that the racket they made might alarm some of the harbor police and that I might be pursued and recaptured.

In order to accelerate my own movements in contending with the strong current, I stripped off and jettisoned all my clothing, retaining only the cherished money belt around my waist. Farther inshore, the tide rift slackened and I was able to strike out with long sweeping strokes direct for the port. As soon as I got near enough to the quays to locate the *Sandon,* I swam directly down to her and climbed up her gangway dripping like a half-drowned rat.

* Williams remained convinced that he had killed Cumshaw. When his account of his experiences was accepted for publication in *The Independent* in 1908, he requested that the article appear anonymously. The editors, however, convinced him that the statute of limitations applied and that he could no longer be prosecuted for murder.—Editor's Preface, "Betrayed," *The Independent,* LXV (August 20, 1908), 407. (Ed.)

As I had surmised, it was past midnight and my friendly quartermaster was on watch.

"Good God, mate!" he exclaimed, as I stood glistening in my naked skin in the glare of the gangway lantern. "Is that you? 'Ow in 'ell did yer get hoff 'er?"

I briefly related my night's experiences.

"Come down for'ard, lad," he said, "but be quiet. We'll gi' you a passage down to the Straits, an' you'll be clear o' the blame Yankee 'ell 'ook."

Fifteen minutes later, I was clad in a dry suit of clothes, supplied with food, a pipe, and tobacco. I then turned into a good, comfortable bunk and enjoyed a sound and dreamless sleep.

Next morning, the *Sandon* cast off her shore-fasts and steamed out of Hong Kong en route to Singapore, 1,450 miles farther down the coast. I had escaped from the *Inquisition!*

## 5 · FOR THE WANT OF A BECKET

*For the want of a seizing the becket was lost,*
*For the want of a becket the sailor was lost,*
*For the want of a sailor the canvas was lost,*
*For the want of the canvas the rigging was lost,*
*And the ship to her beams was in jeopardy tossed,*
*'Twas all for the want of a fathom of yarn.*

Crouching low and huddling close beneath the tattered bamboo
hood that canopied the midship section of the bumboat, we first
glimpsed the towering spars and majestic proportions of the *Late
Commander* riding idly astream in the gradually diminishing distance, while Sam Doss, our turbaned dinghy wallah, ferried us
skillfully across the surging current of the turbulent Hooghly River.

There were four of us in the bunch, Big Mac, Little Mac, Spike
Riley, and myself. We were the only Yankee sailors on the beach
and had been sent down from Calcutta to complete the complement of the *Late Commander*. I had met up with my three companions at the Sailors' Home in Calcutta where I had gone after
being discharged from the American windjammer *Maine*, which I
had shipped on from Singapore.

From the narrow vantage of our crowded and cramped position

beneath the flimsy hood, we commanded a fine view of the lofty windjammer tugging stolidly at her anchor cable, and we could form an estimate of her size, rig, carrying capacity, and sailing powers. The ship was lying well over toward the left bank of the river, and she loomed large against the verdant scenery of the distant landscape.

She was a large, stately, composite British East Indiaman with wooden hull and iron topsides, and had evidently been built during the transition period when iron was gradually displacing wood in marine construction but had not yet been finally adopted by naval architects as a safe building material for sailing ships.

She was a vessel of rising 2,500 tons register and about 5,000 tons burden. She was broad in the beam, full in the bilge, and bluff in the bows. She was evidently built for carrying rather than racing; but the lofty poise of her sturdy masts and the enormous sweep of her towering yards gave token of great sailing power in strong winds and the ability to carry sail in heavy weather. Her lower masts and yards were of steel and her upper or topgallant masts and lighter spars of pitch pine. She had an unusually sharp tumble home to her waists, which gave her somewhat the appearance of an old-time frigate, an illusion which was highly accentuated from a distance by the two rows of grim-looking false ports painted along her sides.

The high-flung fiddlehead beneath her big bowsprit was decorated with the carved figure of a hardened old admiral of doubtful identity, clad in full-dress wooden uniform and grasping a wooden sword with a scowl of graven ferocity.

Such was our first impression of the towering Indiaman riding majestically at anchor and loaded to her Plimsolls with baled jute and bagged linseed consigned to New York.

When the dinghy rounded handsomely alongside, we all sprang nimbly to the grating and made a Yankee hustle up the gangway. At the head of the ladder, we were met by the chief mate, Mister Riggins, who greeted us with that air of gruff civility so peculiar to English deepwater mates of the old school.

"Welcome aboard, me lads!" he exclaimed heartily. "Glad to see you're so spry. Nimble men is what we want here. Go forrard now an' get yoursel's stowed an' stand by; we bend sails tomorrow."

The first order of business next morning after we had disposed of our early refreshment of bootleg and hardtack, was the bending of the sails. We opened the sail lockers and at once proceeded to break out their carefully stowed contents and distribute the well-saved canvas along the decks ready for bending on and hauling up.

Our crew consisted of twenty-two A.B.'s (Able Bodies) and six ordinary seamen together with three mates, four apprentices, and a full list of petty officers. Quite a heavy crew for a modern merchantman, to be sure, but not a man too many, for the *Late Commander,* besides being a very heavily sparred ship, was fitted alow and aloft with old-fashioned dummy blocks and ancient deck appliances.

Before noon, we had all the square sails aloft and festooned along the yardarms. The remainder of the day we spent in hauling out, shackling up, bending on, and reeving off running gear. Spike Riley and I were working together on the main topgallant yardarm assisted by Barney Dent, a superannuated old barnacle who constantly insisted that he was "on'y knockin' 'round ter save fun'ral expenses," but who, nevertheless, clung to everything tangible aloft with a grim resolve that rather belied his oft repeated notions of postmortem economy.

"Be there never a becket no'eres in this ship, mates?" demanded Spike Riley, who with careless freedom was riding astride the yardarm mousing a clip hook.

"Damn th' wan I seen," spluttered old Barney as he promptly ejected a torrent of tobacco juice forward of the yard, regardless of consequences to people or things below. "Damn th' wan I seen, an' I'm three years in the ship. There do be a few loops o' junk on some o' th' jackstays, but God save th' man wot grabs wan uv 'em on a dark night an' it blowin'; he might as well be grabbin' a rope o' sand."

"They ought ter be beckets on these 'ere yards," said Spike soberly, "'cause th' heads o' ther sails bend up so close ter th' jack-stays they ain't no room fer a han' holt, an' if a feller gits tossed onct he's gone."

"They ought ter be lots o' things wot ain't an' lots more wot never wuz an' ain't goin' ter be," said old Barney resignedly. "It's both han's fer th' ship 'ere, an' 'ang on by yer bloomin' eyebrows."

By knock-off time that night, all our sails were bent and neatly furled. Our ship was snug and trim and all ready for sea. After mess, all hands gathered under the forecastle awning and a lengthy discussion ensued on the subject of beckets, manropes, and life-saving gear generally. The deplorable neglect of shipowners to provide such necessary attachments, and the reckless hazard to life and limb to which seamen were being constantly exposed was severely criticized and bitterly denounced, but since no one had any practical remedy it seemed to be a simple case of "bell the cat." So we all turned in none the better or safer for our evening growl.

Bright and early next morning the big paddle wheel Hooghly tug *Warren Hastings* came hooting and thrashing alongside prepared to tow us to sea. We soon had our pilot with his retinue of *kulashi* servants on board, and as soon as the springs of our towing cables had been fully secured the big tub swept on ahead, upstream, and held the ship against the powerful current while we shipped our heavy capstan bars and proceeded to heave up the anchor.

Then to the heavy trundle of our mighty windlass and the merry rattle of the capstan pawls, we trudged and tramped sturdily in unison around the forecastle deck raising chantey after chantey while the mystified natives lined the wooded shore in crowds and listened in silent wonder as we fetched our anchor home.

When our mud-hook had been broken out, we ceased our labors at the clanking windlass, unshipped our capstan bars, and raised the joyful signal "Anchor's Away," for were we not homeward bound? Then the *Hastings* took up the long sweep of both her hawsers, turned our ship's head downstream, and started us for the open sea.

All that day we swept along the muddy current through the tortuous windings of the Hooghly—over the treacherous quicksands at the James and Mary's, across Diamond Harbor, and past the verdant shores of Sager Island. The sun was still mastheads high when we emerged safely through the low reaches of Sand Heads into the broad blue sweep of Bengal Bay.

There the *Hastings* dropped her hawsers, screeched a parting salute on her strident siren, and scurried back to the river mouth. We, with all sail set, stood gallantly away on our westward course.

For the first three days of the voyage, we encountered light baffling winds and did not average over one hundred miles a day. On the fourth day there fell a tense and awful calm. A deep and awesome silence more terrible than the wildest tempest reigned over sea and sky. The terrific heat of the blazing sun seemed doubly concentrated upon our narrow decks. Molten pitch bubbled from the seams and spread over the whitened planking until it resembled the murky floor of a cane press. Tar streamed from our well-set rigging and trickled lazily over the deadeyes. The paint blistered on the waterways, and the sails hung against the masts in wrinkled folds as limp and motionless as the rigid drapings around a bronze statue. Not the slightest sign of atmospheric movement was discernible. A feather dropped from aloft fell straightway to the deck with no more flutter than an iron bolt. The crew sought in vain for shelter from the penetrating heat; the fowls died in their coops; the ship lay in a dense and absolute slick, and all nature seemed gasping for breath.

Indeed, it was an experience to remind us all of the woeful lay of the Ancient Mariner and cause us to ask ourselves and each other with solemn intent, "Who is the Jonah among us?"

Toward evening, however, while the sea and sky were still aflame with the brilliant colors and fascinating hues which combine to make up the enchanting aurora of an Indian sunset, a grateful little breeze wafted over the ship, slightly rustling the listless sails and gently rippling the glassy surface of the sapphire sea like the subdued breath of whispering mermaids.

But shortly after sundown, a low range of black and ugly-looking thunderheads suddenly appeared above the western horizon. They spread with amazing speed and cast an ominous gloom across the glowing sky. Then we knew that one of those appalling bay squalls known as a "Bengal Tiger" was about to envelop us and we prepared to meet it.

These bay squalls are the terror of all Bengal sailors. Rising suddenly after prolonged seasons of blighting heat, they always begin after nightfall and blow with hurricane violence and destructive force. They are invariably accompanied by the appalling phenomenon of terrifying electric displays. Blinding lightning, terrific thunder, torrential rain, and intense darkness are the natural concomitants of a sunset squall in Bengal Bay.

Early in the evening, we furled our royals and skysails and hauled down our lighter staysails. Later, as the tempest loomed larger and blacker and more threatening, we shortened down to a full-set main-topgallant sail and stood by for orders.

It was about ten o'clock when the squall struck us just abeam. The great ship heeled over bodily with rails awash, and fled before it like a frightened gull. In ten minutes, our big main-topgallant sail had been clewed up and hung floundering wildly in the buntlines. While eight men were sent up to furl it, the remainder of the crew were kept on deck with orders to stand by the lower tacks and sheets and see the topsail halyards clear.

At the lofty altitude of the topgallant yard, we stood in the center of a wild and awesome grandeur which inspired us with mingled feelings of fear and admiration. The shrieking wind, the complaining spars, the floundering canvas, the intermittently flaming sky, the pitch-black darkness, the crashing thunder, the phosphorescent crests of the breaking seas, and the fiery streak of the brilliant wake of the ship were enough to inspire the densest mortal with an inward sense of divine magnificence and his own insignificance.

Laying out on the yardarms and striving to shield our faces from the lashing of the blinding rain, we cleared our gaskets and strove to create a wrinkle in the inflated belly of the stiffened sail ballooning over the yardarms. At length, in a momentary lull, the sail relaxed slightly for an instant. Seizing this opportunity, we drove our fingers into the fluttering cloth and with loud yells of encouragement to each other sought to drag it up to the yard. Big Mac and I stood in the bunt, one on either side of the mast, struggling with the refractory canvas. As for the others, I could not tell how they were dispersed along the yardarms, for the vivid flashes of lightning were blinding, and in the mad uproar of the mighty tempest the sound of our voices was indistinguishable.

Finally, when we had almost succeeded in smothering the big sail and all were eagerly striving together on the footrope for a homeward-bound roll, there came a sudden blast of renewed intensity. Although each man clung to the sail with every atom of his power, the canvas was torn from our grasp. Again, the great sail ballooned upward, threshing and roaring madly against the mast above our heads with a force that threatened to bring the rigging down.

Then it was that I suddenly felt an ominous slackening of the footrope and became conscious of a vacant place beside me on the yardarm. By the light of the next flash of lightning, I glimpsed a human shape hurtling through midair fifty yards from the ship, and by the next flash I saw the climbing crest of an onrushing sea break mercifully over an upturned face and a fugitive cap careen wildly away to leeward. Then I knew that old Barney Dent had saved his funeral expenses. He had gone to eternity for the want of a becket!

Next morning, the storm had passed. The sun rose clear and serene, and with all sail set again the ship was slanting gallantly down the bay under the freshening impulse of a brisk westerly breeze. When the starboard watch came below to breakfast, the spare bunk in the forecastle and the vacant place at the mess board were silent reminders of the tragedy of the previous night.

Naturally we were depressed by the loss of our old shipmate, for old "Daddy," as he was always affectionately called by the younger members of the crew, had been very popular. His death filled our hearts with sorrow and inspired us with angry resentment against the miserly, hair-splitting cupidity of our owners which we believed to have been responsible for his death.

"It's jest plain murder, that's wot it is," growled Spike Riley as he prepared to turn in. "Ther greedy vampires 'll risk a sailor's life any time ter save a fathom o' rope. 'Tain't no use pratin' to us 'bout economy. This 'ere ship is seventeen years old and ther firm's built a dozen better ones sence that out o' ther proceeds uv her freights. They keep right on everlastin'ly a-paintin' her bends, an' scrapin' her spars, an' gildin' her trucks, an' varnishin' her poop, but there's never time nor tackle to put on a few hol'fasts aloft! I know ther law can't tech 'em," concluded Spike gloomily; "ther law's a liar mostwise enyhow, but if ther devil don't get 'em in ther long run, then I'd like ter know what in 'ell ther devil's good for!"

"Say, fellers," cautioned Little Mac as the watch proceeded to retire, "don't trust that ol' manrope on ther jib boom. Ther lashin's plumb rotten, jest a frayed-out ol' piece o' junk smeared over with tar. I axed ther bos'n fer a piece o' new stuff ter set it up with the day we rigged ther boom, but he called me down fer it; said I was d—d pertic'lar an' skeery. He 'lowed thet thet thar lashin' had b'en thar five years an' never parted. But you bet I don't trust it. I b'en to sea twenty years, an' I know when ther life's stretched outun a piece o' hemp."

Going down the bright sou'west monsoons across the broad sweep of the warm Indian Ocean, we found time to become better acquainted with each other and to indulge in the few pastimes which a tall-water voyage affords.

Our skipper's name was Grummitt, a hard-visaged, crusty old tyrant as grim and silent as a graven image. His chief executive, Mister Riggins, was a large masterful man of middle age, a thoroughly practical seaman as well as a skillful navigator. He esteemed his two subordinate mates but little because they were both training-ship graduates. Our bos'n, Tom Splicer, was a leather-lunged old veteran with a voice like a human calliope. His mate, Jack

Fidd, was a remarkable combination of legs, lungs, and sea boots.

Among the four apprentices was a young gentleman named Alfred Pengelley with whom I soon formed a strong and lasting friendship. Pengelley was a native of Cornwall and his father was a lieutenant in the Royal Navy. He was a well-bred, well-read, manly fellow about twenty years of age. In spite of the fact that he was entirely unsuited by nature for a seafaring life and was out of place on shipboard, he was the idol and admiration of the whole crew.

Although in point of birth, breeding, and culture Pengelley belonged to a higher social grade in longshore estimation than the rest of us, he never allowed this presumed superiority to be felt. A civil, well-mannered fellow, he always carried himself with an air of quiet dignity and natural courtesy. He was a large handsome boy with frank intelligent eyes and glossy chestnut hair.

Often in the last dogwatch, from six to eight in the evening when our day's work was done and all hands gathered on the forward deck, he would slip forward to witness our impromptu sports. He always enjoyed our games and contests of strength or agility—boxing, racing, wrestling, jumping, or climbing—but he never participated in the games himself.

Pengelley's great drawing card among the crew was his collection of songs. He possessed a magnificent baritone voice and his repertoire of patriotic, naval, and sentimental songs seemed almost endless. He never needed to be urged to sing, for he seemed to consider it his own legitimate contribution to our evening entertainment.

Thus we sang and danced and played the fine weather away, for time passes swiftly at sea. We finally ran out of the pleasant monsoon zones and began to encounter the bleak southerly winds of the approaching Cape. We were greeted by moderate weather and homeward winds directly off the Cape of Good Hope, but the same night we were overtaken by a strong southeast gale. Before midnight our ship was staggering blindly away to the northwest under three topgallant sails with her cro'jack furled and fore and main courses hauled up in their gear. The storm increased in violence during the night, bringing a rapidly rising sea, and in the middle watch all hands were called out to snug her down.

As soon as both watches had mustered on deck, the fore- and mizzen-topgallant sails were clewed up and the flying jib hauled down. When Tom Splicer's stentorian voice was heard bellowing above the storm, "Tie 'em up," I happened to be near the lee fore-rigging; so I mounted the forecastle head and started for the jib boom. Just as I was crossing the knightheads, I saw two figures out on the bowsprit ahead of me. In the darkness, I could not distinguish them but I followed them out.

By the time I reached the head of the bowsprit, my two predecessors were already out on the jib boom footrope waiting for me to help get in the clew of the wildly threshing jib. Just then, a tremendous sea broke completely over the ship and her great bows were flung high in the air until her very forefoot entirely left the water. Then as the sea receded from beneath her, she fell bodily forward, driving boom, bowsprit, forecastle deck, and all completely under water so that she stood for a time practically head downward and stern in air.

Realizing from the first what was about to happen, I locked both arms around the collar of the forestay and clung for dear life. At the same instant, Little Mac's warning about the rotten bolt lashing on the manrope flashed through my mind and I tried to shout a warning to my shipmates out on the boom. But my voice was stifled in the mighty tempest and the next instant I was plunged bodily beneath the brine. Down, down, down I went, clinging desperately to the stay and holding my breath. In the downward wash of the great ship, my feet were swept from the footrope and my body was flung outward at right angles to the bowsprit like a pennant in a morning breeze. It seemed as if my arms would be torn from their sockets. My big sou'wester came off and the chin strap clung round my neck. Although I was holding my breath, I could still feel that the pressure of the water inside the helmet was strangling me. Yet

I inwardly cursed when the strap broke and my valued sou'wester was swept away.

At length the downward motion was reversed and the ship's bows began to surge upward again. Then the tension on my arms was increased by the stupendous weight of the water above me. Finally, however, perfectly familiar with the head-fittings of the bowsprit, I managed to get my feet securely planted on the wooden beading block which held the nib of the stays. This relieved the terrible strain on my arms, and thus I clung until, what seemed an age later, the ship's bows were flung upward again and I felt the cold wind in my face and heard the noise of the storm in my ears. There I hung for a moment choking and gasping for breath.

At last, I pawed the brine from my streaming face and looked forward, and lo, I stood on the footrope alone! Both of my comrades were gone, and the fag end of the sundered manrope lashing furiously in the wind told in eloquent action the way of their going—they had followed old Barney Dent for the want of a becket!

The jib had split and was fluttering in tatters across the headguys, and I made my way inboard as rapidly as possible to report the woeful tidings to those on deck. By this time, the storm had redoubled its fury and although the ship was driving free and still carrying a good pressure of sail the green combers were constantly racing under her counters and breaching the quarter-decks at will. A part of the crew was still aloft furling the fore- and mizzen-topgallant sails and the remainder were engaged in stretching life lines and grab ropes across the deck.

I found the bos'n, Tom Splicer, at the main fife rail bellowing orders, and I seized him frantically by the arm. "Tom," I roared in his ear, "Tom, two men washed off the jib boom when she dipped that time; manrope parted! Flying jib's gone out o' the bolt ropes! Tell the mate!"

I jerked these broken sentences into his ear as rapidly as possible, watching the weather rail meanwhile to dodge the next comber.

"Who was they?" bellowed Tom excitedly.

"Don't know," I retorted, "couldn't see in the dark. I went under too. It's about ten minutes ago."

"O God," he exclaimed with an inward groan, "they're as dead as they ever will be by now!"

Just then, Mister Riggin's big voice came howling through a speaking trumpet. "Clew up the main-topgallant sail! Haul up the fore an' mainsail! Lively there, bos'n; she won't stand this long."

"Aye, aye, sir," roared Tom Splicer, getting into immediate action; and in the tumult and confusion that followed we did not discover until next morning that our two lost shipmates were Stavanger Lars and Geordie Jack, two of our most jovial and popular comrades.

By this time, the fore- and mizzen-topgallant sails had been furled and the hands were straggling down from aloft. So with our large force we were able to man the main-topgallant gear and the fore and main clew garnets simultaneously. When the main-topgallant halyards were started, they refused to run, while the chain sheets likewise remained immobile. The big topgallant sail, with the gear released, was creating a tremendous commotion aloft.

In the blank darkness of the stormy night it was impossible to see from the deck what was wrong. Therefore, responding to the mate's order, I went aloft to find out. When I reached the masthead, I saw at once that the chain tie connecting the yard with the halyard span had snapped just above the truss; the big sixty-foot yard had descended and was now swinging wildly and threatening every moment to bring down the topgallant mast. Through the roar of the storm my voice would not carry to the deck, so I drew my sheath knife and split the distended belly of the sail in as many places as I could reach in order to spill the wind; then I descended to the deck and reported the trouble aloft.

"Can't yer git out on the yardarms an' bend on a preventer line ter steady 'er?" demanded Tom Splicer.

"No," I answered decisively, "all four of the lifts are gone and there are no beckets on the yardarms."

The next instant there came a warning bellow from the poop,

amplified through the resonant trumpet. "Stand by for'ard! Look out to wind'ard!" Glancing over the weather rail, we saw three tremendous seas with towering white crests rushing with incredible speed straight toward the staggering ship.

Every man sprang for safety to his nearest place of vantage and hung on. I leaped to the main fife rail and clung to the collar of the mizzen stay, and an instant later the foremost comber broke with terrific violence over the rail, hove the ship to her beam ends and buried her hulk beneath thousands of tons of water. Before she could rise again and shake off the enormous weight above her decks, the following two seas boarded her in rapid succession.

Just as the last sea swept over the floundering ship, we felt a heavy, startling jolt as though we had struck a sunken rock. The entire hull trembled violently from stem to stern and, after the seas had passed, the ship slowly settled on her port side and lay there as dead and helpless as a derelict.

Then we all surmised the fearful truth. The three thousand tons of jute which formed the major part of our cargo had been idiotically stowed on top of the consignment of slippery linseed. Loosened by two months of constant wrenching, the jute had shifted because of the violent pitching of the hull and fetched away bodily into the wing, thus heaving the ship down rails under and holding her firmly on her beams at an exceedingly dangerous angle.

Then, before we had time to appreciate the awful peril of our position, there came a terrific, rending crash. Flashes of living fire streamed from broken bolts and shattered chain plates, followed by the snarling twang of sundered rigging and the cracking of broken spars. The loose topgallant sail, caught in the intense angle of the ship's list, had at last jumped the main-topgallant mast from its step, and the broken spars in falling had also dragged the mizzen-topgallant mast and topmast with them over the side. A moment later, the fore-topgallant mast, deprived of its after supports, followed them into the sea, wrenching the flying jib boom off at the bowsprit cap.

This seeming catastrophe, serious as it appeared, was really fortunate, for nothing else could have saved us from total destruction. Suddenly relieved of the enormous weight and leverage of her top hamper, the ship gradually rose, lifted her lee rails above the water, and righted herself to windward. Although still far from being on an even keel, she was in a far less dangerous position and more manageable.

Immediately after the supreme crisis was past, we set to work to clear away the wreckage, for the broken spars training alongside and swinging by their numerous attachments were pounding with titanic violence against the ship's hull. Axes, sheath knives, wire pliers, and pinch bars were at once brought into requisition and the dangerous work of cutting and clearing away the maze of tangled rigging both alow and aloft went bravely on. Fortunately, it was accomplished without further mishap to the remainder of our crew.

When the wreckage had been cleared and the broken spars cut adrift, we took in all remaining sail except the main lower topsail and the fore-topmast staysail and brought the dismantled ship head to the wind. Then we clung to the rigging and wished for the day.

At length a dull, somber morning broke over a wild and desolate scene—a heavy lowering sky, a cold drenching rain, and a sadly crippled ship floundering helplessly in the relentless grasp of a howling tempest. The main topsail of itself was not sufficient to keep the badly listed ship head to the wind. To set more sail was impractical as well as perilous. Moreover, the topsail itself was likely to be blown from the bolt ropes at any moment, and in that case the result would have been disastrous.

Therefore, the mate decided to rig up a sea-anchor and endeavor to hold the ship head on to the sea at all hazards. As soon as it was light enough to see, all hands were called down from their several "safety" perches; and, after receiving a gill of rum all around in lieu of breakfast, we were at once set to work to construct the sea-anchor and rig it out.

To accomplish this, our largest and longest studding sail booms had to be sacrificed. Two of these splendid spars, each about fifty feet long, were sawed in two. The ends were then crossed, securely bolted, clamped, and still further secured with heavy lashings. This made a huge diamond-shaped frame exactly like that of an ordinary kite. A heavy crossbeam was then securely bolted and lashed across the center of the frame for bracing. The whole contrivance was then completely covered with two courses of strong tarpaulin securely fastened to the sides of the frame. Next, a seven-hundred-pound kedge anchor was fastened by a short length of chain to one angle of the great kite for ballast. This was to hold it vertically in the water exactly as a kite must be ballasted to maintain an upright position in midair.

One hundred and twenty fathoms of new ten-inch hawser were then broken out for a riding cable. One end of this line was passed through a hole in the center of the tarpaulins and firmly secured to the crossbeam behind the frame. The other end was carried over the bows, brought inboard again through a towing pipe, made fast around the foremast, and finally secured to the towing bitts on the main deck.

All of these ingenious preparations required a good deal of time and were accomplished only by the most strenuous labor and in the face of direst hazard. Fortunately we finished in safety, although it was nearly noon before we were through.

When at length our sea-anchor was complete and all its attachments secured, we cockbilled the huge frame on the weather rail and dumped the whole contrivance overboard. The drift of the ship soon picked up the slack of the hawser and the mighty resistance of the kite suspended upright in the water was sufficient to check her leeway and hold her head fairly to the sea.

This done, we took in our main topsail, lashed two tarpaulins in the lower rigging instead, and left our fore-topmast staysail set to ease the ship's head off the wind sufficiently to enable her to ride the seas.

After another round of grog, we were set to try the pumps. Despite the furious laboring and pounding of the previous night, the ship had not sprung a leak; but the ventilators had been washed away and large volumes of water had poured into the hold. It required nearly two hours of constant labor to drain the water from the bilges; then one weary watch was sent below for rest.

We found our quarters in a woeful condition. The sea had completely gutted our forecastle and every item of our clothes and bedding had been swept away. To make matters worse, the galley, too, had been washed out and no food could be cooked. Most terrible and distressing of all, the hood to our main tank had burst and our entire supply of fresh water had been defiled with brine.

I can never attempt to describe adequately the terrible suffering we endured in the days that followed. The awful pangs of thirst and the unbearable agony caused by the constant chafing of our salt-encrusted clothing were too maddening in their intensity to be told.

In the bottom of an abandoned tank beneath the poop, we found a small quantity of rusty drainings, thick as mush with iron, rust, and slime. All this filthy dampness, muddy and corroded as it was, was carefully scraped together and the bottom mopped dry with rags. And when the last drop of moisture doled out to us in spoonfuls had been consumed and the dirty rags had been sucked dry, we glared and craved each other's blood.

As soon as the storm had blown out and the sea had subsided, we had opened the hatches, gone down into the hold, and rolled as many bales of jute as we could back to starboard against the empty wing from which they had shifted. Thus we had righted the ship. Then we worked three days rigging up jury spars and inventing jury sails to fit them, and after that we made every exertion to reach the southeast trades. Meanwhile, we kept a sharp lookout by day and night for sight or sign of a passing sail, but all in vain!

Early one morning, fourteen days later, the lookout at the military station on the summit of Saint Helena sighted a large ship under jury rig heading toward the island. The wind was light and she was moving slowly and still many miles away. The telescope revealed her in wretched condition. Two black shapes suspended from her masthead as a signal of distress confirmed her plight. Her topsides had been beaten flat to the deck; all her boats were gone; her figurehead had been wrenched from its fastenings beneath her bows; across the face of her fore topsail was painted in huge black letters the one awful word: WATER; and the code numbers fluttering listlessly from her mizzen peak revealed her name as the *Late Commander.*

It was obviously impossible for her to reach the island that day unless the wind increased soon, which seemed improbable. Therefore, a boat was sent out to meet her.

Throughout that long morning we gazed with burning, bloodshot eyes toward that distant peak hanging like a small blue cloud on the northern horizon and prayed fervently for wind. Shortly after noon, we observed a tiny speck between us and the far-off rock. As it grew larger, Captain Grummitt lowered the glass which had long been glued to his eye and cackled in joyous accents through parched and bleeding lips that it was a *water* boat.

As the little craft drew nearer, we saw to our inexpressible delight that it was a lugger, crowding sail and manned by six lusty Negro rowers and a Negro coxswain. We welcomed them alongside with a feeble cheer. Water was doled out to us in moderate doses at first, but we were then allowed to lave our parched and salt-encrusted bodies and wash our brine-starched clothing.

The generous Negroes had also brought us a small quantity of fresh vegetables, and these we ravenously devoured. They then came on board and helped us navigate the ship up to the island.

It was past midnight when we reached Saint Helena and dropped anchor on the little bank in front of Jamestown, the only anchorage the isolated rock affords. Late as the hour was, we were immediately surrounded by a swarm of bumboats crowded with eager visitors of both sexes, and during our stay at the island we never lacked company.

For a full week we lay under the shadow of the famous peak recuperating our strength, trimming our cargo, and improving our jury rig, so that by the time we sailed we were able to show quite a respectable spread of canvas. After a prolonged passage because of our scanty rig, we finally arrived at New York without further mishap or hardship.

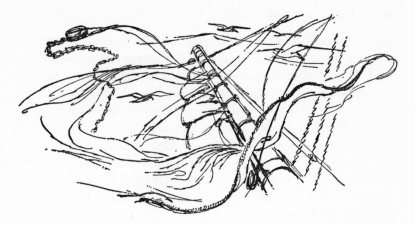

## 6 · THE PASSING OF PENGELLEY

We lay three months in the port of New York discharging and loading cargo and repairing the hull and rigging of the *Late Commander* before we sailed again for Calcutta in May of 1887. Two months later, on the fifteenth of July—midwinter in the Southern Ocean—we rounded the boisterous Cape of Good Hope and began circling boldly away toward the forty-sixth parallel to begin running our easting down.

A week later, we were in the midst of our great easterly sweep toward the eighty-fifth meridian. The prevailing westerly winds peculiar to the zone had gradually increased in force and the sea had risen, so that now we were scudding through the tumult and smother of a mighty gale at a seventeen-knot gait. We were swinging three whole topgallant sails with preventer backstays set up and preventer braces on the cro'jack yards. Running with squared yards and everything bar taut, there was not much to do execpt relieve watches and stand by for emergencies.

For three consecutive days during this superb run, the old ship made a glorious record—over a thousand miles with five thousand tons of case oil as cargo in our hold! Here is an authentic sailing item for amateur sailors and deepwater yachtsmen to ponder over.

On the second day of that great run, we passed two British-

Australian mail steamers. Both were high-diving until the crests of the seas threatened to flood their boiler rooms through the funnel tops. Their propellers churned wind oftener than water.

We were running with an old-fashioned log at that time—a canvas bag and a wooden plug trailed by a sticky line wound on a wobbly reel and held unsteadily aloft by a lurching seaman and timed by a sleepy apprentice with a worn-out sand glass. An honest taffrail log would have recorded us at least eighteen instead of the miserly fourteen-odd knots we were credited with. But sailors never were noted for doing anything remarkable except drinking rum and chewing tobacco.

On the third day of the big run, the wind had attained almost hurricane force, and the sea had risen to mountainous heights and fearsome aspect. Our grand old ship, however, carried on nobly and showed not the slightest symptoms of weakening or distress.

*That night off Good Hope I shall never forget;*
*Ofttimes I look backward and think of it yet;*
*We were plunging bows under, her courses all wet,*
*At the rate of fourteen, with to'gallan' s'ls set.*

*So we'll roll, roll, bullies,*
*Roll as we go,*
*For the kidapore ladies*
*Have got us in tow!*

At four in the afternoon, before changing watches, the Old Man ordered the mate to take in the fore- and mizzen-topgallant sails since, as he declared, the ship was dragging instead of sailing. It had reached the limit of its sailing power, and the surplus canvas was now a hindrance rather than a help. As soon as we had mustered watches, the order was given; clewlines, buntlines, and leechlines were manned fore and aft at the same time. In just twenty minutes, the two big kites were taken in and snugly stowed. The *Late Commander* carried a noble crew! As soon as we had the ship shortened down to a whole main-topgallant sail, the port watch was sent below and the watch on deck was left to clear up the tangle of loose gear washing about the deck and trailing overboard through the scuppers.

The ship continued her racing gait with no apparent slackening of speed after shortening sail, and she rode much easier and made better weather of howling winds and driving sea. When the starboard watch went below at four bells for the second dogwatch, the ship was high-diving and wallowing through the thundering seas at a terrific pace.

According to the common plan in British ships, the *Late Commander's* forecastle was directly beneath the forecastle head, with two doors at one end, the hawsepipes at the other, and a massive patent windlass in the center. After our Act o' Parliament supper of hardtack, "strike me blind," and "water bewitched" had been disposed of, we lighted our pipes and gathered around the big windlass for our usual dogwatch smoke session and yarn-spinning contest.

We were a motley bunch of weather-beaten, hardened sailors, every mother's son a typical man-Jack. Lords of the gale, we reveled in our manhood and our strength and knew no hardship except the misery and degradation of being too long ashore. The British element naturally predominated among us, not because the ship was British, but simply because the voyage had originated in England nearly four years before. All of the original crew had not yet been seduced into desertion by the crimps in the various ports. Still, the inevitable vacancies had had to be filled from time to time until now more than half of our foremast complement of twenty-two A.B.'s were non-British seamen. Only four of us, collectively known as the Yankee Squad, were native Americans.

Seated around the forecastle in various easy and careless attitudes, we were surely an uncouth and unearthly looking group that might have descended from some remote planet and been sent away into these desolate and uninhabitable solitudes where nothing but blowing whales and pinioned sea birds could find contentment or natural sustenance. All of us were fully clad in the height of the prevailing fashion—sea boots and pea jackets, with oilskins and sou'westers ready on hand in case of an emergency call.

Ever since the mutiny at the Nore, a national superstition has prevailed in British ships, both naval and commercial, against striking seven bells in the second dogwatch and rigging the gangway out on the port side. When four bells terminates the first dogwatch at six P.M., the chimes begin with one bell again at six-thirty, two bells mark seven o'clock, and three bells are struck at seven-thirty. Then the usual intermediate one bell at a quarter to eight warns the watch below to turn out and get ready. The final stroke of eight bells ends the dogwatch and calls all hands on deck to muster at the mainmast.

It happened to be Saturday night, and just before three bells young Pengelley came splashing forward through the deck swash to visit the sailors. Pengelley was as welcome as a Christmas morning, for every man among us adored the big handsome young Cornishman. The entire watch arose as one man to greet him and offer him the place of honor in our midst as he pushed his way in. Of course, it was contrary to both rule and tradition for apprentices to associate in quarters with "common" sailors, but no one, not even old Cap'n Grummitt himself, ever thought of reprimanding Pengelley.

Like many other high-minded but hardheaded men, Pengelley's father, being an officer in the Royal Navy, had insisted upon a sea career for his son even though the sensitive lad was unfitted by natural impulse and predilection for the hardships and drudgeries peculiar to the maritime service. Pengelley was a born scholar. He was studious, book-minded, and thoughtful rather than practical. He was as much out of place among a windjammer's crew as a marble statue in a farmer's barnyard. Nevertheless, Pengelley was the light, the life, and the pride and ennobling influence of our whole ship's company. We needed someone better, nobler, nearer the unknown unattainable than our miserable selves. That was why we all adored Pengelley. He never needed to do any sailorizing; we could do all that!

Politely but positively declining any of the vacated seats around the windlass, Pengelley stripped off his dripping oilskin coat and spread it over the horn of the windlass to drain. Then loosing his big woolen lammie at the throat, he stretched himself at full length in precarious comfort along the running board fronting the lower tier of bunks. The strait-laced restrictions of quarter-deck discipline evidently bored him, and he appreciated the homely good will and natural levity of us "common" sailors.

He seemed to be in unusually high spirits that night. His blue eyes twinkled with suppressed mirth and his chestnut hair glistened in the flickering light of the spluttering slush lamp. Although the constant lurching and diving of the ship rendered his recumbent position on the bunkboard somewhat insecure, Pengelley seemed to enjoy the situation. He began describing, with witty embellishments, some of the amusing mishaps to officers and crew which he had witnessed during the day.

The resonant clang of three warning strokes on the big watch bell directly over our heads interrupted his amusing recital and created an uneasy stir among the tired seamen. The short and comfortless dogwatch was nearing its close and we would soon be called on deck to wrestle with the warring elements again until midnight.

"Sing us a song, Pen, before the watch is called," shouted Spike Riley. "Sumpin' sad an' sentimental; sumpin' with a chorus so's we kin all jine in an' blow th' wind. Ain't no ladies present, ye know," the old vagabond reminded us with an artful grin, "so we kin make all th' noise we've min' ter 'ithout disturbin' enybody's nervous systim."

"Let 'er go, Pen," piped half a score of eager voices. "Order for a song! Go ahead, Pen. Sing 'er up."

Always willing, Pengelley at once responded to our request. He broke into the opening verse of the sailors' love song, "Anchor's Weighed," with all the entrancing vigor and glorious fervor of his marvelous voice. As verse after verse rolled out in perfect rhythm and soulful expression, the whole watch would take up the simple and appealing refrain with boisterous enthusiasm, our combined voices ringing and rising above the roar and thunder of the storm, the thousand deck noises, and the raging sea.

Our evening song ended in salvos of wild applause, and at the stroke of eight bells we donned our coats and hurried out on the deck. The night and the sea had assumed truly fearsome aspects. The heavy black wind bags that dominated the sky and shut out the light of heaven had settled over all apparent creation with appalling completeness. The night was as dark as a bottomless pit. Only the phosphorescent gleam of the breaking sea crests and the iridescent and fleeting glow of the splashing side wash afforded an occasional and flitting glimpse of the loom and tension of the bulging sails. The big westerly wind had settled down into a continual, monotonous, bellowing roar. The whitecaps were flecked angrily from the summits of the racing seas and lashed away in great windrows of gleaming spindrift that spread like driven snow flurries in the pathway of the rushing waves.

But everything on the ship held even though the storm seemed to have attained its maximum intensity. So, except for some untoward accident during the night, prospects seemed good that the ship would be able to carry on until morning.

When all hands had assembled at the main fife rail, Tom Splicer communicated the fact with the usual announcement, "Watch is aft, sir." Then, after a brief interval of uneasy suspense, came the welcome, though slightly amended order and admonition: "Relieve the wheel and lookout. Two A.B.s at the wheel. That'll do the watch. Stand by for a call."

That the afterguard was feeling suspicious of the weather and preparing for trouble was quite evident, but it never pays to borrow trouble or spoil your peace of mind either by tragic anticipations or vain regrets. If we could read the inexorable decrees of fate beforehand, the human race would soon become extinct because every individual on earth would break his neck trying to dodge the inevitable.

As soon as the port watch had been relieved and gone below, the starboard watch scrambled for various safety perches above the level of the sea-swept deck. Most of the crowd climbed to the little flying bridge over the quarter-deck and wrapped themselves in the idle clew of the mizzen staysail, which had not been hoisted in over a week. The lookout was kept from the break of the poop, but as I was the "farmer" that watch, having neither wheel nor lookout coming to me, I climbed to the top of the forward house and stowed myself snugly away beneath one of the big boats lashed keel upward to ringbolts in the beam skids. Lying down with my head pillowed on the oaken skid with only my sou'wester for softening, I soon fell sound asleep, entirely oblivious to all my wild and fearsome surroundings.

I was awakened from my slumber by hearing my name called in ordinary and friendly tone. Had it been a watch call, I should have scrambled out in a hurry and shouted, "Aye, aye, sir." But as it was, I simply stretched out my hand, more provoked than alarmed, and felt a presence I could not see.

"Is that you, Pen?" I asked, sensing the identity of my unexpected visitor.

"Yes, it's me, Jim," answered the young apprentice. "Do you like manavlins? I gave the steward a shilling for the dog basket after supper last evening. The small stores are getting smaller now, and we don't get much better food in the half deck than you men do in the forecastle."

"I know it, you young rascal," I answered as I sat up and eagerly accepted a generous section of sea pie proffered me in the dark.

After I had gobbled the cabin leavings, we sat together in shrouded silence beneath the pitch-black darkness of the upturned boat. Round about and overhead and down beneath us thundered the tumult of ship noises and the storm—the rush and roar and hollow reverberations of driving seas; the monotonous, insistent wailing of the wind; the chaotic crash and tumult of an occasional comber breaching the rail, staggering the ship with its sudden impact and stupendous weight and battering the hatch coamings with the fury of a cataract. Overhead, the screaming tempest held high carnival in the vibrant shrouds. Idle chain gear rattled discordantly against the reechoing spars of hollow steel. The groaning yards and creaking blocks and grinding gins and singing boltropes told the terrific strain imposed upon our flawless gear.

Below the heavy deck, responding to every lurch, the throbbing hull labored incessantly beneath the avalanches of water constantly thundering aboard. The submerged clatter of disgorging sluice ports, the hollow chortling of choking scuppers, the occasional pounding of spare spars and loosened deck fittings kept apt and fitting accompaniment to the surrounding tumult. Above the storm, the wind reigned triumphant over all.

"What time is it, Pen?" I finally inquired.

"Six bells went before I came forward," he replied. "Jones is keeping scuppers on the poop, and I'm standing by to call the watch. The second mate has been ordered to make one bell at half past and get all hands out. We're going to take in the topgallant sail before the watch is relieved. It's blowing harder now and we're edging to the northward to get out of the zone and into smoother seas."

"Well, Pen," I said cheerfully, "I guess I'll jump down into the forecastle and try a drag at the pipe before we start gehawking again. A feed like that deserves a smoke for consolation."

"Wait a moment, Jim," urged Pengelley in a pleading tone as he laid a restraining hand on my oilskins. "I want to ask a favor of you."

"Sing out, Pen. It's already granted," I exclaimed, startled by the sudden tenseness and appealing solemnity of his voice. "What can I do for you?"

"Jim," asked the young apprentice seriously, "do you remember the evening we first met in Calcutta?"

"Certainly," I replied. "That was a year ago when all our squad went up to say goodbye to Black Harry and Piringee Katherine."

"Yes, it was a year ago—just a year ago tonight. Do you remember that I told you it was the third anniversary of my apprenticeship?"

"Why, yes," I answered. "I do. I suppose you are trying to remind

me that tonight is your fourth anniversary in the half deck. Your
indenture expires at midnight and tomorrow you will be eligible
for promotion to the quarter deck. From Calcutta you will be sent
to London to pass examination for your new rating. Congratulations, old man!"

I found Pengelley's hand and gripped it warmly in the dark. For
a moment neither of us spoke. Then he broke the tense silence
beneath the sheltering boat with a startling declaration.

"Jim, I am not going to reach Calcutta. I shall never see dear old
England again."

"Say, what ails you, Pen?" I exclaimed, horrified by his suddenly changed demeanor and mysterious talk. "You've been worry-
ing about something and your wits are going astray. Tell me about
it. You know I'm a safe counsellor and even if I can't help you
perhaps I can share the burden with you and help you bear the
strain." I was so profoundly shocked by Pengelley's behavior that
I sat still in mystified silence waiting for him to proceed.

"Do you ever become frightened when you're aloft, Jim?" asked
the boy suddenly, gripping my oilskins nervously as he spoke.

"Scared, you mean? No, of course not," I asserted contemptu-
ously. "The safest place on a ship is aloft, especially on a night like
this. You're out of the deck smother, clear of the wrack, and above
your officers for the time being. And the wind don't blow any
harder upstairs than it does down here. But why such foolish questions, Pen? You aren't afraid of anything, are you?"

"There is only one thing I fear, Jim," replied Pengelley, "and that
is disgrace. I've always been timid about climbing; it's a natural
weakness that I cannot overcome no matter how hard I try. For a
long time, I thought the feeling would wear away by enforced
habit and constant practice, but in that hope I've been sadly disappointed. Ever since the night poor old Barney Dent was flung
from the main-topgallant yard, I've been oppressed by an unspeak-
able horror every time I go aloft, especially on that particular yard.
Sometimes the terror makes me sick and causes me to vomit while

I'm aloft; and then the reaction causes me to vomit again after I am safely on deck.

"Of course, everybody attributes it to seasickness, which is really chronic in some constitutions. In a sense it is seasickness, Jim. It is not actual fright. It is simply my stomach instead of my heart that gets in my mouth at such times, and it could not happen anywhere else except at sea; but it is a condition I can no more avoid or overcome than I can stop breathing and live.

"I know you will consider me silly and superstitious," he went on, "but I know I shall never see the end of this passage, and before anything happens I want you to promise that you will do something for me after—after you reach Calcutta."

He faltered at the conclusion of the sentence, and I knew that his feelings were overwrought. Although I placed no credence in his premonition, I realized that it was useless to try to reason him out of it. If he had been an ordinary, simple-minded old sailor oppressed by silly seasaws and ancient superstitions against capsizing hatch covers, striking the bell backward, or sailing on Friday, there might have been some hope. In that case, if he could not have been reasoned or ridiculed out of his groundless fears, he could have been kicked or cuffed out of them or otherwise left to steep in his own ignorance.

But Pengelley was different. He was a broad-minded, widely read, well-informed young man. I had never known him to harbor spooks or mental hallucinations, nor was he a victim of melancholia. In fact, he had always been regarded as the most cheerful of the four apprentices.

"If it is as serious as all that, Pen," I said, for I was becoming alarmed for his safety by this time, "you had better lay up for a few days or until we run into fine weather again and your nervousness subsides. I am sure Captain Grummitt won't insist on ordering you aloft if your life is endangered by it."

"Jim," he declared firmly, "I can't do that. The other apprentices would despise me and my father would disown me. Please keep quiet about it," he pleaded in genuine alarm. "Simply do as I wish you to."

"But, Pen," I insisted, "you are the bravest boy I ever saw to live through a horror like that for four years just to gratify your father's whim. I am sure he would have withdrawn your indentures long ago and had you sent home if he had been aware of the facts."

But Pengelley was obdurate. All I could do under the circumstances was to humor him and appear to acquiesce in his plans, for he was really laboring under a dangerous mental aberration. His designs would have to be humored in order to be circumvented. I therefore pretended to act in accord with his wishes, but mentally resolved to frustrate his quixotic fancies of filial devotion even if it meant incurring his everlasting displeasure. I inwardly resolved to try not only to have Pengelley relieved, but, if possible, prohibited from going aloft during the remainder of the voyage.

"Well, Pen," I resumed, "don't be downhearted. We'll run into fine weather in a day or two and the danger will be over. Meanwhile, whenever we have to go aloft, you stick close to me. That will encourage you and I will always be there to lend a hand."

"Thank you, Jim," exclaimed the boy with grateful fervency. "But before we separate I want you to promise that in the event of anything happening to me you will send this box to my sister Eunice, at Saint Ives. She knows of you already," he added, thrusting a package into my hands as he spoke, "because I mentioned you to her in my last letter home from New York.

"In this package," he went on, "there is a camphorwood box containing some letters and photographs, some private papers and trinkets, and the gold watch my father gave me when I left home. I know that if I am missing all my effects will have to be accounted for by the captain and owners of this ship. But in that case they would likewise have to be inspected, and the contents of this box are too sacred for that.

"You can get Miss Primrose, the little missionary in Calcutta, to help you. She knows me well and I believe she knows you also. She can manage to have the package sent for you by special dispatch.

Under the canvas wrapper around the box, you will find a letter addressed to my sister. I want you to send it to her together with another letter to be written by yourself."

"Well, I'll take your orders, Pen," I replied, "and all the more willingly because I feel certain I shall never be required to carry them out."

Pengelley wrung my hand warmly. "God bless you, Jim," he exclaimed. "And now I want you to accept these trifles as a token of our friendship." With that, he thrust into my hand a heavy gold watch guard with a solid gold anchor pendant attached as a charm. I recognized the pieces and appreciated their intrinsic value and artistic merit, for I had seen Pengelley wearing them on special occasions.

It was nearing seven bells now, and Pengelley and I both crawled from beneath the sheltering enclosure of the inverted boat and descended to the slippery surface of the main deck. Pengelley went aft to take the time, and I dove into the forecastle to secrete my precious charge before the watch was called.

Returning to the deck, I proceeded at once to locate some of my watchmates and arouse them to the fact that another furling match was about due. I could not think of taking in that big main-topgallant sail, however, without feeling concerned over Pengelley's tragic premonition. There was great danger to anyone working aloft in the *Late Commander* because of the complete absence of any beckets, grab lines, or saving gear of any kind on her yardarms. The harrowing lessons of three tragic casualties on the previous run had made no perceptible mark on the hearts or minds of those responsible. No effort had been made to guard against future tragedies. She lacked even the most basic lifesaving attachments on the yardarms. This deficiency, because of the great girth of her principal spars and the immense spread and heavy weft of her enormous sails, made the *Late Commander* an extremely hazardous ship to manipulate aloft.

I tried hard to invent some lubberly trick, no matter how base, to prevent Pengelley from going aloft that night, but I was at my wit's end and could not think coherently. There was no time to weave a plot or to execute it if found. The stroke of one bell found me still struggling with my inward terrors and with no hope of any design. In a few minutes, both watches were out and Tom Splicer was splashing around the deck roaring orders to everybody alow and aloft.

There was no general muster, but within a few minutes all hands were hauling away on the main-topgallant running gear. Clewlines, leechlines, buntlines, and downhauls were all manned at once and the massive topgallant yard came creaking down handsomely to the topmast cap. The voluminous canvas came floundering, fluttering, and thundering with a tremendous straining and baffling uproar against the mighty tension of the gear.

Amid the momentary excitement and general din, I ceased for a time to worry about Pengelley; and when the tautened gear had been belayed and the braces steadied, I was among the first to lay aloft in response to the imperious order, "Tie 'er up."

Upon reaching the masthead, I assumed one side of the bunt, with Big Mac for a side partner. With a forty-foot hoist on a sixty-foot spar, it was no child's task to bunt that main-topgallant sail. Moreover, it was always a desperate job, especially when running square, because the yard was rigged with old-fashioned quarter clewline blocks, there were no spilling lines, and the buntline lizards on the jack-stays were entirely too long. This left large quantities of slack canvas with which to contend. Consequently, there was always an immense wind bag to smother when the sail was brailed up.

When the watch had mustered along the yardarms and the gaskets were cleared, the huge bag bellied and bellowed above our heads as tense and rigid as an inflated balloon. The wet and hardened canvas was as unyielding as chilled boiler plate. Taking advantage of a momentary wind flaw in a lucky backsend of the ship, we all grabbed the slightly slackened canvas and, shouting encouragement to each other, made a united and desperate effort to smother the big wind bag and strangle it up snugly to the jack-stay.

But in the next dive, the clews filled away again. In spite of the desperate exertions of ten strong men, the sail burst away with an exultant bang. And then, in the extremity of common danger, I heard a faint, wild, despairing cry and felt an ominous slackening of the footrope beneath my feet. Instantly a fearful dread froze my heart. Where was Pengelley? Had he purposely eluded me in the darkness and brought about the terrible fulfillment of his premonition? Trembling at the harrowing thought, I returned to the hazardous duty before us; and, after a few more daring attempts, we finally succeeded in overpowering the raging sailcloth and bunched it up securely on the swaying yard.

After passing the tail stop of the bunt gasket to Big Mac, I clutched the convenient warp of the topgallant backstay and slid like a plummet to the topgallant rail. As I leaped to the deck, I met Jones, the junior apprentice, a muffled and impersonal shape in the darkness. I recognized him by his voice, and he probably knew me by my hasty and vigorous actions.

"That you, Williams?" he inquired.

"Yes, it's me," I responded. "Who fell?"

"Pengelley! He wants you," he replied in a horrified tone. "They carried him into the cabin and the cap'n says he's dyin'. He's been callin' for you." The young apprentice subsided with a smothered sob, and I made my way with bursting heart to the cabin. I pulled the heavy teakwood door open without any preliminary knock and strode unceremoniously into the forward cabin. It was likewise the officers' mess room; and there, bolstered up on a berth mattress on the big mess table lay the broken frame and tortured body of the dying boy.

At the head of the table stood Captain Grummitt, a chastened look softening his wooden features. Beside him stood the steward, striving awkwardly to minister to the last earthly needs of the passing spirit. Ranged alongside the mess board were four able seamen standing in reverent silence. They were the rescue squad that had brought Pengelley into the cabin. Above, in the skylight, the tell-tale compass wobbled unsteadily with the yawing of the ship; the marine clock in the alcove ticked the fateful seconds away with relentless beats; and outside the storm wind howled a mighty greeting to the departing soul.

As I stood near the entrance, sou'wester in hand, Captain Grummitt beckoned me to the side of my shipmate. Stepping quietly to the head of the table, I bent reverently over the dying apprentice and listened attentively to his labored breathing to catch any parting words.

Pengelley lay perfectly still for a while. His hands were cold as ice, his eyes partly closed, and his handsome features, now distorted by mortal anguish, were as white as chiseled marble. Only the painful and irregular breathing and the slight twitching of the pallid lips after each feeble gasp indicated that the spark of life still glowed faintly within.

"Do you know me, Pen?" I asked, pressing his cold hand firmly in mine.

The dark eyes opened slowly and a slight flash of glad recognition illumined the pale features. The bloodless lips moved inaudibly and I bent closer to catch the whispered words.

"You'll remember, won't you, Jim? The package and the letter?"

"Surely, Pen," I murmured hoarsely. "I'll do all I have promised."

"Thank you, Jim," he faltered once again. "I'm glad—you—came. Now—I am—content."

Then the weary eyelids drooped again over the fading orbs, the death pallor deepened to an unearthly whiteness, and for fully a minute the labored breathing ceased. Then, just as Captain Grummitt was about to make an inspection to detect any lingering spark of life, Pengelley's whole body became suddenly convulsed by a raging spasm of supreme agony. His eyes opened wide, staring and sightless. His classical features were fearfully distorted in an excruciating horror of unutterable anguish. His head rocked violently from side to side and raised spasmodically from the pillow in an uncontrollable ecstasy of intense soul-racking pain.

"Lord! Lord! Help me!" he shrieked in the terrifying accents of mortal extremity, and with that great agonizing appeal a surging hemorrhage burst the internal barriers of life. The pent-up flood poured forth from mouth and ears and nostrils in crimson streams, the raised head fell back limply to the waiting pillow, the contracted features relaxed in a smile of ineffable relief, a parting sigh of weary contentment escaped the colorless lips, a settled attitude of eternal repose stole over the stalwart form on the table, and all was still.

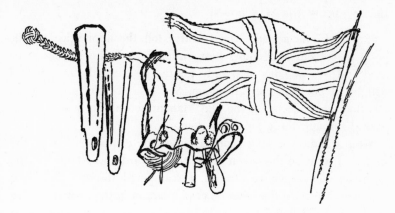

## 7 · BURIAL AT SEA

Alfred Pengelley was dead. Like old Barney Dent and his unfortunate comrades, he had gone to eternity for the want of a becket. I glanced at the marine clock in the skylight. It registered twenty minutes past midnight. I took a towel from the steward and wiped the crimson streaks from the placid face, pushed the glossy chestnut locks from the marble brow, and then, drawing my sheath knife, I cut two metallic buttons from my oilskin coat and pressed them gently over the nerveless eyelids.

Having performed these services, I looked old Captain Grummitt squarely in the eyes as he stood motionless at the head of the table. My look must have conveyed the meaning of the solemn accusation which rankled in my heart.

The Old Man, however, remained silent. With an authoritative wave of his hand, he dismissed the four seamen who had remained mute and sorrowing mourners at the deathbed scene. After they had retired, I helped the steward compose the dead boy's limbs and cover the body with a cotton sheet. Then we both stood by looking to Captain Grummitt for orders.

"You may call the sailmaker now, Williams," said the Old Man. "You'd better remain up the rest of this watch and guard the body from rats and help make the shroud.

"Steward," he added, "you'd better tell the apprentice on the poop to get out Pengelley's best uniform. And also set out some food and two noggins of brandy for the deathwatch. The funeral will be at one bell this afternoon. See everything's ready." With this final announcement, the Old Man turned abruptly and disappeared through the after cabin door.

After standing a long moment in silent contemplation of the shrouded form on the oaken table, the steward and I both left the cabin on our respective errands. I scampered through the flying deck swash toward the petty officers' quarters in the forward house to call "Sails." I found him up and fully dressed. He was seated on the locker in his little cubbyhole of a stateroom smoking his pipe and awaiting my call.

"Mortal man could never endure a fling from that yard and live," he averred as he arose and turned down the light in his little gimbal lamp and prepared to accompany me aft.

When "Sails" and I reached the cabin, we found Pengelley's dress uniform and cap carefully laid out on a settee and heard the Steward busily engaged in the pantry. He soon appeared bearing a platterful of stale manavlins and a decanter containing about four long fingers of red liquor. Then, telling us to call him if necessary, he entered his own stateroom in the forward cabin alleyway and quietly closed the door.

Left alone together, "Sails" and I sat down at the head of the improvised bier, one on either side, and began our silent vigil. For a quarter of an hour not a word passed between us. Only the booming deck noises, the screaming blasts, the tumbling seas, and the constant creaking and complaining of the straining ship disturbed the awesome silence of our deathwatch.

At length, the chiming of two bells aroused us to the pressing duties before us. After an unceremonious tot from the brandy bottle to "splice the main brace," we at once set about undressing Pengelley's corpse and preparing it for burial.

Strange to say, there was not a mark on the boy's dead body to indicate the violent nature of his awful death. Not even an abrasion of the skin was evident. The heavy sea clothes he was wearing beneath his oilskin suit had muffled the mighty blow and protected his body from any external evidence of its terrific impact. All his injuries had been internal. His entire vital system must have been wrenched from its wondrous moorings when he fell.

At last, carefully groomed and dressed in the braided blue uniform, Pengelley's mortal remains lay in state. "Sails" went to his locker and soon returned with a cloth of new duck for the shroud. When we had measured and cut the form, I scuttled away forward to procure weights for sinkers, thus leaving "Sails" to run the short seam. Out of respect to the memory of our late shipmate, I felt that the usual gift of rusty scrap iron would not do. Therefore, in lieu of the two historic round shot so dear to tradition and song, I returned with two prosaic but equally effective dipsy leads which I had stolen from a big chest in the carpenter shop.

When the shroud had been completed and the sounding weights neatly tucked in at the dead man's feet, we left the top flap open at the head to afford a parting glimpse of the rigid features to such of the crew as cared to pay their last respects.

Having fulfilled our grievous task, "Sails" and I finished the remaining contents of the spirit flask and sat down to mark time until relieved. At eight bells, the watches were changed again, as usual, but we still maintained our vigil until relieved by the steward and Chinese cabin boy at four-thirty.

It was my wheel from four to six that morning, but I was excused in order to obtain some much-needed rest. Upon entering the dismal and comfortless shelter of the forecastle, I threw myself disconsolately on the deck and gave way in unrestrained vehemence to the raging tumult of grief pent up within me. When the watch came below at five-thirty for early coffee, I roused up and concealed my feelings as well as possible, partook of the steaming decoction with my mates, and then went on deck to avoid observation and questioning.

Daylight was now struggling through the thick mist. The weather remained unchanged. The storm gave no sign of either abating or increasing in force. I went aft and climbed to the dreary shelter of the monkey bridge, and there, wrapped in the lee cloths of the slack staysail, I stood by for orders. I remained there undisturbed for over an hour until a sudden hail from the poop proclaimed another sail in sight.

A passing ship is always a notable event at sea, but it was a momentous circumstance to our distracted and overwrought crew on that morning. It was a diverting and welcome relief from the depressing effect of our misfortune. All hands, including most of the watch below, were quickly on the alert. All eyes strained eagerly through the driving mist for a glimpse of the towering stranger coming up rapidly astern and overhauling us at a three to two pace. The ship was about a point off our lee quarter, evidently intending to pass us to starboard; and as it approached nearer it soon became painfully apparent that it was swinging a whole main-topgallant sail. In a few minutes, old Captain Grummitt appeared through the companionway in the skylight and took supreme command on the poop. His Galway whiskers pointed aggressively to wind'ard at an angle of forty-five degrees and the fighting instinct gleamed in his eye.

"Loose the main t'ga'n' s'l," he bellowed fiercely, taking the situation in at a glance.

Every sailor loves a race and no true son of Neptune will submit to defeat without a supreme tussle. In an instant, I was over the main sheer pole and making my way rapidly over the futtocks and the top through the crosstrees to the topgallant yard. Hastily stripping the gaskets from the lee yardarm, I crossed to windward and began releasing the weather yardarm gaskets with reckless haste. In a moment the outer, inner, and middle gaskets were clear and flying wildly in the wind.

But then, when I let go the quarter gasket, the big clew dropped, the slack canvas filled with a thunderous bang, and the great mass of bulging cloth struck me squarely in the face and toppled me over backward from the lofty yardarm. Just how it happened, I do not know; but the "Sweet Little Cherub," which according to our own encouraging song "ever sits up aloft" and watches over "poor Jack," must have come speedily to my rescue. The next instant, I found myself hanging suspended, head downward, by the crook of my knees, from the footrope. Strange as it may seem, no one on deck noticed my terrifying predicament. For a moment I hung like a trapeze performer, my heart palpitating, my body almost palsied by the horror of my plight. But at length I recovered sufficient presence of mind to grasp the footrope with my hands and thus draw myself up to a sitting posture on the hemp rope.

For a moment I sat clinging to the neck of the buntline block beneath the yard with both hands and quivering with the reaction of mortal terror. Then I heard Mister Riggins, our big beef-eating mate, roaring some unintelligible order evidently calculated to accelerate my movements. The sound of his voice enraged rather than inspired me to activity. The overpowering fear which had lately paralyzed and stifled me now gave way to an overmastering passion of savage, all-consuming rage.

They were rubbing it in too thick! In my tense mood, I feared neither man, devil, nor destiny. Clambering angrily to my feet on the swaying rope, I drew my sheath knife and with one vicious slash cut the tail stop of the bunt gasket. The liberated sail expanded with a tremendous roar and the ponderous yard threatened to leap from the truss under the mighty impulse suddenly exerted upon it.

"Hoist away now and sheet home; and be damned to you!" I shouted excitedly, no longer dominated by the superstitious reverence of a "common" sailor.

Then I stepped proudly off onto the topmast cap and looked over the quarter for a glimpse of our pursuing rival. She was close upon us now, not more than half a mile distant. From my lofty position, it was easy to make her out as an American ship fully as large as the *Late Commander* and far speedier. Her lithe, light, lofty, tapering spars, her snow-white canvas, and the inevitable gilt streak around her bends, following the graceful lines of her faultless sheer, all proclaimed her nationality as well as though she had her colors flying and the name of her hail port painted on her foresail.

Then the grinding of the tie in the masthead and the ringing of the chain span in the big iron gin abaft the mast told me that the halyards were tautening and that the crew on deck were preparing to masthead the yard. I looked down at the long wild sweep of the narrow deck and saw the men, both watches included, trailing along on the topgallant halyards. The yard surged up a few inches under the preliminary pull. Then, after a brief pause, "Broken Nose" Cockney's strong, sonorous voice arose in the inspiring strains of an old American chantey—a courteous tribute to our fleeter rival:

> *A Yankee ship come down the river;*
> *Blow, boys, blow.*
> *He luffs her up till her tops'ls shiver;*
> *Blow, my bully boys, blow!*
>
> *A Yankee ship, she's a Yankee clipper;*
> *Blow, boys, blow.*
> *A Yankee ship with a Yankee skipper;*
> *Blow, my bully boys, blow!*
>
> *This Yankee ship she's bound to China;*
> *Blow, boys, blow.*
> *Hooray, my boys it's time to jine 'er;*
> *Blow, my bully boys, blow!*
>
> *"Now how d'ye know she's a Yankee packet?"*
> *Blow, boys, blow.*
> *"They fired a gun; I heard the racket;"*
> *Blow, my bully boys, blow!*
>
> *"An' how d'ye know she's bound to China?"*
> *Blow, boys, blow.*
> *"The Stars and Stripes float out behind 'er;"*
> *Blow, my bully boys, blow!*
>
> *"An' who d'ye think was the skipper of 'er?"*
> *Blow, boys, blow.*
> *"Oh, Jimmy Long Jackson, a South Sea rover;"*
> *Blow, my bully boys, blow!*

*Oh, Jimmy Long Jackson's a Yankee sailor;*
*Blow, boys, blow.*
*Oh, Jimmy Long Jackson's a South Sea whaler;*
*Blow, my bully boys, blow!*

The inspiring strains of the good old chantey restored my mental and nervous poise. Standing proudly on the topmast cap and hauling up the slack of the running gear with both hands, I joined with wild enthusiasm and reckless abandon in singing the simple words and exhilarating refrain of the historical hoisting song.

As verse after verse of the measured stanzas came wafting over the mastheads, I sang the loudest and boldest of anybody until the crunching of the sheaves and the straining of the well-stretched hemp told that the parrel was up to the collars and the yard was home. Then I quickly stopped the gear and descended safely to the deck.

By this time our morning visitor was nearly abeam and sailing past us as though we were windbound. Her graceful lines and lofty rig showed up to splendid advantage as she rolled majestically in the mountainous sea, and the bright sheen of her coppered bilges emphasized the finely chiseled lines of her shapely bottom.

The two skippers were exchanging signals by now, and we soon learned that our fleeting consort was the ship *North American,* bound, like ourselves, to Calcutta. She had left New York ten days behind us. She reached Calcutta about a week ahead of us, thus beating our time by nearly seventeen days.

We were wearing our colors at half-mast in honor of our dead, and when informed by code of the reason of our mourning, the American skipper dropped his own colors to the half peak and signaled, "Condolences." The two captains then continued to exchange messages in code for some time longer, but as we had no translation they were uninteresting to the crew.

But what did interest us was the amazing burst of speed developed by that stately American ship in passing us at sea. It seemed incredible that after our immense, almost record-breaking run of the previous few days the *Late Commander* could so easily be beaten. And, more remarkable still, the setting of our enormous main-topgallant sail appeared to better our chances not one iota. The American ship apparently gained at exactly the same rate she had before the sail was set. In an hour, she had dipped us a blurred and indistinct farewell and disappeared from sight in the skydrift ahead. It seemed as if the corpse of Pengelley lying stark and cold in his shroud held like lead on the oaken keel of the *Late Commander.*

There is always a weird and awful solemnity attending a burial at sea that does not inhere to shore funerals. Not that shore people as a rule grieve less or mourn less sincerely for their dead; but there is an all-pervading significance inseparable from the tragic formalities of a sea funeral that seems to bring the living into closer relationship with the mysterious unknown. The vast solitudes of the sounding sea, the endless wastes of troubled waters, the solemn unknown depths of silent darkness below, and the limitless expanse of vaulted and ever-changing immensity above—all conspire to oppress us with an unutterable fear of the mysterious transformation from the conscious persistent present to the cold, placid, impenetrable silence of eternal separation.

We may visit and decorate and venerate the graves of our loved ones who die ashore. But where are the graves of those lost or buried at sea? A land funeral appeals mainly to our corporeal feelings. Our sympathies and inward senses are deeply and perhaps overwhelmingly disturbed by the enormity of our bereavement; but a burial at sea staggers human imagination and depresses the spirits of men by the incomprehensible and awful grandeur of the eternal solitudes surrounding the event.

Then, too, a burial at sea is an astounding event in the experience and memories of a sailing ship's crew from which they never recover during the remainder of that voyage and which they never forget during their lives. Among the surging multitudes of men on shore, the passing of an individual is soon forgotten and his absence is never felt for long. But within the limited community of the "rank and narrow ship," where all must live and do or, perchance, all die together, a sudden vacancy is immediately and sadly felt. Sailors at sea are more than kindred to each other; shipmates are often dearer than brothers.

Pengelley's funeral having been set for half-past twelve that Sunday afternoon, preparations advanced accordingly. During the forenoon, the members of the crew had been permitted to file around the bier on the cabin mess board and view the silent features of their late shipmate—a privilege which, according to my own experience, is rarely extended under such circumstances in the merchant marine. When all had passed, "Sails" and I closed the flap reverently over the still face and sewed it carefully in place, shutting out the light of this transitory existence forevermore.

Punctually at the stroke of one bell came the order from the poop to shorten sail. It would have been impractical to heave to while running square before that mountainous sea; therefore, we merely lowered our main-topgallant and fore- and mizzen-topsail yards and let the sails hang floundering in the buntlines during the funeral exercises. When the running gear had been belayed, the entire crew, except the mate on watch and the two helmsmen, were mustered aft to witness the burial. Then the closely shrouded form was brought from the cabin by the three remaining apprentices and Mister Denham, our third mate. They placed their burden on a rude catafalque of boards erected on deck in front of an open waist port.

Captain Grummitt then mounted the little monkey bridge extending from the break of the poop to the spur of the mainmast. With Prayer Book in hand, he proceeded to read the immortal ritual, "For the dead who die at sea," with as much feeling or sympathetic inflection in his tones as he would have displayed in reading over the stated text of a ship's manifest. Just before the final passage was reached, the Old Man paused, and at the raising of his right hand the bos'n and carpenter obediently elevated the inboard end of the burial plank and prepared for the final and eternal plunge. Then at the conclusion of the brief service, the Union Jack, with which the shrouded form had been draped, was reverently withdrawn and carefully folded, the funeral plank was tilted at an acute angle, and all that was mortal of Alfred Pengelley plunged downward to its everlasting resting place at the silent unsounded bottom of the eternal sea.

*We sewed him in his hammock; an able seaman's shroud,*
*As we sailed along the low lands, low, oh, low.*
*And we sunk him where the green seas were booming long and loud,*
*For we sunk him in the low lands, low, oh, low,*
*We sunk him in the lonesome sea.*

A few days later, we ran out of the stormy southern zone into the bright and glorious region presided over by the humming constancy of the sou'west monsoons. Then, contrary to all our previous experiences, all the humdrum drudgery of ship cleaning, souji-moujeing, painting, holystoning, and scraping was dropped and not resumed until lifelines, preventer backropes, flemish horses, and full-arm beckets had been rigged in their proper places throughout every one of our yards, upon our massive bowsprit, and on the flying jib boom. Then, the *Late Commander* was the most completely equipped ship in the matter of saving gear I had ever seen.

At last, after the needless sacrifice of four human lives, the awful lesson had struck home. Who shall answer in the Day of Judgment for these wanton crimes? What difference is there in kind between murder for revenge and murder for aggrandizement? We cannot, by statutory law, punish the unscrupulous shipmonger who willfully jeopardizes human lives to enhance his dividends; but the Higher Law, the innate sense of right and wrong, recognizes no difference between murder for revenge and murder for greed.

It was the night after our return to the famous "City of Palaces" (and mud huts), and we were all comfortably seated round a table in the guest room at Piringee Katherine's spacious and well-appointed bungalow in the New Market Road. There were four of us in the bunch: Big Mac, Little Mac, Spike Riley, and myself. The *Late Commander* was posted at the British shipping office to pay off the next day. With the enthusing prospect of twelve months' pay under our lee and nothing to do but enjoy ourselves, we could be gentlemen, at least for a week. We felt and behaved as though we had been nominated Rajahs for life; hence, we relaxed at the table with a decanter of prime Three Star, glasses, a box of imported Manila cigars, and a bevy of highly "educated" young Maghees to fan and wait upon us, to perform for our entertainment, and to anticipate and gratify our every wish.

Little Mac, the literary enthusiast of the group, was industriously scanning the previous day's issue of *The Hooghly Lyre.* "Here ye are, fellers," he piped suddenly, pausing with finger posted on a paragraph in the "River Column." "We're here at last. Listen. 'Arrived: *Late Commander;* Grummitt; New York; 133 days. 90,000 cases r.p. to Bying & Selling; Hooghly Moorings, Budge-Budge.'"

"Glad they found it out," grunted Big Mac dryly.

"Yeah," assented Spike Riley with a cheerful grin. "I never thought enybuddy noticed us coming up th' river 'ceptin' them rotten o' bramlykites. But I don't reckon them reporter fellers is much diffrunt from bramlykites; they all feeds on th' same carcasses enyhow."

"Bramlykites is right, Spike," chimed in Little Mac, still scanning the paper with renewed interest in his quest for news. "Here fellers, jest hark to this."

## KILLED BY CARELESSNESS

There were tears in the kindly eyes and deep sorrow in the voice of Captain Grummitt, master of the stately, well-found clipper, *Late Commander,* as he told in feeling accents and with fatherly compassion of the accidental and deplorable death at sea on July 23rd of Mr. Alfred Pengelley, late senior apprentice on that ship, and eldest son of Lieutenant Edward Pengelley, R.N., of Saint Ives, Cornwall. Apprentice Pengelley was buried at sea on Sunday, July 24th, with full maritime honors. His bereaved relatives have been duly notified of the sad event.

Captain Grummitt attributes the unfortunate and distressing accident to the carelessness displayed by one of the able seamen among the crew in improperly seizing a becket to the main topgallant yardarm from which Mr. Pengelley fell.

It is the general belief prevailing among the officers of the ship and concurred in by Captain Grummitt that Mr. Pengelley's fall was caused by his grasping an insecurely fastened becket, thereby losing his balance on the footrope beneath the yard.

Mr. Reuben Riggins, the courteous chief mate of the *Late Commander,* was most diligent and obliging to a representative of the *Lyre,* and spared no pains in exhibiting and describing the various kinds of lifesaving appliances with which this ship is so thoroughly equipped throughout.

Since all the topgallant and royal and skysail yards had been lowered to the deck in obedience to port regulations, a close and complete inspection was easy. Judging from the personal examination of the *Late Commander's* yardarms afforded the representative of the *Lyre,* there can be no ship on all the seven seas in which the members of the crew have been better safeguarded from accident. Her life-saving equipment must be maintained at a very considerable expense to her enterprising but careful owners.

A long moment of silence prevailed over the group as Little Mac, having concluded, pushed the paper aside and sat regarding us with a questioning stare.

" 'S that all?" asked Big Mac tersely, breaking the silence.

"Ain't that enough?" retorted Little Mac. "I wonder how much a fathom them reporter fellers gits fer stringin' lies. They kin shore string 'em faster'n a So-So gal kin string beads."

"Wal," put in Big Mac slowly, "I wuz jest waitin' fer yer to git to whar' Ol' Man Grummitt growed a par o' wings and flew away when yer stopped readin'. It wuz a kind uv a disap'intin' finish, thet's all. Th' Ol' Man, hisself, is a shore enuf three skys'l yarder when it comes to stringin' reporters. Don't blame thet pore reporter chap. He's on'y a dummy. Ol' Grummitt's got him plum lassoed, tied, and fair locoed. He'd swar th' monkey gaff wuz th' martingale ef Ol' Grummitt on'y said so."

The facetious criticisms of my mates no longer interested me. The reading of the passing of Pengelley had brought back to mind my last promise to him. Rising from my place at the table, heedless of the remonstrances of my erstwhile cup companions, I made a suitable excuse and left the room. Passing out to our sleeping quarters in the courtyard in the rear of the house, I dug into my sea chest and brought out the cherished box entrusted to me. Then I walked quietly around to the big front gate, hailed a passing cab, and jumping in instructed the gherry-wallah to drive to the Priory.

I presume the Sultan of Turkey and myself were about the last two callers Miss Primrose was expecting that particular evening. I fear her previous acquaintance with me had not tended to exalt me in her personal esteem; nevertheless, she greeted me graciously and invited me into the sanctuary of her cozy little study.

Miss Primrose was the daughter of an English clergyman. She had come out to Calcutta some few years previously as a volunteer missionary among the merchant seamen who, I am ashamed to say, were the most benighted heathens in the Indian Empire.

But if the sailors were bad, it was largely because the hypocritical Holy Joes sent out to reform them were their moral superiors in appearances only. A great deal of moral latitude, not to say license, was permitted in Calcutta at that time. Everything was cheap—rum, women, and tobacco. The merchant sailor was allowed to do pretty much as he pleased in pursuing his peculiar ideas of personal enjoyment. He might get drunk in The Numbers, riot in the Checkers, and then proceed to clean out the "German Barracks" without fear of serious interference or arrest on the part of the East India Police, most of whom were recruited from the maritime contingent themselves. But the only real difference between a sailor and a Devil-dodger was that the former was exactly what he professed to be while the latter pretended to be what he was not.

Of all the revivalists in the degenerate environs of Sailor Town, Miss Primrose was in a class by herself. She had but little in common with the corporate brotherhood of "seamen's friends." Laboring principally alone and largely on her own resources, she had accomplished more in the short period of her humble ministry to convert and regenerate depraved and dissolute seamen than all the other moral and social forces on the Hooghly combined. Drunk or sober, every sailor on the beach saluted Miss Primrose when she passed, and there was no seaman so degraded as to offer her the slightest offense.

This was my first visit to the Priory, and I am now proud to add it was not my last. Miss Primrose had already heard of Pengelley's death and was eager to hear from one who could give her first-hand information. Seated together in the seclusion of her quiet little room, I told her the broad facts concerning Pengelley's sorrowful end and stormy burial.

After I had concluded my recital, Miss Primrose sat for some time weeping softly. When she had regained her composure, we conversed for a while on other topics. Then I handed her my treas-ured package and told her the purpose of my visit. Removing the wrapping, Miss Primrose drew forth a large envelope addressed in Pengelley's bold clear hand to "Miss Eunice Pengelley, St. Ives, Cornwall." Miss Primrose held the envelope for a few moments and then sat back waiting for me to speak.

Then, in unconscious obedience to her silent invitation, I related all that had taken place under the longboat that dreary night, of Pengelley's dreaded premonition, and of his terrifying death on the cabin table. I told her, too, of our close friendship, of the pleas-ant liberty days we had enjoyed together during our long stay in New York, and of how we used to attend church together every Sunday while in port at Old St. Paul's on Broadway. Finally, I re-ferred to Pengelley's request that I write his sister and send, with Miss Primrose's assistance, his last letter and the keepsakes.

When I finished, Miss Primrose stood up quite abruptly and came toward me. Her eyes were dry now and she seemed quite cheerful. "Why, Mr. Williams," she exclaimed, "you are not a bad man after all. I am afraid we have all misjudged you terribly. And now," she continued amiably, "we'll just have a cup of tea and some refresh-ment together. Then you shall write your letter to Miss Pengelley."

At Miss Primrose's order, a *kulashi* servant came silently into the room and set a small collation table with a pot of fragrant Ceylon tea, wheat bread and ghee, and preserved fruits. He stood by and

served us; then quietly withdrew taking the simple table service
with him.

Miss Primrose then opened her secretary and produced writing
materials. It was no easy task for me to write that heart-burning
letter, but I finally succeeded to the best of my ability. It com-
prised six closely written pages, and it was drawing near midnight
before I finished. My mind was weary, for heavy writing was not
in my line. The composition of that missive caused me more mental
and spiritual anguish than any I have ever attempted since.

That night, under Miss Primrose's earnest persuasion, I slept at
the Priory. A bed was arranged for me in the "Boys' Dormitory,"
and I passed the night in peace. And it may be interesting to note
in passing that it was within the cloistered shelter of that same
Priory nearly two years later, that is to say, on July 4, 1889, that
I wrote another letter, one afterward signed by twenty-five able
seamen and two bos'ns in a certain ship. Addressed to the Rev.
Father Hopkins (†), Seamen's Chaplain, it resulted in a thorough investigation and reform of the hypocritical sky-pilot system prevailing at that degenerate period in Calcutta. A vigorous and effective
overhauling of the Sailors' Home management likewise ensued.
The pernicious crimping system which long had corrupted the
Home officials, degraded the seamen, and disgraced the port was
completely abolished. God grant that Pengelley's fearful death
may have been the beginning of a righteous purpose.

The Yankee squad disbanded that time in Calcutta. We never
came together again. Big Mac shipped for Australia and his ship
was lost on the Great Barrier Reef near the entrance to Torres
Strait and all hands perished. Little Mac went to New Zealand,
married in Port Littleton, and raised a pair of Yankee twins who,
according to a fraternal announcement reaching us, were named
after Spike Riley and me. Spike Riley made one voyage in a country-wallah among the Indian Islands; then becoming disgusted
with the trade shipped for England. I remained on the beach a few
months longer driving a gang of coolies in the graving dock at
Howrah across the Hooghly. Then, I, too, felt the call of the sea.

## 8 · THE WRECK OF THE "WILD ROSE"

Among the stately fleet of loftily sparred windjammers that lined the Esplanade, the *Wild Rose* was the most noticeable of all. Among the entire fleet of fifty sail, she was the only bark; all the others were full-riggers. She was likewise the smallest—only 760 tons register—a mere fishing smack in size compared to her broad-winged competitors. She was the only ship occupying a berth at the government dock; all the others lay astream in the Hooghly moorings. And, last and most noteworthy, she was the only wooden ship moored in Calcutta. All the others were steel-hulled and steel-sparred racers.

Like the rest of the fleet, the *Wild Rose* was a British vessel, but a British deepwater ship built of timber had become a *rara avis* by the late 1880's. Iron was abundant in Great Britain; timber was scarce. Therefore, wooden ships were seldom built except for special service.

The *Wild Rose* had arrived in Calcutta with a cargo of salt. Salt quickly cankers in a steel hull unless specially and very expensively stowed. Hence the appearance of a solitary wooden ship on the scene. Salt was, moreover, a government monopoly in India; therefore, the *Wild Rose* was carefully berthed at the government dock to protect the British revenue.

118

I was a gay young ropeyarn in those days and a good judge of windjammers. My fancy in ladies and ships always favored the smaller ones. The smaller they are the easier they handle and the less gear it takes to rig 'em. When the *Wild Rose* hoisted her "Seamen Wanted" sign in the fore rigging, and it was officially announced that she was about to clear, I made a beeline for the shipping office to file my application and leave my discharges.

When the crowd of expectant seamen lined up for inspection and service, my friend, Mat Doran, and I were the two first men selected. The following day, we were ordered aboard. The ship cast off her moorings and dropped down to Garden Reach where we lay astream several days, our time occupied in sending up our topgallant and royal yards, bending sails, trimming ballast, and otherwise preparing for sea. The *Wild Rose* hailed from Liverpool, was owned in West Hartlepool, and was bound to Delagoa Bay in Portuguese East Africa to load a cargo of wool for London.

With ballast and stores aboard and everything taut and snug, we took our pilot and towed down the turbulent Hooghly behind the big river tug *Warren Hastings*. At Sand Heads, we spread our great wings for a pleasant passage down the broad Bay of Bengal and across the indigo expanse of the Indian Ocean to the coast of Africa.

Our trip to Delagoa Bay was fair and uneventful. The *Wild Rose* was a well-found, able vessel, though not overly fast. Our skipper's name was Foss. He was managing owner and was a superb master. Officers and crew were always on the best of terms. From a sailor's point of view, there was nothing on earth to complain of, and everyone on board looked forward to a speedy voyage, a safe and happy conclusion, and good pay to dissipate among the rosy-cheeked barmaids of the London pubs.

Delagoa Bay was a great, open, unsheltered roadstead entirely unprotected from the rigors of the violent storms that periodically blew up from the Cape of Good Hope with destructive force, leveling everything in their wake along the land. At the time, the Bay was a barren, dreary, irregular indentation on the African seaboard entirely destitute of artificial improvements or harbor facilities of any kind. The place was important only as the one possible outlet for the exportation of the agricultural products of the surrounding region.

The ships always rode at anchor with springs on their cables and with their topsails furled in stops. Then, in case of an approaching tempest, they could quickly break out the stops, sheet home the sails, slip their cables, leaving the anchors behind, and drive off to sea where they could ride out the storm in deep water. When the weather abated, they could return to their mooring place, pick up their deserted cables, and resume loading as before.

It was all in the day's work, and the *Wild Rose* was compelled to clear out to sea twice to ride out the severe storms during the long six weeks her lading was in progress.

The bales of wool were lightered out to our moorings and steved by native African Kroo-boys, great, long-limbed, powerful fellows, and wonderfully efficient stevedores. Whenever there was an easterly wind from any angle, a tumultuous surf would disturb the Bay and often we would be compelled to suspend operations. During these "lulls" the Kroo-boys would all jump overboard and tumble about gleefully in the boiling surf. On such occasions, I, too, used to dive over the side to enjoy the strenuous frolic with them, for I delighted in rough swimming. Those big, long-geared savages could beat me two to one swimming in level water, but not a mother's son of them could beat me riding the surf.

I got to be real chummy with all of them during our stay in the Bay, and they urged me to go ashore with them when the ship left, pick out some wives, and settle down to the kingly life of a native chief. But that was only one of many remarkable chances to become rich and numerous which I have felt constrained to forego. When our last bale of wool had been stowed and our hatches battened, we found our anchors and cleared for merry England with glad and valiant hearts.

It was summer in the Southern Hemisphere, mid-December, and we skirted boldly around the eastern coast of Madagascar and rounded the dread Cape of Good Hope within easy code signaling distance. We enjoyed fine weather and favorable winds all the way. The southeast trades in the Atlantic were unusually light that year, and we made rather a long passage to the Line. But once across the Equator and clear of the doldrums, we picked up the brisk northeast trades and our good old bark kicked up her heels and came romping toward home at a racing gait.

We sighted the Lizard on the southern extremity of England in the last days of February and stood across the chops of the Channel toward Plymouth Sound. Then we steered boldly up midchannel for the Strait of Dover.

After we had proceeded well up the Channel, the wind suddenly veered to the northeastward, the weather became much colder than it had been, the winter sky became thickened with heavy, leaden cloud rifts, and a whirling snowstorm became imminent. That afternoon we shortened down to lower and upper topsails, single-reefed courses, lower staysails, and spanker, and began to beat.

Just at dusk, we met the *Niobe,* a large, full-rigged steel ship bound from Calcutta to London with a cargo of jute. Thereafter, she became our chance consort, nearly always within sight. For ten long dismal days and fearful nights, we split tacks with each other on every leg. For ten fateful days the northeast wind prevailed with varying force but constant fury. Ten times both ships, by dint of superhuman exertions on the part of their devoted crews, attempted the passage of the storm-bound Strait; and as many times we were driven hopelessly back in a tumult of howling wind, tumultuous sea, and stinging snow.

When the last despairing attempt had failed and our devoted ship turned reeling and groaning in every frame and fiber of her battered hull before the pitiless blast, every man on board realized that the battle was lost. Our noble bark was doomed. The drenching spray constantly sweeping over our bulwarks had frozen as it struck, and our waists and channels were at length weighted with accumulated masses of packed ice. Our sails and running rigging, stiffened and panoplied with clinging sheets of frozen snow and sleet, were almost unmanageable. The hull was strained and leaking in every seam, and the exhausted, embattled crew was no longer able to man the pumps.

It was near midnight and the blinding snow and impenetrable darkness shut out all possibility of observation or hope of assistance from shore. In this hopeless extremity we made torches of oakum dipped in slow-burning colza oil and set them on poles at the gangways. Then Captain Foss mustered all hands aft on the poop for the fatal conference which is always the last act in a marine disaster before the final crash. Then, and only then, custom and maritime law require the master to share his responsibility with his crew. When disaster is inevitable, the master must take counsel with his crew.

Captain Foss was over sixty-five years of age at that time. He was a kindly, considerate old master and a prime seaman. He knew every fathom of the English Channel as intimately as he did every nautical problem in his well-thumbed epitome. When the crew had mustered around the binnacle light, Captain Foss set our position before us in simple, unassuming, but tragic terms. The impossibility of forcing a passage through the turbulent, storm-torn Strait in our present extremity was apparent to all. Our only thoughts must be for ourselves; we must wreck the ship as judiciously as possible to save our lives.

Ten miles below us, the captain explained, was an open cove with a sandy beach near a fishing village on the French shore. Beyond that lay a ridge of merciless grinding rocks. If we went astray on those pitiless rocks, the master solemnly warned us, all hands would perish. But by bracing our yards and laying our course directly for the sands, we could beach our ship without dashing her hull to splinters. We would also be within reach of help and some of us might be saved.

The soundness and resourcefulness of the Old Man's reasoning was inescapable. In the flickering light of the lonely binnacle lamp, we unanimously voted to defer entirely to his intimate knowledge and experienced judgment. The short and solemn council ended, we trudged heavily forward to execute the skipper's orders to shorten sail and prepare to strike.

Glancing backward from the break of the poop, we beheld the storm-shrouded figure of the Old Man as he stood unsteadily near the wheel, his weather-beaten, careworn features and venerable gray beard faintly illumined by the feeble glow of the binnacle light.

"Cheer him, boys! Cheer him!" yelled Jack Wadhams, our leather-lunged old bos'n.

Then in one death-defying voice, we sent up three rousing cheers for Captain Foss that rose clear and undaunted above the midnight tempest, the screaming mastheads, and the sifting snow. We saw the Old Man raise his grizzled head, and a grim smile of confident determination lit up his graven features as he waved his appreciation. Then we knew our battle with Death and the elements was more than half won.

Our ship was soon shortened down to two lower topsails, fore- and main-topmast staysails, and spanker. We braced our yards sharp up on the port tack and hove to long enough to get our longboat down from the top of the forward deck house and launch it. Then we rigged up a boom for an outrigger to hold the boat off the ship's quarter and prevent it from being stove when we went a-wreck. We made fast the slack of the boat line on deck so that we could pay out as required to keep the boat clear of wreckage when we struck. Then we were ready for the great adventure.

When all was in order, we checked our yards and drove headlong for the deserted beach. Just as we were squaring our yards for the final drive, we heard a muffled and indistinct hail, and for a moment in the obscurity of the night and the snow we saw our old consort in adversity, the brave *Niobe*. She, too, was under short canvas, was burning naphtha torches, and, like ourselves, was preparing to drive for the beach in a last forlorn extremity.

After running before the wind for half an hour, we hove to again and made several casts with an armed lead. When the depth and nature of the bottom indicated to the Old Man that we were in the right position, he took his bearings accordingly and ordered us to square the yards for the final drive. Then we paid out on our boat line to give it plenty of scope to clear the inevitable wreckage.

As the devoted ship was driving toward her doom, Captain Foss came to me where we were all now assembled on the poop for safety. Laying his hand firmly on my shoulder, he drew me a little aside from my mates. "Thee's a bowld swimmer, lad," he said gravely. "I saw thee strivin' wi' the big black fellers down on the coast, an' de'il a wan o' 'em could best ye i' the tumblers. The wather's a wee bit chilly 'ere-abouts," he added significantly, "but someone has to fetch to the boat when we're a-wreck or aw 'ands mought perish.* I canna order thee in this case, lad," he said appealingly, "but will thee do it as a seaman's duty to 'is mates?"

We could faintly hear the ominous rumbling of the distant boomers on the beach by now, and I removed my stiffened oilskins and began to undress, for I realized that amid the raging surf a heavily clad man would soon become waterlogged and helpless. I therefore stripped myself to bare poles. I then strapped my sheath knife and belt securely around my naked waist so that in case I became entangled among the wreckage I might cut myself clear, for a sailor without a knife is as useless as a soldier without a musket.

Mr. Burns, our old first mate, fetched a blanket and wrapped it about me, and during the short remainder of that fateful passage I stood shivering in the gangway as I watched the heavy combers rearing over our bulwarks and breaching furiously across our sloping decks.

The roar of the boomers became more distinct and insistent as we neared the fatal cove. Through the blinding obscurity of the driving snow, we caught occasional fitful flashes of flickering lights darting like restless fireflies about the beach. The vigilant Coast Guard was alert and sensible of our distress. As we entered the

---

* Since in the tangle of wreckage it would probably be impossible to haul in the boat to the ship, it was necessary to have someone carry a life line to the longboat. (Ed.)

mouth of the cove, the lights became more distinct, and we could faintly hear voices shouting unintelligible instructions in French.

When we were well within the inlet and could distinguish the brilliant white crest of the agitated beach, Captain Foss ordered the helm hard aweather, and the lee braces let go. The bark, answering obediently the turn of her rudder and the new impulse of her squared canvas, veered southward, struggled forward through the wild surf a few moments longer, then struck with terrific impact on the hardened sand. Picked up by the relentless onrush of the next comber, she was tossed forward again as lightly as a shuttlecock flung from a battledore and thrown on the implacable sand again with a still mightier crash that threw every man on board to the deck. Her massive hulk, wobbling like a stricken roebuck, was raised momentarily again in midair on the crest of a mighty surge. Then, impelled forward and downward with the velocity of an alpine avalanche, her great frame struck with stupendous violence, ploughed deeply through the sodden bottom, and hung motionless.

The masts and rigging swayed violently a few times and then crashed over the side with all their enormous weight of towering spars and tangled gear. The ship rolled heavily to her bilge, a dead and useless thing, and the unfeeling elements began their eternal destruction upon her helpless form as though she had always been theirs to destroy.

Then, just as the ship had stranded, a wild, despairing cry was borne to us on the wings of the relentless storm. Its meaning was easily defined. The *Niobe* had not been as fortunate as the *Wild Rose*. The fateful tidings of the loss of the *Niobe* came to those of us who still survived a few days later. Being a narrow-hulled, steel ship of deep draft and speedy design, the *Niobe* had stranded far out on the brow of the sandbank as she attempted to make the entrance, and her bow plates were stove. Then she slipped off into deep water again, carrying every soul aboard down to the eternal depths with her, including the unfortunate captain's wife and daughter, who had sailed with him on that last fatal voyage. The *Wild Rose*, a sturdy wooden ship of broader beam, shoaler draft, and greater natural buoyancy, had easily cleared the brow of the shoal and driven well up to the head of the inlet. Thus we had a fighting chance.

As soon as the ship had permanently stranded, we turned to our longboat which had been towing bravely astern during our daring drive for the cove and which lay tugging wildly at its hawser. Captain Foss's methods had worked successfully. The boat lay safely attached to the hulk, clear of the wreckage, but twenty fathoms away. A small lifeline was soon secured around my waist and I was ready for my own part in the desperate adventure.

"Now go in, lad!" Captain Foss shouted in my ear, "an' God go wi' thee!"

Then I mounted the rail and plunged into the raging surf. The shock of the plunge soon passed, for the water was not as cold as the air. But the task before me as I began that struggle against the destroying elements was one to appall the heart and bewilder the head of a braver and stronger man. The boat was twenty fathoms from the wreck and in the tumultuous surf there was imminent danger of being carried beyond it. Great quantities of fine sand churned up from the bottom mingled with the agitated water and blinded and choked and distressed me. Stray pieces of vagrant wreckage pierced and bruised my body and lacerated my flesh. Straggling bights of rope and stray wisps of shredded rigging constantly ensnarled me and hampered my movements. Rearing combers broke over my head repeatedly, submerging me and nearly stifling out my life. But every time I struggled to the crests again and was nearer to the coveted boat.

At last, when in danger of being carried beyond, I managed by the desperate effort of a despairing man to grasp the boat line. After a series of cruel buffetings and a mad scramble with the storm-tossed boat, I finally secured a drowning man's grip on the stem and clambered painfully over the gunwale. Then I fell battered, bleeding, blinded, and exhausted among the naked thwarts and wished I was dead.

I could distinctly see the people on the beach by now. Women as well as men flitted excitedly about with flaming torches in their hands. I could plainly hear their animated cries and eager shouts, and I longed to be with them where I might find warmth, food, shelter, and solace. I could cut the hawser with my sheath knife and let the boat drive ashore! No one would ever know! I could throw my belt away in the roaring surf and leave no trace of my perfidious deed—the hawser parted!

Obsessed by this cowardly desire, I crawled forward to execute my treacherous design. Then I glanced at the stranded wreck and beheld my helpless shipmates clustered hopefully around the mizzen fife rail. The forlorn appearance of that group expectantly waiting for the sound of my voice reacted upon my conscience like a challenge from the grave, and I shrank back abashed and ashamed.

With trembling hands, I took the lifeline off my waist, made the end fast to a thwart, and then hailed the ship. "Wreck ahoy!" I shouted. "All fast in the boat! Ready to haul out!" The exertion of my lungs and the sound of my own voice inspired and warmed me wonderfully. I was back on duty again. Soon I felt an insistent tug on the heaving line, and a strong voice from the wreck hailed me to "haul out." I tugged away lustily on the life line and soon brought alongside "Dido," the cabin boy, gasping, choking, and strangling for breath but safely enclosed in the center of a ring buoy. I dragged him half-drowned into the boat.

By the time the buoy had been hauled back for another venture, "Dido" had recovered sufficiently to help me haul out his principal, the cook. And so, one by one, all the living among the crew were hauled safely into the boat—thirteen in all saved, and five missing. Captain Foss was the last to leave, and we dragged him into the boat completely exhausted and near collapse.

At an order from the mate, I severed the five-inch line which held us to the boom. Rising on the crest of a giant comber, the boat sped toward the wild but welcome shore like a bird suddenly released from a snare. But just as we swung away from our mooring, a wild shout arose from the stranded ship. Straining our eyes through the stinging snowstorm, we could faintly discern by the dying glow of the smoldering torches the familiar form of our loyal old bos'n, Jack Wadhams. He was riding desperately astride the end of the spanker boom and beseeching us not to desert him.

The boat, though now adrift and plunging toward the shore in the surf, was still head on toward the wreck, because in that riotous sea it would have been madness to have attempted to turn it about. We had intended to allow the boat to drift ashore stern first, using our oars only to prevent broaching. We therefore made every effort to pull straight toward the wreck in response to Jack's frantic call. But from the very first, it was sadly apparent that our struggle was hopeless. Still, as long as the loom of the ship remained in sight, we never relinquished our futile efforts at the oars or missed a single stroke. But the gale and waves were too strong; hope departed with the vanishing sight of the stranded hulk.

As our boat neared the storm-strewn beach, two-score strong-armed lifeguards and husky fishermen rushed into the raging surf up to their shoulders and grasped the gunwales. We threw away our now useless oars as, with an exultant shout, a mighty heave, and a homeward-bound rush, the brave French seamen swept our heavy boat bodily ashore with all its occupants and launched it high and dry beyond reach of surge and tide.

The kind-hearted fisherfolk, as poor as they were, actually fought each other for the honor of caring for us. But finally we were amicably distributed among them and all our wants were ministered to with solicitude and Christian kindness.

At the earnest entreaties of Captain Foss, the big Coast Guard lifeboat was run down to the beach, manned by a picked crew of burly oarsmen, and launched in a final attempt to regain the wreck and rescue Jack Wadhams. For more than an hour, the courageous Frenchmen battled frantically with the raging elements, but at last they were beaten back.

The next morning the storm had subsided and the snowstorm had passed. Everyone in the village was down on the beach to view the remains of the ship, now plainly visible in the near offing across the cove, and to salvage such odds and ends of stray wreckage or cargo as might have drifted ashore.

The hulk of the *Wild Rose* had broken up during the night. The quarter section and stern part of the vessel had been wrenched forcibly away from its fastenings by the tremendous battering of the sea and was now turned at right angles to the main body of the hull, which was already immovably imbedded in the sodden sand. We found Jack Wadham's body with his arms wrapped tightly around a neatly rolled spare topsail which had been washed out of the lazarette when the wreck broke in twain. In the course of the day, the bodies of our remaining four lost shipmates were likewise washed up with the tide. All were bruised and battered almost beyond recognition by the remorseless sea.

The following day was Sunday—for we were wrecked on Friday, the sailor's day of ill omen—and the morning sun broke bright and glorious. Then, all the inhabitants of the village, men, women, and children, turned out in a body and marched in solemn procession with us to attend the strangers' funeral. They lie, today, buried on the deserted brow of that barren slope overlooking the boisterous Channel where the once sturdy frames of the good *Wild Rose* lie grounding in the sullen sands.

One of the best men I ever shipped with was a he-goat; and one of the worst hounds was a brute called, for courtesy's sake, a man.

The bark's name was *Helaroara*. The Captain's name was Larruper, and because he always wore a red skullcap, the boys dubbed him "Old Antichrist." Tom Swattem was bos'n, and the Mongolian pot wrestler was designated on the ship's articles as Ah-Chuk but otherwise nicknamed "Chink."

I was the oracle of the forward end. Whenever anything came on board for which no name or use could be found, it was always brought to me to be officially christened and assigned to its proper place in the sphere of natural economy—usually over the side where there's plenty of room for everything.

At Iloilo in the Philippines, somebody brought two Malays on board in exchange for a couple of advance notes and a bottle of *canea*. I named them Johnny Hilo and Patsey and the names stuck. Johnny got a job in the cockpit tarring the anchor chains and Patsey found steady employment holystoning the 'tween decks. That's all they were good for and they were not much good at that.

At Honolulu, we got a pig, a quaint, inquisitive little cuss who soon became a general favorite. I named him Dennis and appointed him Head Squealer, and assigned him to duty at the forecastle door to call the watch every morning at breakfast time. Dennis made a most efficient and reliable squealer, but unfortunately we lost him overboard in a gale one dark night before we had time to test his chops.

At Penang on the Malay Peninsula, the most esteemed acquisition to our floating menagerie was the biggest and ugliest dog ever pupped. I never saw his color anywhere else so, of course, I don't know the name of it. As to his breed—well, refer to Darwin.

I labeled him "Bos'n" out of compliment to my esteemed friend Tom Swattem, and I assigned him to gangway duty so I might get a chance to snooze in my anchor watch. The dog made much the better bos'n of the two.

My hero, the goat, came on board at Port Louis in the Isle of France where we loaded chemicalized railroad ties for Rangoon. I christened him "Billy," but the boys maliciously surnamed him "Stink." Billy was no ranik or destitute Paddy West send-off, but a full-rigged, respectable seafaring goat of the noble "butt in" breed. And he carried all his belongings with him.

Billy always wore a mixed suit of brown, yellow, and white goat hide with a jet-black patch pasted across his memory pane. His chief pride lay in a long pair of formidable and aggressive-looking horns and a splendid set of Yankee Doodle whiskers.

Billy also brought with him an appetite and a disposition, and he was richly perfumed with a doubly distilled and highly concentrated odor. He greeted me with a vigorous nod as he ascended majestically over the side with the strong assistance of a block and strap. We shook—er—horns cordially, and I volunteered to escort him forward and introduce him to his shipmates. The main deck was only about fifty-seven feet wide,* but after a long series of Alphonse and Gaston antics, during which Billy continually insisted that the right of personal precedence should be given to me, we managed to squeeze through and reach the forecastle head.

The day happened to be Sunday, and when I introduced Billy to

* A breadth of beam not meant to be taken literally. (Ed.)

the boys, who were loafing under the forward awning, they made way for him with splendid unanimity. Billy nodded pleasantly all around, and then I showed him his quarters under the forecastle head.

Owing to my own ignorance of goats at that time, I had considerable difficulty in explaining to Billy the great importance of preserving the windlass bitts intact. It was also a hard matter to convince him that the Manila lanyard which I bestowed upon him was to preserve him from personal injury in case of accident.

I visited Billy after supper and offered him a couple of pantiles and a chew of tobacco, all of which he gratefully accepted, especially the chew, for although Billy reeked some he did not smoke. After bidding him a cordial good night, I went below and turned in.

About eleven-thirty that night I was awakened by a most unusual commotion on the main deck. An unearthly discord of excited barking and bleating, prancing and pawing, and mingled sounds of strife and struggle rent the quiet midnight air. I jumped out on deck and there beheld my two protégés, Billy and Bos'n, engaged in a life-and-death encounter over the question of mascotship. Billy was rearing and prancing on his hind legs looking for an opening and Bos'n was dodging warily around trying to secure a strangle hold.

In the wind-up, Billy carried the day, or rather the night, by butting his husky rival overboard through an open side port into the harbor, where he was eagerly gobbled by a vigilant shark. That settled the question, and the next day Billy was elected ship's mascot by unanimous consent. Although somewhat aggressive in his habits and a little reckless in his general deportment, Billy made an excellent mascot, and the ship encountered nothing but fair winds and good fortune from that day forward.

Billy was a proud goat, somewhat disdainful in his demeanor toward common mortals and promiscuous in the bestowal of his belligerent attentions. He never took anybody's backwash, and he never starved for the want of a mouth. He was very discriminating in the selection of his friends, but beyond that no respecter of persons. In bestowing his favors, he never drew the line anywhere from the taffrail to the knightheads.

The only two people on board with whom Billy could by any means be persuaded to associate were the emasculated little cabin boy, whom the captain carried for a football, and myself. As for the rest of the crew, aft or forward, Billy only regarded them as a set of animated tenpins to be bowled over at will. His pet aversion, however, was Ah-Chuk, the cook, a feeling which was strongly reciprocated by the Chink himself. Many were the impromptu set-tos which occurred between them.

It should be recorded here, however, that this feeling of mutual antagonism was entirely owing to the characteristic perverseness of the Chinaman and not to the inherent offensiveness of the belligerent goat.

Although there was a great deal of pride in his character, Billy was not particular in the matter of diet. He *could* eat scupper-nails, but other things seemed to agree with him better. I hate to cast any reflections on the personal traits of an old, esteemed shipmate, but for veracity's sake I must admit right here that I never let Billy know where I kept my oilskins and sou'wester.

The mutual animus which existed between Billy and the cook began at Mauritius and ended on the way to Rangoon in a manner which I shall relate. Since Billy's name did not appear on the ship's articles as a regular member of the crew, it was assumed by the afterguard that he was mascot by sufferance only, and no allowance was made for him in whacking out the daily rations "under the Act." For this reason, I had earnestly entreated Chink to set aside the yam parings and other galley refuse for the special delectation of his goatship. But this he obstinately refused to do and persisted in laboriously throwing them over the side.

"Me no come fleedee gloatee," he chattered testily when I urged this point upon him for the fortieth time. "Me no likee gloatee! You likee him? You fleedee. Gloatee stinkee! Tamn gloatee!"

"Damn you, too, ye bloody heathen," growled old Tom Grunt, bristling up. "You didn't come ter feed enythin' 'cepting yer own dirty face! Yer coffee is merlasses, yer tea is all slops, yer soup is all shadders, yer duff is all putty. Bah! Ef I was a goat, I'd butt ther stuffin' out o' yer mizable hide."

But criticism only served to make Chink more obstinate, and the luscious leavings which Billy craved so ardently still continued to go over the side. Driven desperate by the pangs of hunger, Billy had already made several predatory raids on the galley lockers which Chink had cruelly repelled by deluging him with hot water, a treatment which served neither to improve the creature's over-wrought temper nor to diminish his appetite.

While we were engaged in sluicing down one morning, I observed poor Billy nibbling reflectively at a tattered corner of the forehatch tarpaulin and casting, meanwhile, a wistful eye on a pan of luscious flapjack batter which stood alone and unprotected on a corner of the galley mess locker. I appreciated Billy's cravings and was seized with a desire to help him. Looking in the galley door where Chink was flip-flopping about in great haste with his break-fast preparations, I called out: "Chink, lay aft quick. The steward wants you."

Chink threw off his checkered apron with an angry gesture and started aft on the double, grumbling volubly in his own unintelligi-ble jargon. Presently he came shuffling back looking more vexed than when he went.

"Stewee no wantee me," he snapped angrily. "What for you lie me? Sailorman too muchee liee!"

"That's all right, Chink," I responded cheerfully, "he will want you pretty soon. Go ahead."

When Chink got back to the galley, there stood Billy with his forehoofs braced securely upon the ledge of the mess locker, his long face immersed nearly to his eyes in the sacred cabin batter, and slobbering away to his heart's content. Chink emitted a yell, something between a death wail and a Comanche war whoop, and made a savage lunge at Billy with a convenient pothook. Billy beat a hasty but dignified retreat before the advancing weapon and came on deck with smacking chops and dripping whiskers.

Captain Larruper, a strict disciplinarian in all things, was above all an especial stickler for punctuality at mealtimes, and particularly at breakfast. Whoever was responsible for a late breakfast would remain the object of his unbridled wrath for the remainder of the day. No one knew this better than Chink, who had had the misfortune to fall under the ban of autocratic displeasure more than once for slight lapses of duty in this regard.

Seven bells was drawing near and there was no time to waste, so Chink stirred up his pan of bewildered judy paste just as it was, and he proceeded with his flapjacks. Now, the weather was warm and Billy was shedding badly; consequently, he had inadvertently dropped some of his superfluous hairs in the startled batter. That morning the old man had flapjacks for breakfast with whiskers on 'em.

Shortly after seven bells, there came a muffled bellow couched in wild and blasphemous accents from the direction of the poop, which indicated in set terms and with certain uncomplimentary allusions to his physical, mental, moral, and spiritual make-up that the cook was wanted aft. It was no joke this time; he was wanted, sure enough.

I am not brutal enough to describe in detail the excruciating episode which followed, but when Chink was suddenly projected from the forward cabin door and left to roll helplessly in the lee scuppers, Billy and I both felt that our wrongs had been in some degree avenged.

But the final taming of Ah-Chuk occurred some days later. By some obscure and unfathomable perversity of his Chinese mind, the episode of the bewhiskered pancakes only increased the cook's obstinacy. If the crew fared badly before that event, we fared infinitely worse afterward. If the coffee had been boiled molasses before, it became tar syrup thereafter; if the tea had been slops, it degenerated into dirty water; the "shadow soup," which had long been a standing menace to the peace and loyalty of the whole crew, soon became a synonym for hot bilgewater; and the plum duff, which had hitherto been made without plums, was now made, as nearly as possible, without flour.

Protests and pleadings at the galley door were alike unavailing. Threats or violence of any kind were out of the question, the cook being a ship's officer according to statute, and none cared to invoke the penalties of maritime law upon themselves by mutinous conduct. In this dilemma, Billy and I artfully put our heads together and rigged up a purchase calculated either to produce better grub or to put the almond-eyed grub-spoiler out of commission.

Our opportunity came one day when I happened to observe our mutual *bête noir*, the Chink, at the top of the ladder leading down into the halfdeck. He was industriously pounding the dusted lining from inside the staves of an empty barrel of flour in order to obtain every last grain. Now, like most other independent characters, Billy nearly always disdained friendly advice. On one point, however, he was always fully in accord with my views. That was, that anything I held my cap in front of deserved butting into, no matter whether it was the cabin window or the samson post.

Chink was leaning well down, head and shoulders inside the barrel, intent only on his task, the wide cloths of his baggy trousers flapping gaily in the wind like the after-leech of the spanker. Such a splendid opportunity to secure revenge was not to be lost, and I promptly called Billy's attention to it by holding my tar-stained watch cap about three feet astern of Chink's other end. Billy took the hint and landed on the most exposed portion of Chink's anatomy with the force and vengeance of a battering ram.

Chink went first into the barrel and then through the bottom. He then whirled end over end and round and round down the steep ladder into the halfdeck, where he landed with a crash. There he skirmished about, his movements actuated by the lurching of the ship, still tightly jammed in the close-fitting barrel, as snugly restrained as though in a strait jacket.

Chink managed to get some control over his surroundings after a while, and, thrusting a scared, flour-besprinkled face through the bottom of the barrel, he looked up appealingly at Billy and me.

Billy was rearing and tramping, impatiently waiting for the next round.

"Take l'off! Take l'off!" wailed the cook from his cramped position.

"Take what off?" I exclaimed exultantly. "Take it off, yourself, you heathen fool."

"No can do, Jimmy, no can do," he pleaded. "Him gloatee too muchee bobbery."

"Why don't you feed him, then?" I asked coldly.

"Me fleedee, me fleedee, plenty fleedee," he promised eagerly. "Take l'off, take l'off. Me by-m-by fleedee."

"Will you save all the scraps for Billy if we let you up?"

"Yes, yes; me savee, plenty savee."

"Will you stop spoiling our coffee with burned molasses?"

"Yes, yes."

"Will you put more tea in the water?"

"Yes, yes," consented Chink, wagging his head eagerly.

"Will you put more raisins in the duff and more peas in the soup?" I went on heartlessly.

"Yes, yes."

"And look a-here," I urged sternly, "will you promise to stop scalding Billy with hot water and calling him names in that outlandish gibberish o' yourn?"

"Yes, yes! Me stoppee. No more scaldee Missee Gloatee. Nice gloatee! Take l'off. Take l'off."

"What do you think, Billy?" I asked. "Had we better let up on him?" Billy wiggled his horns distrustfully, but turned away from the hatch, thus indicating that he was willing to give Chink another trial.

"All right, Chink," I said finally, "we'll let you off easy this time. But next time you try to starve or scald any of us you'd better stand by for an easy place to jump overboard."

Billy and I then went forward to enjoy a laugh that would have cracked the ribs of a clinker-built whaleboat, leaving Ah-Chuk to extricate himself as best he could. Whatever else there may have been to complain of on board the *Helaroara* after that, the grub, if not all that could have been desired, was certainly all that could be expected. I actually began to get some of the wrinkles out of my belly.

It was at Rangoon that Billy distinguished himself as a snake charmer and undoubtedly saved some of us from a horrible death. It happened on a Sunday afternoon when we were all enjoying an afterdinner siesta beneath the forecastle awning. I was just dozing off into a comfortable snooze, entirely oblivious of any lurking danger, when all hands were startled by an unusual commotion on the main deck. I could hear Billy's sibilant bleat tuned to an intense and frantic treble, followed by a rapid and intermittent stamping of hoofs.

"What in the blazes is the row wi' Billy now?" yawned someone next to me. But Billy's wild bleat persisted sharper than ever, while the accompanying ca-chug, ca-chug, ca-chug of his hoofs plainly told us that a life-and-death struggle was in process on the main deck.

I could not bear to leave my old chum in trouble alone, so I ran down the forecastle ladder, closely followed by all hands. There, not six feet from the starboard forecastle door, we were horrified to see brave Billy engaged in a desperate battle with a deadly snake. The huge reptile was writhing, twisting, hissing, and darting with lightning-like movements, while courageous Billy, with all four limbs locked together beneath the center of his body, was valiantly trampling it.

"It's all up with poor Billy," I moaned as I dashed for a handspike to help him. Before I could return to the scene, however, Billy had successfully chopped the monster into mincemeat with the sharp edges of his hoofs.

To make a safe job of the snake, I brought the handspike down on the creature's head. Then I turned to Billy, who was quivering with feverish excitement. I found that he had been fanged in several places. I quickly ran aft to the steward and begged a stick of lunar caustic from the medicine chest. With this, I treated Billy's wounds and poulticed them with a mixture of pine tar from the bos'n's locker and mud from the banks of the Irrawaddy River.

For two weeks, Billy's life was uncertain. He was drowsy and listless and refused to eat. But his strong constitution and the constant ministrations of his devoted shipmates finally pulled him through. A month after his hideous ordeal, Billy was prancing and plunging about the deck as rampant as ever.

There was not gold enough in all India to buy Billy from the crew after that. He was ceremoniously decorated with a new collar and adorned with a brass knob on each of his horns. He was likewise officially entered on the Admiralty crew list as "William Butts, Mascot."

I could easily use up a ream of paper writing the authentic history of Billy's exploits, but one more episode of his antics should be noted. It was the crowning achievement of his career and one that endeared him to us even more than the charming of the snake.

Captain Larruper was a burly, bellicose brute weighing fully two hundred and fifty pounds. Our half-starved little cabin boy weighed about two hundred pounds less—just the convenient weight for handling. Unfortunately, the Old Man had no dumbbells with him on that voyage, so he spent most of his leisure, which was nearly all the time, practicing on the boy in order to reduce his weight.

One fine morning—we were in the Pacific at the time—I was relieved from the wheel at eight o'clock. I started forward to breakfast followed by my constant companion, Billy. Walking on the lee side of the poop deck, I was incensed by the sight of Cap'n Larruper busily engaged in his usual morning pastime of knocking seven bells out of the cabin boy with the knotted end of the mainroyal brace. He stood near the head of the starboard poop gangway, leaning over the writhing boy whom he held securely between his massive legs while he applied the rope remorselessly.

So deeply engrossed was he in his fiendish exercise that he did not notice our approach. In passing, I paused to scratch my head and rather absentmindedly dangled my watch cap about three feet abaft the Old Man's position.

Instantly there resounded a shrill bleat, a scurry of hoofs, and Billy suddenly landed full tilt on the Old Man's stern post with a thump that must have sprung his rudder head. The Old Man shot over the boy, cleared the break of the poop, performed an awkward flip-flop down the gangway ladder, and landed on the main deck with a mighty jar.

When I saw Billy proudly prancing with bristling horns on the break of the poop and loudly bleating his defiant challenge to the fallen tyrant to renew the conflict, I could not help regarding him as the noblest brute I had ever seen in command of a ship.

Of course, Billy was court-martialed. The Court was just *aching* for revenge. I voluntarily appeared as Billy's advocate. In pleading for his life, I reminded the Court that to kill a ship's mascot, except for food, would be to violate the most sacred of all ancient maritime traditions. It would certainly tend to jeopardize the success and good fortune of the voyage, if not of the ship itself. I dwelt long and feelingly on Billy's many fine qualities and noble deeds, including the taming of the slovenly cook who had insulted his majestic master by insolently serving him a filthy mess of flapjacks. I laid special stress upon Billy's heroic exploit in killing the snake at Rangoon. In this connection, I asked the Court which it would prefer—to be butted by a playful goat or bitten by a deadly snake.

The Court stroked its whiskers thoughtfully, relented somewhat, and finally decreed that thereafter Billy's antics should be restricted to that portion of the deck space between the foremast and the forecastle head.

I got separated from Billy on the coast of Chile where we went to load nitrate. While lying at Pisagua, it suddenly occurred to five of us that we had important business in Antofagasta which lay about three hundred miles up the coast. The route overland lies through a wide strip of alkali soil where no water exists and where transportation facilities were nonexistent. We had no money to buy horses, departing without pay as we did, so I had to leave Billy behind because I could not lug water enough for both of us. But I kissed him between the horns before I slid down the jib downhaul, and urged him to ever remain as he was, a good, game goat.

I suppose that in the nature of things Billy must have long since gone to his account. I never learned the way of his going, but I am ready to wager that William Butts gave a good account of himself in the last round.

## 10 · JOSEPH O'BRIEN, IRISHMAN

When we came down to the Philadelphia waterfront that cold winter's morning in January, 1889, under convoy of a boisterous horde of loud and truculent boardinghouse "runners" who ever hovered about our serried flanks and harried the laggards along with foul epithets, base objurgations, kicks, cuffs, threats, and blows, I thought that as a spectacular exhibition of sheer wanton brutality and a fair sample of the Great American Crimping System in practical operation our treatment was about the limit.

So we hurried mutely along like a terrified herd of stampeded steers, a straggling score of unfortunate send-offs, unkempt, unwashed, unshorn, and unknown. When we reached the tender, the ship was lying abreast the ballast wharf, "riding short," with her topsails loosed, her Blue Peter fluttering nimbly at the fore, and the inevitable tugboat lying impatiently alongside ready to tow us to sea.

As soon as we had tumbled over the side and stowed our dunnage below, we were promptly ordered by our bellicose bos'n, Tom Bellows, to "lay aft to muster!" We shambled meekly to the quarterdeck and lined up along the starboard rail. As soon as we had been officially reviewed and critically surveyed by our future bull drivers, we were carefully counted, like a herd of steers, and gruffly ordered to "go forrard, 'n' turn-to, get out ther hawser 'n' man ther win'lass!"

When we started down the river with the tug panting hoarsely at the end of our long, fourteen-inch warp, the wind blew keenly from the north'ard, the mud-colored river ice hung in heavy pendent masses from our chain bolts and bobstays, the hoar frost clustered in fantastic sprays of gleaming white crystals along the twisted strands of our tautened shrouds, and the heavy masses of gray, somber clouds, rolling sullenly overhead, told ominously of coming snow.

About four o'clock in the afternoon, having got things, alow and aloft, worked out into something like proper shape for handling, we were mustered in the waist again to go through the ancient and time-honored ceremony of "picking watches" for the voyage. This venerable custom, as old as the history of maritime ventures, is extremely simple. It merely consists in lining the crew along one side of the deck and then allowing the first and second mate to choose one man each for their respective watches. They continue to select alternately until all men have been chosen. Each mate depends, of course, on his own individual judgment to secure the best men for his watch—just like a crowd of boys choosing teams for a game of ball.

But in this instance, we were destined to witness an astounding and unparalleled departure from immemorial practice. Our chief mate, Mister Thomas Swindell (†), had lately been sent out from Liverpool as a "company's man" to join the ship. A somewhat protracted and painfully enforced experience with this gentleman and his methods fully confirmed our first impression that he was a swindle by nature as well as by name.

When we had all lined up, our second mate, Mister Jesse Jones (†), —a very active and capable officer of the practical school—stepped to the cabin door and reported to his superior: "Crew is aft, sir." After a period of seemingly unnecessary delay, Mister Swindell stepped from his room carrying the shipping articles tightly rolled in his right hand. He was a long, lean, lanky-looking gantline with a sallow complexion and a bristling mustache which stuck to his upper lip like a bunch of "bag o' wrinkle" tacked onto an outrigger. He had a weak, characterless, unsettled countenance, and his obvious efforts to coax it into assuming an austere, commanding expression were extremely ludicrous. To complete the physical peculiarities of this quarter-deck paragon, he had a shambling uncertain gait like a day-old calf, which he was forever trying to develop into a plausible imitation of the Liverpool swagger and the Western Ocean roll.

Mister Swindell waddled up and down the line of assembled men twice or thrice with an air of ungainly dignity. He regarded us individually and collectively from a pair of pale blue eyes that stared wide open and bulged outward like a pair of hawsepipe plugs. At length, seemingly satisfied that he had made a profound impression, Mister Swindell took up a position at the after end of the line, unrolled the articles with official deliberation, and, after clearing his throat a few times, raised his harsh, cackling, dissatisfied voice. "Now men, I will read all your names from the articles just as they have been entered. Each man will respond to his name by answering, 'Here, sir,' leave the line, step across to the mizzen hatch coaming, and take his place in the watch to which he has been assigned. The first man called will be in the port watch, of course; the second in the starboard watch, and so on alternately throughout the list. Now do you understand?" he demanded, sweeping his goggle eyes along the straggling line.

He was answered by a series of affirmative grunts from the bewildered crew and a defiant snort of open indignation from his colleague, Mister Jones. "No, sir! I'll be d—d if I understand you; neither does anybody else," he blared out. "This proceeding is a mockery on custom. It is irregular, unwarranted, and unreasonable, sir. I never heard of such methods before in picking watches. According to your plan, you're going to ruin the whole crew; for, as you're going, you're apt to read a majority of the A.B.'s into one watch and a majority of the deck swabs into the other. Mind you, sir," roared the irate second mate, "if I get too many hoodlums in my watch I'll pass some of 'em up to you for combing out, and I'll take down some of your A.B.'s by way of exchange. I ain't goin' to do your dirty work for you!"

"I think, sir," said Mister Swindell in his most conciliatory tone when Mister Jones had relapsed into silence, "that it is the first duty of a second officer to abide by the orders of his superior."

"Yes, sir," retorted Mister Jones warmly, "and it is a first officer's duty to learn his business and abide by the dictates of established custom. You're tryin' to upset the whole maritime code and make us learn all our duties over again."

Mister Swindell ventured no reply to this outspoken piece of personal sarcasm, for the energetic second mate was obviously more than a match for him at any point of the compass. So he adopted the only sensible course open to him short of deliberately yielding to the second mate's protest. He resumed his place at the end of the line and proceeded to read off our names as though apparently determined to carry out his original program at all hazards.

Early in the process, I discovered to my delight that I had been read into the starboard watch. Everything went along smoothly until Mister Swindell called out the name "Joseph O'Brien." We were all astonished to see a huge Negro quietly disengage himself from the line and start across toward the second mate's row.

"Here, you black sweep," snarled Mister Swindell, stepping forward angrily and extending a restraining arm to stay the Negro's progress, "is your name *Joseph O'Brien?*" (†)

"Yas, sah," answered the big black, demurely showing his gleaming ivories. "Yas, sah. I'se de on'y Irishman in de ship."

The subdued murmur of suppressed merriment which resounded around the quarter-deck was promptly echoed from the narrow bridge where our good skipper, Captain John Richards (†), unnoticed by Mister Swindell, had been quietly pacing forward and back directly over the mizzen hatch, an interested spectator of all that had taken place within the last half hour.

Mister Swindell's countenance drooped amazingly when he found that his novel proceedings had been the subject of autocratic review, but he went through the rest of his rigamarole with the best grace possible. Then the starboard watch was sent below until four bells. But from that day forward, Joseph O'Brien became a marked man, a subject of abject and unrepining servitude upon whom Mister Swindell delighted to pour out the vials of his unbridled and unrestrained wrath.

About midnight, the storm which had been threatening for the previous forty-eight hours burst upon us with all the fury of a blizzard. It struck in first from nor'-nor'east with a driving mist of swirling snow, but the wind gradually tacked around to nor'-nor'west. There it stuck and settled down to good steady business, bringing blinding snow, clinging ice, freezing spray, and sweeping seas. The *Main* (†) was an able, well-found ship; but with a new and untried crew, most of whom were obviously untrained, Captain Richards did not deem it prudent to run her before the storm. So we shortened her down early in the encounter and lay to until morning.*

That night Joe O'Brien distinguished himself and proved himself a typical deepwater shellback from backbone to breakfast time. The general verdict, both fore and aft, was that "he was a brick," an unstinted estimate which even Captain Richards endorsed. But little moles have little eyes, and Mister Swindell's stunted mind refused to appreciate as all the rest of us did the tremendous nature which dwelt within that mighty Negro. In the person of the dusky, unassuming, hard-working giant, he recognized only the innocent cause of his own ridicule when picking watches. His official dignity had been lowered and he lusted for revenge.

We ran out of the storm next day and squared away with every inch of canvas set toward fine weather and the glorious brimming trades. It was then we were treated to an exhibition of O'Brien's manly character and wonderful presence of mind. Among our cargo was a certain consignment of five hundred barrels of lubricating

* The *Main*, built by Russell and Company in 1884, was a relatively new ship. Its gross tonnage was 1,691; its dimensions, 256 by 38 by 23; its port of registry, London. (Ed.)

oil. This shipment had arrived late, was rather indifferently stowed, and in the hurry of departure was entirely forgotten. But the storm had loosened things up below decks and the casks, wrenched clear of their defective blocking, had lost their original alignment and threatened to take charge.

As soon as we got into fine weather, therefore, the starboard watch was sent below to shore up the bulging tiers of casks and block them off anew. The barrels were piled precariously in tiers on their bilges in the after 'tween decks. The forward tier extended flush to the after part of the mizzen hatch coaming; forward of that there was only a narrow standing space on the 'tween deck hatch covers.

We set to work as carefully as possible to collect all the props and wedges which had worked adrift so that we might use them to block off the casks afresh and then further secure them with shores set against the deck beams. In wiggling one of the props, however, to disengage its end from under the bilge of a bottom cask, somebody set the whole outside tier in motion. Instantly, with a low ominous rumble, the whole weight of the barrels started slowly toward the clear space where we all stood in the hatchway.

There was sudden panic. We all started fighting, swearing, tearing, and grappling for the narrow iron ladder leading to the main deck and open air, but up which only one man could climb at a time. All, did I say? No, not all, for from out of the depths of the cavernous hatchway arose Joe O'Brien's stentorian voice, ringing loud and clear and decisive above the babel of cowardly hubbub around the ladder.

"Doan' run 'way dar, yo' wuthless no 'count landlubbers! Whar yo' gwine ter run? 'F yew tries ter git out, der bar'ls sho' come down 'n' kill all han's! Git back yer' yo' lazy swine, 'n' help me hol' on 'tell some han's git sho's roun' de bar'ls! Calls yo'se'f sailors, hey? I calls yo' swabs!"

These gentle objurgations were not uttered in a pleading tone, but with the authoritative voice of one who really commands by divine right and who must be obeyed. Looking sheepishly astern, we saw that Joe O'Brien had coolly interposed his mighty frame between us and death, and that while we had been struggling panic-stricken for the exit, which none of us could hope to attain, he had stood calmly and heroically at the post of duty with his herculean shoulder planted snugly against the bulging center of the forward tier. By exerting all his mighty strength, he had actually held the moving avalanche of casks in check and averted catastrophe.

So we ran back, shamed out of countenance by Joe's heroism. While some of us braced our shoulders beside his against the center barrel, the rest sought diligently to block off the tumbling tiers of rolling barrels. Thus we were saved.

During the long six weeks from Henlopen to the Cape, we had ample time to get acquainted with Joe O'Brien and to appreciate his stalwart character. Physically speaking, he was the most magnificent specimen I ever saw. Full three feet broad across the shoulders he was, and over six feet in stature. But his girth was so great and his form so massive that his height was not apparent until you stood beside him. Then you found he was a giant, and you felt your own insignificance.

Whenever he stripped off for a bath, all hands, including the Old Man, turned out to look at him. He was certainly a grand array of special humanity; framed like a giant, muscled like an ox, a perfect Hercules in ebony.

An enterprising bunch of sporting men at Liverpool tried to induce him to enter the prize ring. But the big, good-natured stupid was too kind-hearted to fight.

"What I wanner fight fer?" he argued when pressed on the subject. "De Book say God He make man in He own image, an' I ain' got no right ter poun' God's image all ter pieces, has I?"

Although he declined to fight, Joe could certainly wrestle. In fact, I think if he had made wrestling his specialty he would have been an easy champion. Often in the dogwatches, I used to struggle with him, mainly to learn his grips and holds, for I stood about as much chance of throwing him as I did of capsizing the Rock of Gibraltar. I was often black and blue from the severe turns he gave me.

Joe hailed from Cameron County, Kentucky, and he was a relic of slavery days. But he was proud of his parents and loyal to his country. The Negro, generally speaking, although the worst oppressed and least respected of human beings, nevertheless links his fortune, his fate, and his future with the land of his birth. With the Negro, patriotism is a passion, and regardless of ancient abuses or existing prejudices or persecutions he ever remains loyal to the flag under which he was born.

Going down the trades, Joe was the life of the whole ship. He was a marvelous storyteller—as amiable and good-natured as he was mighty and masterful. In the evening dogwatches, he used to sit on the samson post with the crowd grouped around him and spin some of the most amazing sea yarns on record. Meanwhile, his hearty guffaws would resound fore and aft as he laughed at his own jokes.

Captain Richards carried his family with him. As a rule, petticoats were not appreciated by sailing ship crews, but Mrs. Richards was a rare exception. She never got in the way, she didn't try to run the ship, and she never enticed the Old Man to chase us aloft just to see how much we looked like monkeys.

They had a beautiful little daughter about five years old. She was a happy, darling little somebody, and to know her was to love her. Her name was Bessy Rose, but because of her ruddy cheeks, her sandy tousled hair, and cheery disposition, the boys dubbed her "Rosy."

Between Rosy and Joseph O'Brien there existed a mutual admiration and cheerful comradeship which no one could rub out, much less define. Nearly every day, in fair weather, little Rosy would come toddling to the forecastle door and get someone to help her over the "stop water" at the sill. "I wanner see Joe," she would lisp with childish eagerness, and make straight for her chum's bunk.

Sometimes she would get the watches mixed and come forward when Joe was at work somewhere between the chain locker and the truck. In that case, she would plead pitifully to be elevated into Joe's bunk, and there she would scatter the contents of his ditty box or curio bag all over the blanket and then fall asleep in the midst of the articles.

If Joe happened to come below and find her there, he would stand and gaze at her with a degree of admiration that amounted to worship, and then tiptoe quietly away so as not to disturb her.

One day, as we neared the Cape of Good Hope, Mister Swindell altered the course to check the yards and then forgot to correct it. Little Rosy was playing about the poop because the weather was so boisterous that her mother had forbidden her to go forward. She was amusing herself as best she could down on the lee side, and an able seaman named Henderson and I were securing all movable objects about the poop in prospect of heavy weather. The wind was from the westward and blowing strong and free. The old ship was surging along at a twelve-knot gait when suddenly the spanker vang tautened by the raising of the gaff as we mounted a swell and the little girl somehow got tangled in the coil of the fall. She was raised over the rail, and with a startled little scream she disappeared under the quarter and splashed into the sea.

Instantly, O'Brien let go the wheel and sprang to the taffrail.

"Get back there, you black sweep," yelled Mister Swindell, "and secure that wheel!"

"Damn de wheel, sabe de baby!" thundered Joe as he breached the taffrail and dove into the swirling smother of the ship's wake.

Henderson and I cut away two life buoys just as Captain Richards rushed from the chartroom and glanced with an ashen countenance astern. The little girl was still afloat. Her skirts had blossomed out and formed an air cushion, thus sustaining her for a time. Joe was striking out for her with the vigor of a tiger shark.

The Old Man grabbed the wheel and rolled it hard down. "Weather main braces!" he thundered excitedly. "Back the main yards, ease away the head sheets, and let fly the clews of the foresail! For God's sake, men, be quick!"

The boys forward had not seen the accident and were naturally startled by such a sudden flow of excited orders. But I ran forward with the awful tidings: "Man overboard! Come out quick, boys, Rosy is overboard!"

And lay out quick they did. Never have I seen men respond with finer alacrity, for any man aboard would have died for Rosy. By this time, nearly two months out, the crew had been combed out and well drilled in their duties. So they manned the clew garnets and braces with a vim and vigor that was astonishing. The sparks fairly blazed from the burning block scores as the great yards swung round against the lee backstays with a rush that threatened to bring our rigging down. Meanwhile, some of us had cleared away one of the quarter boats so that we were ready to launch it by the time the ship came head to wind.

But a big ship under full sail cannot be checked quickly, no matter how lively her crew, so we must have been fully two miles from Joe and the baby before we got her head around. We dropped the boat and pulled away, our sixteen-foot oars bending like withes and groaning against the oaken tholes beneath the strain of our eager strokes. Never in my life did I lay back on an oar with such unreserved good will as I did that day.

Mister Jones sat in the stern-sheets steering with one hand and helping on the stroke oar with the other. "Give way, men," he urged excitedly, "for God's sake, give way." And give way we did. When we reached them, Joe had the little girl encircled in one of the life buoys and was treading water beside her. We took the child into the boat and Joe hopped in as nimbly as a schoolboy vaulting a four-foot fence. Then we all stood up in the thwarts and tossed oars as a signal of triumph, and we heard three ringing cheers from the ship in response.

The Old Man had tacked ship during our absence and was now standing back against his course to pick us up. So we soon ran alongside and were hoisted up. As the gunwale of our boat mounted to the ship's rail, Mrs. Richards stood with eager outstretched arms and streaming eyes ready to grab little Bessy Rose.

Captain Richards stood there, too, and as we scrambled out of the boat he reached out and grasped O'Brien's dusky palm and wrenched it cordially. "God bless you, Joe," the Old Man exclaimed fervently. "You stay with this ship and I'll make you as good a man on the company's list as I am. Go forward now and get a dry shift. I'll send the steward to you presently."

On our way across the Indian Ocean, Mister Swindell kept up his brutal unruly hazing of O'Brien. We were all astonished at the big Negro's patience under such intense provocations.

"Why don't you lick him, Joe?" some of his watchmates inquired one evening after O'Brien had been subjected to a day of unusually severe hounding. "You can knock seven bells out of him easy. You lay him out once and he'll respect you and leave you alone."

"Yas, Ah know Ah kin lick him," answered the big giant, "but what's de use o' dat? He de mate, ain' he, and Ah's gotter min' he orders, ain' Ah? Ef he shob me roun' some Ah doan' min' dat, long's he doan' hit me. Ah hopes ter Gawd he doan' hit me, cause Ah doan' 'low no man ter hit me, no matter ef he am white, 'n' 'f he hit me I 'fraid I break he neck."

After that we all knew that Joe was conscious of his strength and that he had no reason to fear the mate. Still, we all expected something to happen before the end of the passage, and happen it did, though not until we reached Sand Heads at the mouth of the Hooghly River.

We reached Sand Heads early one fine morning just as the sun rose across the eastern shoulder of Sager Island and met the pilot brig bearing down to meet us. We backed our yards to get the pilot on board and then squared away again for Diamond Harbor on our way to Calcutta.

We had belayed our braces and were trimming our lee foresheet to the strains of that good old foresheet chantey, "The Bowlin'."

> Haul away the bowlin',
> The packet ship's a-rollin';
> Away, haul away,
> Haul away, Joe!

*Haul away together,*
*We'll either break or bend 'er;*
*Away, haul away,*
*Haul away, Joe!*

*Oh, haul away, my bully boys,*
*We're sure to make 'er render;*
*Away, haul away,*
*Haul away, Joe!*

*Oh, once I had an Irish girl,*
*And she was fat and lazy;*
*Away, haul away,*
*Haul away, Joe!*

*And now I've got a Yankee girl,*
*She nearly drives me crazy;*
*Away, haul away,*
*Haul away, Joe!*

O'Brien stood beforehand, near the bollards, dragging away like a hoisting horse at the big bight of wet coir. He was singing lustily with a voice like a calliope, when Captain Richards suddenly ordered the starboard watch to the cro'jack braces. Joe belonged to the starboard watch so he dropped his hold on the foresheet and started to lay aft with his fellows as ordered.

Then Mister Swindell saw a chance to distinguish himself, and he seized it like a monkey grabbing a hot chestnut. He had been in uncommon bad humor all the morning. He had been busybodying about the deck as eager as a hound with two tails in search of trouble, and he found it. When Joe dropped the sheet, the mate leaped forward and struck him a stinging blow in the face with his flat hand. "Get back there, you damned black sweep," he shouted, "and attend to your duty! I'm onto some of your Black Ball moves!"

The big Negro seemed more surprised than hurt. He turned slowly around and looked with astonishment at his tormentor. Then the inward hatred born of four long months of constant and unwarranted persecution and unmerited abuse seemed to leap into his sluggish mind. His eyes blazed like live coals; his teeth gleamed between his snarling lips; his whole physiognomy changed in an instant. He cast aside notions of duty and became what nature made him—an ungovernable savage, a mad African giant.

He sprang at the mate with all the fury and prowess of an infuriated beast. "Mister Swinnell," he roared, as he grasped the terrified chief by the middle with a grip like the clutch of iron clamps and raised him high overhead, "Mister Swinnell, Ah got one mo' move what you' ain' got onter!" For one awful instant he held the struggling mate aloft and then slammed him with frightful violence to the deck, where he lay writhing and groaning like a stricken ox, powerless to rise.

As the chief mate lay gasping beside the iron hatch coaming, Mister Jones walked over and stood looking down at him with infinite scorn. "There ye are," he cried exultantly; "that's what ye get for trying to fool with my watch. Lay aft, O'Brien."

Shortly thereafter, we saw the big twin-screw Hooghly propeller tug *Dalhousie* coming out between the heads to greet us and tow us up the river to Calcutta, or rather to Budge-Budge, seventeen miles farther down where our cargo was to be discharged. We were to go to Calcutta afterward to load.

The big monster ran down to us with a deafening salute from her siren, passed our mail on board in a watertight can buoy, and took us in tow on two big steel hawsers. We threaded our way cautiously across the treacherous quicksands at the James and Mary's, the confluence of the Hooghly with the mighty Ganges, where should the ship's keel so much as kiss the bottom she would be sucked down, down, down to only God knows where.

But everything went smoothly, and we passed safely up the turbulent river. It was now the hurricane season, and the port regulations required every ship arriving to strip; that is, to send down all their lighter spars above the topsail yards, unbend all sails, unreeve their running gear, and rig in their jib booms.

We reached Budge-Budge about four that afternoon and dropped anchor abreast the pontoons. There were no docking facilities, so all merchant ships were moored to stationary holdfasts established on the shores, and cargoes were then transferred ashore over pontoon bridges. An hour after our arrival, the mud pilot came down with a horde of coolies in a mooring lighter, and we hove up and warped into a berth between the rows of great mooring buoys.

We had unbent and stowed all our sails and unrove our running gear coming up the river, but we did not have time to strike our spars. By the time we got our mooring chains crossed and shackled and set up, it was dark; therefore, the striking of our branches was deferred until the following morning.

Early next day, we started to work in earnest to get down our yards and strike in our flying jib boom. Our activities were accelerated by a telegraphic announcement from Bombay that a cyclonic storm had developed in Diamond Harbor and was traveling up the Hooghly at a fearful rate, driving a big "bore" or tidal wave in its advance.

So we worked desperately to get down our spars and secure them before the tempest arrived. We had gotten our main and mizzen upper yards landed and secured, and were at work on the fore. As previously indicated, the *Main* was a large, heavily sparred ship, and her fore and main topgallant yards were sizable spars, weighing, perhaps, three tons each. They were altogether too heavy to be trusted on a single gantline, or yard rope, so it was necessary to get a couple of heavy twin blocks up to the masthead and rig a double purchase for lowering them down.

O'Brien and I and a couple more seamen were sent up to rig up the gear and sling the yard. As soon as we got the yard unparrelled and slung "a-cockbill," we all descended to the deck except Joe, who remained aloft to see things clear and guide the yard on its way down.

When we started to slack away, we found that our tackle fall was too short by a hundred feet, so we tied onto the end a four-inch line which had outlived its usefulness but like everything else on shipboard was considered good enough for the occasion. Just after the knot which joined the old rope to the new slipped around the barrel of the capstan, the old decayed line sundered with a resounding snarl, and the remainder of the rope, suddenly released from its strain, shot upward and went dangling among the shrouds.

There were at least a dozen men standing directly below to receive the hanging spar, and had it descended by the run as it started to some of us would have been fearfully maimed or killed and the deck, of course, would have been stove. We all jumped away from the foot of the mast in mortal terror, but suddenly the descent of the swinging spar was checked, and Joe O'Brien's big voice thundered from the crosstrees: "I got 'er boys, but Ah cain hol' on long, so make has' down dar!"

Two men sprang into the shrouds with strands of rope and wracked off the running parts of the tackle, making it temporarily secure. And at the same moment the cyclone struck.

From down the river came the awful roar of howling wind and thundering water. Around the bend in the river, just below where we lay, came the bore, the monstrous tidal wave of the Hooghly. Tearing onward with an indescribable roar, towering high above the river banks, inundating both shores, and scattering death and destruction for miles, its bristling mane swept toward us with irresistible fury.

Overhead the darkness was appalling. The rapid flashes of lightning and the deafening reverberations which followed seemed to shake the whole universe. Just as the big black cloud hung directly overhead, it burst asunder with a tremendous crash. First came a lurid blinding flash followed instantly by a clap of terrific thunder. The ship surged and swayed in her moorings as though she had been struck by a broadside of artillery, and every man on board was knocked prostrate by the shock.

Then came the roaring tempest in full blast—a mighty rush of wind which nothing could withstand. It seemed to blow the breath from our bodies. The odor of brimstone was as strong in the air as though a barrel of it had been burning on deck. Orders could no more be heard than the chirping of a sparrow. We had to crawl along the deck on our hands and knees, groping and clutching whatever we could find to hang on by, for in that mighty outburst a man would have blown away like a wisp of straw.

It would be altogether inadequate to say it rained. The cloud just seemed to settle around our mastheads, and the contents, lashed by the wind, were hurled in blinding sheets into our faces.

Then came the immense tidal wave. All ships are moored bow and stern on the Hooghly by cables. The mooring chains are shackled by native divers to stationary "holdfasts" under the water. These "holdfasts" are secured by heavy leading chains attached to mushroom anchors deeply planted ashore, and they are held clear of the bottom by hollow iron buoys. The mooring chains are always extended crosswise of each other, fore and aft, and then set taut on the windlass, thus holding the ship in a practically immovable position while she is being loaded or unloaded. *

When that big tidal wave swept beneath us, it raised the ship bodily about twenty feet in the air. It thus became necessary to release the forward chains on the windlass to allow the ship to rise, for otherwise the chains would part under the strain and the ship would be destroyed. So we struggled forward to the windlass room, threw off the riding pawls, opened the controllers, and released the compressors just in time as the mountainous wave swept under our stern. As the ship mounted upward like a cork in a flurry, the ponderous anchor chains, suddenly released from the restraining clutch of the windlass, flew through blazing hawsepipes with a tremendous rush. The clattering wildcats spun like buzz saws, and the sparks streamed from beneath the restraining clutch of the friction bands. Three times our stately ship rose and fell in that wild surge of destructive water. But she hung to her moorings. In half an hour, the storm had passed, the blazing sun came out on high, and dense clouds of miasmic steam arose like a dense fog above the drenched and reeking jungle.

The shores along the cyclonic pathway, for a hundred miles or

* The picture on the endpapers, "Calcutta in the Days of Sail," painted by Charles Robert Patterson who sailed to Calcutta in the 1890's, depicts the mooring methods Williams describes. (Ed.)

more, were strewn with examples of the dynamic power of the elements. River wreckage, shattered houses, uprooted trees, dead bodies of men and animals, and general destruction and devastation prevailed. One merchant ship was torn from her moorings by the towering tidal wave and carried inland for more than a mile. She was finally launched in an upright position in an open field where she lay for years afterward as one of the great curiosities of the port.

During the confusion of the storm, we had forgotten all about our dusky shipmate, O'Brien. When we had our mooring chains hove taut, we returned to our former task of sending down the fore-topgallant yard, which was still dangling among the shrouds. Fortunately, the wrackings had held and the swinging spar had done no damage. Looking aloft, we were astonished to see Joe's bulky form still seated in the crosstrees, his back braced against the masthead, and his big hands still clutching the lowering tackle fall.

"Come down, O'Brien," sang out Mister Jones. "What are you sitting up there for?"

There was no response. The huge figure sat silent and motionless.

"There's something wrong with him," said Mister Jones uneasily. "Jump up there, a couple of you, and see what the trouble is."

Henderson and I ran aloft to investigate and discovered to our horror that Joseph O'Brien was dead! He had been struck by lightning while clinging to the fall. Above his head, the royal mast was split and splintered from truck downward to the cap. His hands had been badly burned and lacerated by his desperate clinging to the rope, and the white bones gleamed ghastly through the shredded flesh. The last moment of his life must have been a trial of supreme agony.

When the broken rope had snapped and shot upward, he had somehow contrived to catch the flying line below the crosstrees, and, bringing it upward, had secured a half turn around the outrigger. Then, lying back with all of his immense strength, he had arrested the fall of that great pitch-pine yard and undoubtedly saved a number of limbs and lives.

We communicated the woeful tidings to the deck, and more hands were sent up to help us get the body down. A marlinspike had to be used to pry open the implacable grip of the huge fingers on the rope. We lowered Joe's remains in a cargo netting and stretched them on the main hatch to prepare them for burial.

We planted Joseph O'Brien ashore at Budge-Budge in a grave dug by his shipmates and consecrated to the purpose by the Rev. Mr. Macgreagor, the kind-hearted old Scotch clergyman who presided over the spiritual welfare of the parish.

Never was mortal man laid to rest with more heartfelt sorrow. The day of the funeral, there was not a dry eye on the ship. Even Mister Swindell seemed to be affected by the sad event. He hobbled out on deck with two lame legs, his head in a bandage, and one arm in a sling, and stood decorously with chastened face and uncovered head. The poignant grief of little Bessy Rose was pitiful to behold. Small and young as she was, she was an intelligent child and realized what had befallen her adoring champion and valiant savior. For many days after the funeral, the bereaved girl mourned over the death of her chum and would not be comforted.

We could not find a coffin in India large enough to hold Joe's body, so the Old Man ordered the carpenter to make one. A splendid job he did, too. The Old Man went to Calcutta and bought eight silver handles and a silver plate with which to decorate the casket. Mrs. Richards, with the assistance of Miss Primrose, brought armfuls of flowers and decorated the coffin.

When all things were ready, we placed the heavy casket on an improvised bier which we had rigged on the quarter-deck. There for two hours Joseph O'Brien's body lay in state. The colors were draped and lowered to half mast, and all work on board suspended for the day just as though a great king had died. And a king he was in deed and in fact—not born to the purple, but a king by divine right if ever a man was, far superior to his fellows in every attribute of noble manhood, a brave seaman whose noble life and heroic death had sanctified him in the hearts of his shipmates.

While Mr. Macgreagor read the solemn and impressive funeral service, we stood with bared heads and heavy hearts. Then four able seamen shouldered the heavy casket, draped in the American and British colors, bore it to the gangway, and lowered it reverently over the side into a waiting dinghy. Then we formed a solemn procession on the roadway and bore our shipmate's body to its final resting place.

And above his lonely grave we planted a great teakwood cross extending three and one-half feet above ground. And at the top of the shaft was carved, with rare skill and ingenuity, a beautiful wreath, a shower of sprays radiating from a central star, and below it a foul anchor and a broken rope. And across the arms in heavy relief arose this quaint but sincere inscription:

JOSEPH O'BRIEN
IRISHMAN

The ship *Main*, of London. Williams served in this vessel from January 10, 1889, to June 13, 1889. (*Mariners Museum*)

The *Governor Tilley* of Saint John, New Brunswick, a ship very similar to the *Macedon* in dimensions, tonnage, and year of construction. *(Courtesy of The New Brunswick Museum)*

## 11 · SPIKE RILEY'S REVENGE

Spike Riley and I were cronies for years. We wore the same oil-skins, ate from the same mess kit, drank from the same pannikin, and slept in the same bunk—in turns—voyages on end. Together, we toiled through many a dirty night at sea, and engaged in many a happy frolic ashore. Sworn brothers, boon companions, and bosom friends, Spike and I went down the world together looking fate in the face and taking things as they came without complaint.

Spike Riley was born somewhere in Rhode Island. He was a good deal older than I, old enough in fact to be my daddy. I met Spike on one of my first sea voyages and subsequently sailed on many a vessel with him, including the *Late Commander*. He was a long-geared, cadaverous individual with a slight stoop and a resonant nasal twang. The Britishers ashore called him "Yank," and the Yanks dubbed him "Razorback," but I always hailed him as "Spike," and the name stuck to him.

From the first, there seemed to be a natural affinity between Spike and me. He was long and slim and I was short and thick—extremes meet, they say. Spike was not a handsome man. He said it was his watch below when good looks were served out. But though his features were not in his favor, Spike's heart was in the right

161

place. He was an openhanded, warmhearted, rollicking sailor of the old school—courageous to the backbone and generous to a fault. A good shipmate, a true friend, and an able seaman—I could not say more in Spike's behalf.

But Spike Riley, even though my best friend, was always my evil genius. I never met the old villain without painful consequences to myself. At Calcutta, as I am about to relate, he got me "broke" on the police force. In Colombia, he got me shot at by a mob of ragged revolutionists. At Valparaiso, I came near being knifed by a jealous *caballero* through the unintentional conduct of mischief-making Spike. At Rio, he got me marooned during a yellow fever epidemic and I had to stay there six weeks. In South Africa, he got me chased through the bush for fourteen days by the Cape Mounted Police, mistaken for a diamond smuggler. In that case, however, the tables were nicely turned on the crafty old plotter, for the error was eventually discovered and he, in turn, was chased over the Barrier, compelled to swim through the surf in Table Bay, and forced to hook a desperate passage to Sierra Leone to escape from local jurisdiction.

In London, he got me involved in the big sailors' and dock laborers' strike, and I came very near doing a long term on the treadmill in consequence. At Singapore, he had me nearly slaughtered by a drunken crowd of Limejuicers for refusing to drink the Queen's health on Her British Majesty's birthday. And last and worst of all, in America he induced me to squander my hard-earned substance in riotous living for three days and then got me shanghaied!

But for all these injuries and many more which Spike deliberately and maliciously inflicted upon me, I freely forgive him in recognition of one heroic act of devoted friendship. One dark stormy night off the Cape of Good Hope while we were aloft furling the main-topgallant sail in a howling gale of wind, Spike Riley saved me from death and nearly lost his own life in the effort.

I was working on the sail when it suddenly "ballooned" before the wind and struck me squarely in the face, breaking my hold on the jack-stay and knocking me from the footrope. "I am gone," I shouted, as I felt myself falling, for I fully expected to lose the number of my mess then and there.

"Not yet, Sonny," yelled a familiar voice beside me, and I suddenly felt myself clutched in the steel embrace of one of Spike Riley's long, wasp-like arms, while with the other hand he clung tenaciously to a becket on the yardarm with a desperate resolve that defied grim Death. God bless the man who made the seizings on that becket strong enough for double duty, for I know Spike would have gone to eternity with me before he would allow me to have gone alone. Is it any wonder that I should love this old wind-jammer who dared so much for me, or that I should tolerate his natural failings out of sheer admiration for his noble virtues?

I was still quite young and strong in the summer of 1889 after being discharged from the *Main* in Calcutta. In those days, men of my build and training were in special demand by the British Indian authorities as policemen; so, in an evil hour, I went up and "shipped" on the Calcutta police force. Having been duly examined and found qualified, I deliberately took the Queen's Oath, accepted the Queen's shilling, donned the Queen's uniform, and proceeded to enforce general compliance with Her Majesty's statutes. My first official exploit was to arrest Spike Riley for fighting and disorderly conduct.

My beat included the lower end of Flag Street and The Numbers, the toughest section of Sailor Town. The Numbers was the local name bestowed upon a continuous row of disreputable rum-shops on a little side street. They all adjoined each other and were consecutively numbered from one to twelve; hence the name, The Numbers. These places were conducted by natives and frequented by beachcombers and liberty men ashore for a frolic. The bars were protected by long rows of steel rods extending from floor to ceiling, just like the tiers in a jail, to prevent the turbulent customers from making impromptu raids on the stock. The drinks were passed out between the bars to the thirsty tars after the money had been first handed in.

About ten o'clock one sultry July night shortly after my appointment, I was hastily called upon by an excited baboo to quell a disturbance in The Numbers. Upon arriving at the scene, I found Spike Riley in the middle of the street. Hatless, coatless, barefooted, and belligerent, he was loudly proclaiming his unfaltering devotion to the Stars and Stripes and his unquestionable ability to lick anything under the British flag—lion and all!

I approached Spike with all the confidence and familiarity of an old esteemed shipmate, hoping thereby to pacify him and coax him down to the Sailors' Home. Spike did not recognize me at first, but he did recognize my uniform. He went for it like a frenzied bull infuriated by the rustle of a red flag.

Then followed a struggle such as the rounders of the Hooghly Beach have never witnessed before or since between a minion of the law and a legal offender. I had youth and strength on my side, but Spike had height, reach, and a wiggling way. I got dozens of different holds on him, strangle holds included, but he wormed his way out of all of them with the graceful celerity of a freshly captured eel. At every fresh attack, he bit, gouged, tore, butted, clawed, and scratched with the savage instinct of an enraged tiger, employing all the barred and brutal tactics of prohibited rough-and-tumble rowdyism. Meanwhile, I fought back for all I was worth, except that, prompted by a misplaced spirit of old-time chivalry, I refused to use my baton on him.

It was in the midst of the rainy season, and we rolled and wrestled and tumbled and tussled together in the middle of the sodden mire and slime of the filthy unpaved street. The brutal struggle finally settled down to a dumb contest of physical endurance, and here chances were in my favor. Spike eventually collapsed from sheer exhaustion and sullenly submitted to the handcuffs. Just as I was snapping them on his wrists, he glanced up with a venomous glare and recognized me for the first time.

"I'm damn glad it's you, Sonny," he snarled savagely, "'cause I'd hate like hell ter give in ter one o' them blasted Britishers. But, say," he demanded fiercely, "what 'n hell are you doin' in this line o' business, anyhow. Y're an all-fired disgrace ter the country yer come from!"

There were no patrol wagons in Calcutta in those days, and Spike obstinately refused to walk. I could not club him into compliance after he had been handcuffed, so I shouldered the old scamp and carried him bodily all the way to the station compound. When I finally presented him at the rail, our old Scotch captain stared in unfeigned astonishment at us both. I was bareheaded, battered, and bedraggled. My once immaculate white uniform was literally reduced to a tattered array of mud and blood-bespattered rags. As for Spike—he was chiefly clothed in lamplight!

When the captain had made up his mind as to which of us was the officer and which the offender, he gravely adjusted his spectacles and proceeded in his slow methodical way to record Spike's name, rating, and hail port, and enter the long list of criminal charges which I glibly preferred against him. He mumbled something through his thick beard in indistinct undertones about "Greek meeting Greek," and consigned Spike to cell Number Nine for the night.

When court convened next morning, I was punctually on hand newly arrayed in a trim white uniform, and conspicuously decorated with a luminous black eye. Before the Commissioner, I urged nearly every crime on the calendar against Spike short of highway robbery and murder.

Spike's defense was a general denial and a countercharge of treasonable duplicity on my part. He stoutly asserted that I was a notorious liar as well as an arch traitor, that I had willfully forsaken Old Glory for the bloody banner of Old Albion, and was hence unworthy of credence.

The Commissioner sentenced Spike to thirty days on the stone pile and fined him fifteen rupees. Since Spike did not have the rupees, that meant thirty days more for default—not a pleasant prospect by any means. When my anger had assuaged somewhat and the first sting of my many bruises had worn away, I felt sorry for Spike and repented of my severity toward him. In this mood, I "fixed it" about the rupees. I also pleaded so hard and eloquently in Spike's behalf that the Commissioner at length agreed to reconsider the severe penalty imposed and to mitigate Spike's sentence.

Eventually, Spike got off with ten days and a severe reprimand that might as well have been delivered to the Hindu idol, Juggernaut. But would you believe it, the hardened old ingrate returned no thanks for my friendly intercession. Instead, he went off to sea vowing to "get square" with me—and he did! He shipped in a country-wallah bound for Mauritius and was gone for several weeks. Meanwhile, I continued to wear the Queen's uniform, canvass my beat, and fight the Queen's battles.

One night a riot broke out in The Numbers. A roistering crowd of tipsy sailors had taken charge of the entire district, and a whole battalion of reserve officers was sent out on a riot call to quell the disturbance. When order had been restored and all the ringleaders of the tumult had been escorted to the chokee to receive their dues, the rumshops were all closed by special order, and I was left alone to patrol the forsaken beat.

By eleven o'clock, the streets along my post were as silent as a graveyard. For over an hour no sound reached me save the echoes of my own footfalls or the dismal howl of a lone jackal reverberating through the distant jungle. At length, however, I heard the sound of footsteps. By this time, I had learned to distinguish instantly between the firm, decisive walk of an honest man and the stealthy, uncertain tread of a prowling thief or murderous footpad.

The approaching steps had the right ring about them. They indicated to my practiced ear the long, firm stride of a tall man intent on business and prepared to defend his right of way. The loneliness of my midnight vigil, however, rendered me inquisitive. The approaching footsteps excited my curiosity. Somehow they sounded familiar.

I stepped out to the corner of The Numbers and gazed down Flag Street. I was soon confronted by a tall apparition dressed in a white duck suit, cork tobie, and alligator shoes, and twirling a Malacca stick and displaying an amiable grin. It was Spike Riley!

"Hello, Sonny," he hailed cheerily as he extended his fin, "I came up here lookin' fer you. Glad ter see you're still on the force an' lookin' so fine! I hear yer pounded the stuffin' out o' some o' them blasted Britishers in The Numbers tonight. Bully fer you, Sonny! Don't spare the baton on 'em. They need it an' it'll do 'em good. We licked 'em twict, an' we c'n do it ag'in!"

"But," he confided soberly, "I'm on the sober tack myself now. Ain't teched none o' that darned rotgut sence that night yer run me in. So, ye see, I kep' out uv it. I hope ye won't hold any grudge ag'in me fer the mean scrap I put up ag'in yer that night. Yer know, Sonny, I was plumb locoed that time an' didn' reckernize ye. An' besides, you know how hearty I hates that Limejuice uniform, drunk or sober!"

I assured Spike that I held nothing against him on that score. I entertained nothing but the kindliest feelings toward him and was, therefore, delighted to see him again. Spike informed me that he had returned from his recent voyage that very day. He had several weeks' pay under his lee, and he had come up to my post to apologize and to treat me to a little friendly blowout.

I agreed to meet Spike in Bentinck Street as soon as possible after being relieved at midnight. After another cordial handshake, Spike went ahead to make arrangements for the party while I resumed my beat in eager anticipation for the joyful peace party about to ensue. I now began to look forward with the pleasantest fancies to our supper of reconciliation. I counted the minutes with restive impatience until my relief arrived, and swore at him roundly for being ten minutes late.

As soon as I had made a hasty report to my superior at Headquarters, I hailed a passing gherry and drove at once to Bentinck Street without even pausing to change from my uniform into civilian attire. As my chariot dashed around the corner, Spike was on the alert and hailed us to heave to. I ordered my Jehu to pull up. Jumping eagerly to the curb, I encountered my comrade, who stood with both hands extended in an attitude of exuberant welcome. He was wearing a broad grin that threatened to part his jaw tackle fall.

At the corner of Chowringee Road and Bentinck Street, obliquely opposite the Hotel de Europe, was a very snug and well-appointed café conducted by a bustling good-natured Dutchman and his frau. The frau was too big to bustle much, but she was good company and could appreciate a joke. Whenever she laughed, which was very often, she always reminded me of a vat full of soft soap riding on a handcar. It was pleasing to see such a huge section of vibrant humanity having a hilarious time all at once, and her mirth was highly contagious.

This was the place which crafty Spike had selected for his nefarious plan to get revenge by encompassing my moral ruin and gaining my official decapitation. Pursuant to orders previously issued by Spike, our genial German Boniface had made elaborate preparations for our special entertainment and comfort.

An eight-course dinner was ready for our delectation, and two gorgeously turbaned Hindu *kulashis* were prepared to serve it. The big silken punkah waved back and forth overhead with a vim and rhythmical precision of sustained movement during our repast that plainly showed the punkah wallah's exalted opinion of Sahib Spike's respectability.

The night was hot, even for Calcutta, and Spike ordered up four bottles of imported stout to top off our banquet. English ales and heavy brews are not generally recommended for Americans sojourning in Far Eastern climes. They are heady as well as heavy, and very likely will leave you helplessly and hopelessly sprawling on your back in the windup if too freely indulged in. Spike, who had an axe to grind, pretended to be on a sober tack and modestly confined himself to one bottle. I, poor deluded toper, polished off the other three with incontinent recklessness.

We sat facing each other, spinning old sea yarns for a couple of hours. Meanwhile, the insidious English brew was extending its deadly, overpowering influence over my mental and physical sensibilities.

Suddenly an "educated" Maghee injected herself onto the scene. She proceeded to entertain us with an astounding series of sinuous and tantalizing contortions, her alluring antics, sensuous gyrations, and enticing gestures shamelessly emphasized by the flimsy texture of her gaudy drapery. Finally, having apparently exhausted the suggestive possibilities of her lascivious exhibition, she sank down suddenly at the piano and began pounding out an inspiring medley of wild bacchanalian airs that roused my morbid and muddled senses to an exhilarated and frenzied pitch of wanton enthusiasm. Then, she shunted off into a soft, sensuous, dreamy Oriental air that seemed to paralyze all my remaining sensibilities and nearly lulled me to sleep.

For a while I saw Spike in duplicate; then I saw him in triplicate; and in the end I appeared to be the central figure in a revolving apartment with the ceiling where the floor ought to have been and where all the furniture seemed to be dancing about in inverted and most disorderly fashion. I have a hazy recollection of passing through silken portières into a secluded alcove and of lying down on a softly upholstered couch. For a few fleeting moments, I experienced a sort of dumb appreciation for the perfumed atmosphere wafted about me by the slowly waving punkah suspended over my head; after that came oblivion.

When I awoke, the daylight was laughing at me through the latticed window and my aching head and throbbing temples were spinning both ways at once with the velocity of a gyroscope. I began to grope around uncertainly for the other portions of my anatomy. My physical being appeared to be intact, but in other respects I seemed possessed of far more losses than leavings. The more I searched the less I found. My lofty helmet was gone. My badge and weapons were gone. My belt and boots were gone. The bright brass buttons which had adorned the front of my natty coat were gone. My bracelets and whistle were gone, and—*dammit*—Spike Riley was gone!

On further inspection, I discovered a label attached to a forsaken buttonhole on my coat lapel bearing this inscription:

Dear Sonny:

I forgot to tell you that I shipped in the *Dundee* yesterday and must go down the river this morning in an early tow. Am sorry to leave without saying goodby, but hated to disturb your peaceful nap. I'm taking some of your running gear to keep you from losing it. See you in Liverpool.

Spike

There are certain sad moments in the course of every man's life that he is always loath to recall and would gladly forget if he could. This was one of those profanity-inspiring incidents with me. If I could have laid my hands on my whilom betrayer that morning, the gallows would have had no terrors for me. I made some base but futile remarks that were not complimentary either to Spike Riley or his besotted ancestors. But what is the use of continuing? You cannot express meaning or relieve your mind by trying to convey your feelings in printed words.

The following day, I went over to Howrah, across the Hooghly, and shipped in the *Allanshaw* (†). About three months later, I found myself in Demerara, British Guiana, where after a good deal of haggling I managed to get paid off. Then I reshipped in the Newfoundland brig *Plymouth* to Barbados, where after further struggles I got paid off again. After that, I secured a homeward-bound berth by way of Antigua in the American bark *Atlantic* (†), and I eventually arrived in New York after a two years' absence with fifteen dollars and fifty cents.

I was hopeful that I might find Spike Riley in port and was determined to lick him on sight. It was three years more, however, before I encountered him. I had entered the mouth of the noble Penobscot River on board a four-masted schooner carrying two thousand tons of coal for the city of Bangor. We warped into our berth alongside the coal dock just before nightfall, and the skipper obligingly paid us off. As soon as we had shifted into our long togs, the whole crew went ashore in search of something strong, although Bangor is in the original prohibition State of Maine.

Approaching one of the many open rumshops that graced the waterfront and disgraced the town, we were attracted by the mingled sounds of a boisterous Irish parliament going on within—everybody talking and nobody listening. We entered the place expecting to witness a good free-for-all fight and quench our month-old thirst at the same time. An excited crowd of half-drunken mariners were arguing about nothing in particular. At the far end of the long bar stood a familiar-looking lean individual who was belligerently laying down the law with both fists and making more noise than anyone else. Walking down the line I squared off directly in front of this demonstrative customer and took a good look at him. Stow me for ballast! It *was* Spike Riley!

"Oh-ho, Spike," I exclaimed excitedly, "so at last we meet again!"

"Well, shiver me timbers, Sonny," he responded boisterously. "Where in hell did yer drop from? I b'n inquirin' all 'round fer you. Yer lookin' fine. When d'ya leave the force? Horn right in an' have suthin' fer ol' times' sake."

I paid little attention to Spike's blandishments and still less to his invitation to drink. I was looking for trouble and had already begun to shed my coat. The very act, however, reminded me of Spike's rough-and-tumble tactics that wet night in the muddy slums of Calcutta. As I had just bent a brand new shore suit and did not feel that I could afford to invest in another, not even for the gratification of my long-cherished revenge, I decided to use discretion and stall for the time being in the interest of personal economy. I made surly and uncivil answers to Spike's questions and gruffly invited him to meet me down on the dock the next morning when I could get my overalls on as I had a matter of important personal business to discuss with him.

"All right, Sonny, I'll be thar," he answered cheerily. "But you jest hold on here a minute." With this mysterious hint, he vanished through a side door. Presently he returned, bringing with him a canvas ditty bag. Dipping his hand through the nittles, Spike fished blindly about among the miscellaneous junk in the bottom of the bag and finally withdrew a fistful of badly corroded brass buttons.

" 'Ere they be, Sonny," he exclaimed exultingly, extending the brazen symbols toward me in his open palm. "Yer see, I saved 'em fer yer! The shoes wuz a leetle too big, but I managed to wear 'em out. The tobie wuz too big, too, so it jest nacherly blowed overboard goin' down the Bay o' Bengal that time; and somebuddy swiped the other things out o' my room in Filmore's boardin' house in Liverpool.

"I'd hate like hell ter see you wearin' them John Bull buttons ag'in, Sonny," he added earnestly. "They'd look all right with eagles on 'em, but no decent Yank ain't gonna be a liveried jumpin' jack fer ol' Blood an' Guts an' stay a friend o' mine! If you've got enythin' ag'in me on that account, Sonny," he snarled with a vindictive leer in his eye, "we might as well have it out right here so's all han's kin see fair play."

Never in my life have I been swayed by such strange commingling of passions as raged within me. Pride, anger, baffled ambition, vengeance, admiration, loyalty, and friendship all clamored for supremacy within my breast.

My first impulse was to tackle Spike regardless of consequences and prove to the riotous assemblage that I could lick him on the spot. But as I gazed belligerently into his bronzed face and caught the submerged but kindly twinkle of his merry blue eyes, my heart misgave me. I relented. The dismal vision of that stormy night in the Southern Ocean arose in my disordered mind, and I seemed to hear again the blasts of the mighty tempest shrieking through our straining rigging. Again, I felt the stupendous impulse of the mighty sail floundering wildly in the restraining grasp of the tautened buntlines. I recalled the horrible, choking sensation as I felt myself being hurled bodily from the lofty yardarm into blank and merciless space. Again, I felt that strong grasp around my back and heard a faithful voice yell out clear and sibilant above the crashing storm: "Not yet, Sonny!"

A big lump arose in my throat, but I gulped it down. With an impulsive motion of wild contempt, I flung the brazen emblems of British tyranny through the open saloon door into the middle of Union Street. Turning, I grasped the eager outstretched hand of my old shipmate.

"Er—Spike," I stammered lamely, "you saved my life once, and—"

"Aw, stow that gammon, Sonny," he snarled testily, towing me along toward the bar. "What're ye gonna have?"

## 12 · AN INDIAN HURRICANE

Never shall I forget that strenuous Easter Sunday, the 5th of April, 1890, when a terrific windstorm blew across the Indian Ocean, when two of the best built men-of-war and three modern mail boats were literally swamped, when a score of stately merchantmen were driven into the solitary depths, and when hundreds of able seamen lost the number of their mess.

I was out in that storm and weathered it with the worst bunch of raniks that Paddy West ever sent to sea. I was about twenty-six years old then and I just gloried in storms. Fine weather never made a good sailor.

I was in the ship *Macedon* (†), a Bluenose clipper hailing from St. John, which I had signed on in New York early in February, 1890, after my Caribbean cruise in search of Spike Riley. Her captain's name was John W. Hurley, one of the worst brutes that ever crossed blue water.* He carried his wife, the owner's daughter,

---

* The *Macedon* was built at St. John, N.B., in 1877; her gross tonnage was 1,530. Williams' statements in this chapter concerning brutality on the *Macedon* are supported by facts. The following account of the voyage preceding that described by Williams appeared in the London *Times* of February 21, 1888:

A Naval Court at Hiogo has investigated what are called the Macedon atrocities. This vessel sailed from Philadelphia to Japan, and on arrival at Hiogo it was found that every one of the 13 seamen had been attacked by scurvy, and that five had died from the disease or from accidents caused by

with him. She was the dearest and sweetest little creature in petticoats that ever graced a ship's poop. It may be wrong to say so, but I fear it is true that I loved her better than Hurley did, and I am sure she had more respect for me than she had for him. Whatever I did that fateful day in April, I did for her sake, for a man will gladly risk his life for one whom he loves.

In the forecastle, we had eighteen hands, fourteen languages, and only four men who could steer. In heavy weather, we only had one man that could steer, so while we were running our easting down I spent all my spare moments, which was nearly all the time, at the wheel.

The *Macedon* was a timber ship built at St. John. She had the heaviest breasthooks, the highest sister keel, and the sturdiest frames of any ship I ever knew. She also had a "swallow-tail" stern and the biggest and clumsiest old-fashioned windlass ever built—the same kind Noah invented when he built the ark. She had tiller ropes instead of a modern steering gear, and you had to use yourself some at her wheel to keep her straight. That's the reason some of the boys couldn't steer her: they were not strong enough.

She had sturdy pitch pine masts with sixteen bands, a splendid gang of lower rigging, and bows like Sheba's breasts. She was not what we call a handsome ship; she was built to carry rather than to sail, and she was full to the hatches with case oil.

The mates were a pair of huge unflinching bulldozers, and they hunted and hounded the crew to desperation. Yet they were both splendid seamen who always treated me with respect; and, I think, all hands would have been treated better had all hands been sailors.

The most sensitive barometer in the world is the human barome-

---

compelling them to work when rendered unfit by illness. Charges of cruelty against the mate and boatswain were made and they are now on trial for manslaughter, charged with triceing up a man suffering from scurvy to the mast, forcing another when ill to work aloft, whence he fell, receiving injuries from which he died, and dragging a third along the deck on several occasions, more especially on the day of his death. The Court found the charges of cruelty proved against the mate and boatswain. The evidence revealed shocking inhumanity to members of the crew . . . and neglect of the statutory precautions respecting the distribution of lime juice. (Ed.)

ter. A sailor can always tell when a great storm is brewing by the tingle of his nerves, the color of the sky, the oily smoothness of the sea, the strong smell, like gurry-weed, and the low flight of the mollyhawks and gonies.

Such were the conditions the day before Easter Sunday, 1890. All that day, we drifted along in company with two other vessels over the glassy sea, an American ship and a German bark, and all day we kept within signaling distance. But we all knew a cyclone was brewing and did our best to prepare for it. On our ship we bent a brand new main lower topsail. Of "OO" cotton canvas it was made, the strongest fabric known, and sewn onto hempen bolt ropes as thick as a man's arm.

At eight o'clock that night, Mister McElroy, the second mate, came forward and met me outside the starboard forecastle door. His voice was calm and subdued, but his manner was grave and solemn. "Jim," he said, "there's a terrible storm coming up and we can't get out of it. Try to assemble the crew and we'll shorten her down before it strikes. The glass is down in the chain locker."

So we got together as well as we could and shortened her down. Then we watched a-wait for the coming roar. During the night, we had a constantly rising sea, but no wind. The mighty tempest was pushing the whole ocean ahead of it. When we went below at four o'clock in the morning, the storm had not struck us yet, but, except for the main lower topsail, full set, the ship was under bare poles.

About ten minutes after we got below, we heard a tremendous commotion on deck. The ship's bows arose in the air until she seemed to stand on her stern post. Next, we heard a heart-rending cry which told us that someone was in mortal anguish.

The ship had "pooped" before the on-rushing sea because she had no wind to drive her out of the smother. A tremendous sea had breached across her stern, from aft forward, washed away everything movable about the decks, dashed the two men at the wheel overboard, and crushed one poor fellow to death against the starboard bulwarks.

I rushed out of the forecastle door and started aft for the wheel.

Just as I got into the narrow alleyway between the afterhouse and the waist, I encountered the big wooden binnacle and the upper half of our wheel which had broken off at the spindle. This group of furniture, drifting on the crest of an on-rushing sea, struck me full and by and knocked me down. As soon as I could recover, I climbed the poop ladder and took charge of the broken wheel.

Ten minutes later, the cyclone struck us, butt end on, and hove our sturdy ship down to her rails. The force of the wind was so terrific that no man could speak. It seemed to blow from all points of the compass at once, and the sea suddenly swirled up into mountainous heaps of crested smother and boarded us in all directions.

I pulled off my sea boots and threw them away in order to get a decent footing on deck in my stocking feet. Although we were within the Tropic of Capricorn, the temperature fell amazingly and the weather suddenly became cold.

A hurricane is a revolving storm. It may be a mile or a hundred miles in extent, but its peculiarities are ever the same. It revolves with terrific rapidity and force and at the same time travels ahead with amazing speed, precisely as the earth spins on its axis and follows its given orbit at the same time.

But there is a law of storms as well as a law of motion, and it is a seaman's business to know those laws. It is known to navigators that in the Northern Hemisphere a cyclonic storm will always revolve from left to right, while in the Southern Hemisphere it will always revolve in the contrary direction—from right to left. Therefore, if you ever get caught in a hurricane north of the equator, heave your ship to on the port tack; if south of the equator, heave to on the starboard tack. Lay a watch, a chronometer, or a clock down on the table, face upward. Observe the trend of the hands. A northern hurricane will revolve with the hands; a southern storm will revolve against them. Such is the law of hurricanes.*

A ship hove to drives sternwise and sideways; therefore, our judgment tells us to lay her on the tack whereon the tendency of

* Williams was obviously confused in describing the direction of the winds. See Editor's Preface, page 15. (Ed.)

the wind will be to force her toward the margin of the storm. A ship on the wrong tack will be sucked into the center of the tempest, and in the vortex of an able-bodied hurricane no ship can live.

The average life of a cyclonic storm in the open sea is about sixteen hours. Sometimes it may be diverted from its course or caused to collapse by meeting an immovable obstruction—an island, for instance. But we were away to the northward of Saint Paul and Amsterdam heading for the Strait of Sunda, and there was nothing to obstruct our hurricane. So it hurled and swirled and grew and raged for full thirty hours, from four o'clock Sunday morning until ten o'clock Monday forenoon.

After the first shock of the big storm struck us, the raniks bolted into the forecastle to a man and barricaded both doors. This left only four hands on deck, outside of the captain, the officers, and old Alec Rolling (†), our Negro cook, who was also a thorough sailor. We tried to take in the main lower topsail, the only canvas we had set. But we did not have enough men to haul up the buntlines, and the sail split with a roar like a cannon the moment we started the sheets.

Then Captain Hurley came out of the cabin and handed me an axe. "Go up, Jim," he said, "and cut down that topsail or we'll be dismasted."

"Aye, aye, sir," I answered obediently as I took the axe. "I'll cut her down if I can."

As I was crawling over the iron sheerpole on my way aloft, I saw Mrs. Hurley gazing at me with such a pitiful look that I knew I could, and I did. I cut the sail from the yards, though it was an awful job; and when I came down, Mrs. Hurley, still gazing through the cabin window, paid me with a smile.

Our next job was to get our ship to the wind. So we lashed the foot of our leg-o'-mutton spanker to the boom, loosed the brails, and hoisted the head about halfway aloft. Then we rolled the broken wheel down and let her come to. Heaving to in a storm is always a dangerous expedient, but it often has to be done. Just as the laboring ship came to the wind, three tremendous seas boarded her and hove her down under thousands of tons of water. I could feel the wooden fabric struggling like a live creature under my feet. When she arose she was partly dismasted—her jib boom was gone at the cap and her fore-topgallant mast, still clinging by the stays, was pounding her with fearful violence in the sides. The forward house was stove in, and all five of our boats and our windmill pump were gone. Sheer legs, skids and all, and four of our craven raniks had been swept into eternity like chalk off a slate.

Fore and aft we did not have a strip of bulwarks or an ounce of movable property left about the decks. For miles astern, the sea was covered with driftwood—the flotsam and jetsam and planking wrenched away from our gallant ship by that awful storm.

By dint of strenuous and exhausting effort, we managed to chop away the jib boom guys and topgallant lanyards and let the crashing spars go adrift.

We had two jury masts and a spare jib boom lashed in the waist. The lashings got adrift and the big spars fetched away and took charge. Oh, what a mess! One spar was obliging enough to wash over the side and thereby saved us a lot of trouble, but the other was a terror. It floated endwise and sideways and backward and forward with awful velocity, and there was no way to control it. At last, however, after a two-hour tussle, we got it aimed between two of the timberheads where the bulwarks were gone and, getting together on the other end, we gave it the grand rush overboard.

About the same time, the spare jib boom got loose from its fastenings. Wafting astern on the crest of a mighty sea, it crashed through the forward cabin like a battering ram, butt end first, drove for fifteen feet of its length into the house, and crushed the steward to death in the pantry.

It afterward became a part of my job to get rid of that big stick. I went down onto the main deck with a bowline around my waist and got a strap around the spar. Then I rigged a tackle to the main fife rail, and the men standing on top of the house hauling on the fall dragged the big twenty-one-inch spar out of the bulkhead. I then got another strap on the heel of the spar and hooked onto the mizzen-topsail halyards. They hoisted the big stick up and dropped it over the stern, and whoever found it had a fine jib boom.

About four o'clock that afternoon, when everything had been done to save the ship, I was sent to the wheel. I was the best wheelsman on that ship for I somehow knew her motions and how to anticipate them. The ship was head to wind now, her yards braced in the line of least resistance, and nothing set but the head of her leg-o'-mutton spanker.

I had only half a wheel, for the first sea that boarded us had broken it off at the spindle. We did not dare to lash the wheel for fear the sea would destroy our steering gear. So I had to stand there, lashed to a stanchion, until ten o'clock the next forenoon without food or water, sleep or relief. And all that live-long Easter night I cursed those raniks from the bottom of my soul.

Next morning, about ten o'clock, Captain Hurley came to the wheel. The binnacle was gone and I was steering by the wind. "Jim," he bellowed close to my ear, "Jim, the glass is rising and I think the storm is about blown out. I want to get the topsails onto her and see if we can't drive her out of this region. Do you think you can keep her off without broaching? I'll send another man to the wheel if you want him."

"No, Captain," I shouted against the wind, "one bad man is better than two good ones on an occasion like this. Besides, you will need all the hands you've got left on the braces. When you're ready, sir, let me know, and I'll keep her off to a dot on the chart."

Captain Hurley struggled forward against the wind and smother to give the necessary orders. The fore upper and lower topsails were loosed, hoisted, and sheeted home. Then the Old Man stood on the forehatch and waved his hand as a signal for me to keep her away.

Never in my life did I have such complete confidence in myself as I did that moment. I eased the ship away gradually as fast as the laboring seamen at the braces checked in the yards. As the big ship fell off gradually before the wind, I watched the climbing seas and the men at the braces in the waist without the quiver of an eyelid. Throughout the whole maneuver I don't think she shipped a bucketful of water. I felt absolutely safe and fearless. I also felt manly and proud: proud of my power and ability to do what I was doing with that broken wheel, for the safety of that ship and all within her were delivered into my hands that day.

At last the yards were squared, the two big topsails puffed out their cheeks, and the *Macedon* blew away before the wind like a startled albatross. About an hour later, the storm subsided almost as suddenly as it had arisen. Then the lashings were taken from my waist and I was relieved. Stiff and sore and hungry I was, but not fatigued; I even think I could have managed another hurricane had there been one handy.

When I was relieved from the wheel that morning, Captain Hurley came and laid his hand on my shoulder. Speaking as kindly as though I had been his only son, he said: "Jim, you'd better go below and have a rest."

"Thank you, sir," I responded as I started forward. But the Old Man grasped my arm and turned me aft again.

"Come down here, Jim," he said, and he led me to the after companionway. I descended with him into the cabin. The floor had been flooded with water which had now drained out the scuppers, but the carpets were wet and sodden.

Captain Hurley tapped the spirits cask and handed me the best noggin of brandy I ever drank. Then he brought out cabin biscuit and a tin of preserved meat and gave me food, for it had been impossible to cook anything for two days. When my hunger had been satisfied, he told me to lie down and sleep. I sprawled out of my dripping oilskins and turned in on the big couch in the after cabin.

Mrs. Hurley brought a pillow and a quilt from her stateroom and tucked me away just as mother used to do. Then I thanked her and went to sleep. When I turned out and went on deck, the sea had subsided, the ship was under all the canvas it was possible to set, and we were driving away to the east-north-east for the Strait of Sunda before a moderate gale.

We rigged up the flywheel pumps and pumped her out to the

stirring strains of that ironical old pumping chantey, "Fire Down Below."

> *There's a fire in the fore hold, fire down below;*
> *To me weigh, heigh, heigh, ho.*
> *There's fire in the main hold, the cap'n didn' know;*
> *There's fire down below.*
>
> *There's fire in the foretop, fire in the main;*
> *To me weigh, heigh, heigh, ho.*
> *Fire in the win'lass and fire in the chain;*
> *There's fire down below.*
>
> *There's fire in the forepeak, fire down below;*
> *To me weigh, heigh, heigh, ho.*
> *There's fire in the cockpit, the bos'n didn' know;*
> *There's fire down below.*
>
> *There's fire up aloft, there's fire down below;*
> *To me weigh, heigh, heigh, ho.*
> *There's fire in the galley and the cook he didn't know;*
> *There's fire down below.*
>
> *There's fire in the whole ship, the mate bein' drunk;*
> *To me weigh, heigh, heigh, ho.*
> *The cap'n went below and he found 'im in 'is bunk;*
> *There's fire down below.*

The night after the hurricane, we raised the white light on Anjer Point, the northwestern extremity of Java, and then came the inevitable long calm, about the longest and smoothest one I ever encountered. Sometimes a calm will wreck a ship quicker than a storm, for she will lay and roll herself to pieces when she has no wind to steady her. But that calm was absolutely smooth and quiet. It seemed as though the hurricane had carried all the wind out of the Indian Ocean. The sea was perfectly still and aggravatingly limpid.

So, for fourteen days, we lay and drifted between azure sky and a glassy sea. Every night we saw the first gleam from the tower of the white lighthouse, and every dawn we saw it extinguished. One tide would drift us in toward the Strait; the next would drift us back again. Around us floated hundreds of immense island trees which had been torn up, root and branch, and sent adrift by the irresistible power of that storm.

Eventually, a fair wind sprang up from west-sou'-west and wafted us in through the Strait. And so, with the smoking volcano looming up on our larboard hand, Java Island to starboard, Sumatra away to leeward, and Borneo clothed with verdant waving trees just visible in the distance, we dropped our mud-hook abreast the tall lighthouse at Anjer Point.

Next day, one of our old sailing chums, the American ship, moved past us completely dismantled, and proceeded up the bay to Batavia for repairs. They had saved their monkey gaff and lashed it to the stump of their broken mizzen mast for a signal pole. They spoke to us as they passed and reported that they had lost four men and the skipper. The German bark was never heard from again.

We made such temporary repairs as we could at Anjer, and then proceeded on our way across the China Sea without any bulwarks, without fore-topgallant mast or jib boom, and with our wheel lashed up with oaken billets in place of spokes.

We reached Japan on the 19th of June. Our cargo, we discovered, was worthless. The working of the ship in the hurricane had crushed nearly every case of oil in the hold and we had to discharge our consignment through the bilge pump like so much sea water. We remained at Hiogo for three months and two days unloading and loading.*

There were thirteen sailing ships and seven men-of-war in the port—a sight that will never be seen there again. Among the war fleet was the old American frigate *Omaha* (†), at that time flagship of the Asiatic Squadron; the wooden corvette *Alliance* (†), and the old composite gunboat *Palos* (†), the first warship that ever passed through the Suez Canal. She died on the Asiatic Station and never returned to her home port.

---

* Hiogo, now spelled Hyogo, is today a part of the modern city of Kobe, located on Osaka Bay. (Ed.)

Among the foreign warships were the French composite frigate *Triomphante* (†), an old tub with a fake ram and a bow-chaser under her martingale. She was accompanied by her consort, the corvette *Chasseur* (†), manned principally by Martinique Negroes. There was also the German gunboat *Wolf* (†), and an English fighting ship, the name of which I somehow forget.

All our raniks were driven over the side and paid off, with the jib downhaul, during our stay at Hiogo, and we sailed away from that interesting port late in September with nearly a full crew of Japs. Owing to the lateness of the season, it was decided to take the Cape Horn passage on our return.

So we completed the circumnavigation of the globe on that voyage. We reached New York on the 20th of March, 1891, 176 days out from Japan, just fourteen months and fifteen days from the date I joined the ship. It was the biggest pay day I ever had—$257.

We were obliged to lay in the lower harbor and strike our topgallant masts to pass under Brooklyn Bridge. Then we docked at Pier 19, East River, and went to the British Consul to be discharged. When we were lined up at the shipping office and Her Majesty's Consul was about to hand me my written discharge, Captain Hurley took it from his hand, dipped a pen into red ink, and dashed across the face of the document these words: "Helm Excellent, John W. Hurley." That was the very highest recommendation which the law permitted any shipmaster to bestow upon a merchant seaman, and I could not have felt prouder of that discharge if it had made me the ruler of a nation.

A couple of voyages later, when I returned from Calcutta on the *Elbe* (†), I was told that Captain Hurley had committed suicide by poison in Australia. He was certainly a notorious villain. He treated his crew like dogs and his wife like a slave. She left him at Kobe and paid her fare home by way of San Francisco. His sailors left him wherever they got a chance. Yet in spite of his calloused, almost inhuman nature, I could not help feeling grieved over the news of his death, for he appreciated a sailor's work when he saw it done and he treated me as an equal when I did it.

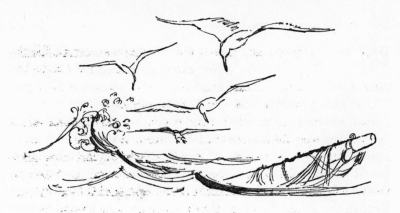

## 13 · SHIPWRECK

I read the wonderful adventures of Robinson Crusoe in my boyhood with absorbed interest and youthful delight. I never dreamed then that I was ever to be cast away on a rock that was absolutely bald and barren, entirely devoid of all vegetation, a rugged little peak in the midst of the bleak and distant Southern Ocean whereon never a tree, a shrub, or even a blade of grass found root, and where the solitary prospect was enlivened only by the discordant screaming of the multitudes of hovering sea fowl that came there to breed.

Yet such was to be my misfortune. With a solitary companion, I was destined to be marooned on that desolate peak for eighty-five days, with only the dismal moaning of the cold westerly winds, the monotonous booming of the sea, and the mournful croaking of albatrosses, cape pigeons, and mollyhawks to remind us that we were still on the earth and of it.

But to begin properly, I must first explain how I came to meet my old shipmate, wreckmate, and rockmate, "Good Old Summertime." It was midwinter in Philadelphia. I and my three companions, "Fingers," "Fourth o' July," and "Bluenose" Jim, had just been paid off from a short West India voyage the previous day. We were plodding along through the accumulated snowdrifts piled high in

Dock Street. It was about five in the morning and, except for the dazzling glare diffused by a few carelessly placed arc lamps, the district was as dark as a coal locker.

Our main objective was the Dutchman's Café, which always opened early for the consolation and comfort of the marketmen and fish venders who did business in Dock Street. We hoped to procure something warm to counteract the ill effects of our homeward-bound debauch the night before. Just as we rounded "Gaff Topsail Corner," we saw with astonishment in the light cheerfully streaming through the glazed panels of the Dutchman's door an odd-looking figure. In shirt sleeves, a battered old straw hat, and bare feet, he was breezily shuffling a sailor's hornpipe in the snow.

"Hey, Cundel, whadda ye think o' thet ol' walrus?" asked Nosey with a spluttering laugh.

"He looks like a hard case," I answered. "Let's take him in and christen him."

"You're a great 'un on names an' notions, Cundel; whatcher gonna call him?" laughed Nosey.

"I guess we'll dub him 'Old Summertime.' He seems to be pretty spry for a morning like this, and he certainly reminds us of warm weather."

"Bully fer you, Cundel," shivered Nosey with a pleased chuckle. "You'd oughtta be'n a Baptist parson."

As soon as we reached the inveterate dancer, Nosey walked up and slapped him familiarly on the shoulder. "Bravo, old sport!" he exclaimed. "Come on in and get christened. Seen any polar b'ars knockin' 'round this mornin'?"

"Say, young feller, who in thunder be yew tryin' ter take a rise out uv?" demanded the itinerant dancer belligerently, pausing in the middle of his two-step and straightening up in a menacing attitude. "Yer take me for a dod-rotted idjit, don't yer? I ain't nobody's goldarned fool. I got these 'ere all-fired chilblains on me feet, an' I'll melt all th' snow in Dock Street ter thaw 'em out. Got 'em frostburnt wunst 'cause uv ol' Blow 'Em Down Baker. Th' stingy ol' pirut kep' us driftin' 'round in an ice field off th' Horn fer 'leven weeks ter make us buy out his rotten ol' slop-chest duds, an' every man Jack aboard got frosted. Dod-blast his flamin' ol' fisog! Wish I had 'im 'ere now!" Whereupon the hardened old harlequin resumed his interrupted hornpipe livelier than before.

I had likewise had my feet frostbitten once under similar circumstances and had been tormented with chilblains for years, so I really sympathized with the poor chap and sincerely wanted to help him. I could tell by the cut of his jib as well as by his remarks that he was a thoroughbred sailor of the old tall-water school, and those observations attracted me to him all the more.

"Come on in, old chum," I said persuasively, "and have something hot to warm you up. We're all sailors, too, so you needn't be bashful."

"All right, Sonny," he answered cheerfully. "I'm with yer. Yer gotta excuse me this mornin' fer talkin' kinda loud. My feet burn so like blazes I can't take no comfort an' it gits me kinda cranky sometimes."

We accepted his apology and entered the Dutchman's Café in a body. We seated ourselves comfortably around one of the bar tables, our new member in our midst, and under the warm influence of a cosy fire, the genial glow of the chandeliers, and sundry liberal potations of hot spiced Jamaica, he soon thawed out and became quite loquacious. Soon the smarting of his feet and the cruelty of Old Blow 'Em Down Baker were forgotten. He was a rather spare-built, wiry man of about three or four and forty. He possessed strongly developed features—an aggressive chin, a bright pair of kindly, twinkling blue eyes deeply set beneath shaggy brows, large, bony hands, and agile, muscular, well-trained limbs. It required only one glance to recognize him as a case-hardened old barnacle, a genuine sailor of the sail.

As soon as our guest had been coaxed into a suitable frame of mind to appreciate the humor of our intentions, Nosey signaled me to proceed with the christening ceremony.

"Stand up, mate, and get christened," I commanded good-naturedly, taking our new comrade by the arm. "We've all been baptized except you."

"I be'n baptized wunct," he protested dubiously, as though he did not entirely grasp my meaning. "My name's Charles R. Page (†), 'n' I hails from Worcester, Massachoosetts."

"Yes, I know, old chap," I said as insinuatingly as possible, "but this is only a nickname—a highway christening, just like crossing the Line. You see, we've all got nicknames. Here's Fingers, and Fourth o' July, and Bluenose or Nosey for short, and Cundel, that's me. Now you don't want us young fellows to call you Mister Page, do you?"

"Call me Mister! Wal, I guess not. I ain't no Mister on shipboard, an' hanged ef I want ter be one ashore. Git out yer articles, boys," he exclaimed hilariously. "I'll sign up with ye. On'y gimme a stylish name so's folks 'll respec' me when I go ter meetin'!"

Then we all stood up and clinked glasses in turn with our new club member while I recited with mock solemnity the ancient ducking formula we used on all greenhorns crossing the Line. "In the name of Father Neptune and Mother Aphrodite, and by the handle of the Great Horn Spoon, I christen you 'Good Old Summertime'!" Thereupon, we all resumed our seats; and, after saluting Old Summertime as a new acquisition to our clan, we drank to his health in unison, and then proceeded to enjoy ourselves after the ancient manner of men of our kind.

In the course of the desultory and somewhat boisterous conversation that ensued, Old Summertime suddenly leaned across the table, attracted by some chance remark of mine, and scanned my face with intense interest.

"Say, youngster," he asked in a serious tone, "whar d'you hail from?"

I told him. Then he straightened up with a flash of recollection in his face. He inquired, with increasing interest, my name. I replied in full.

"Say, boy," he exclaimed joyfully, "yew don't mean ter say you're ol' Uncle Jim's son, do yer?"

"Yes," I replied, "I was named after my father."

"Why bless yer, son," he exclaimed warmly as he took my hand and closed upon it with a grip like a rigging screw. "I wunst sailed with yer daddy in the ol' *Hudson*."

During the remainder of our stay ashore, my father's old ship-mate became my constant companion and most honored guest. Such was the beginning of our mutual acquaintance and the first source of our intimate friendship.

About two weeks later, Old Summertime and I found ourselves on our way across the Western Ocean in a big Bluenose bark bound for Dunkirk with a full cargo of barreled oil. She was not a bad ship as Nova Scotiamen go, but she was old-fashioned in her rig and very heavy to handle; and from the first day of that mid-winter passage we encountered terrible weather.

That wild Western Ocean passage was, I think, the worst I ever experienced. Throughout the long thirty-eight days of the voyage, we never wore a dry stitch, nor in any one watch ever got as much as two hours below without a call. Night and day, all through the voyage, we constantly labored alow and aloft, reefing and furling frozen sails, pounding ice from our rigging, or pumping ship for our lives. It was certainly a drill to be remembered.

About the fourth or fifth day out, one of our crew died. He was a poor Norwegian sailor who had been shanghaied and sent to sea by some unscrupulous blood-money crimp for the sake of his ad-vance note when he should have been sent to a hospital for the sake of his health. The first night out, the unfortunate wretch laid up, and the captain, perceiving at once that he was really ill and not shamming, as is often the case under such circumstances, or-dered the man removed to a spare room in the half deck. There he could receive better attention and care from the steward and be clear of the turmoil of our crowded and washed-out quarters in the forward house.

Every possible attention was shown the sick man, but in spite of all that we could do for him in our rough but sympathetic way he finally succumbed. On going to his room one morning with a basin of hot broth, the steward found him dead. He had evidently expired several hours before, for he was as stark and stiff as a capstan bar. There was nothing for us to do but sew him up in a canvas shroud, present him with a gift of scrap iron, and give him the shortest possible shrift to Davy Jones's Locker.

Old Summertime and I were detailed to make the shroud and prepare the corpse for burial. The body was fully dressed in a substantial suit of heavy Norwegian pilot cloth, for in those old-time windjammers there was never any artificial heat in any of the deckhouses except, of course, the galley. When the mate came with the necessary material and sewing gear, he surveyed the corpse for a moment in unruffled silence and then, turning to Old Summertime, he said: "See here, Page, you're kinder schooner-rigged, an' that pore feller won't need them heavy togs when he goes below. It's a damned shame to waste good comfortable gear on dead men in weather like this. You'd better take 'em off'n 'im an' wear 'em yourself."

The suggestion seemed sensible, so, laying aside all superstitious and sentimental considerations, we set diligently to work to undress our late shipmate. But the body was so stiff and inflexibly set in the unbending grip of *rigor mortis* that we could not undress it in the usual way. So, with the fertility of resource often displayed by seamen in an emergency, we ripped up the seams with our sheath knives and got the dead man stripped in that way. Old Summertime later sewed them together again with sail twine and thus found himself possessed of a warm and serviceable winter suit. And I do not think he was ever oppressed by any uncomfortable reflections conjured up by the gruesome remembrance of its origin.

In due time, we arrived in Dunkirk and delivered our cargo "in good condition," as specified in the bill of lading, received our hard-earned francs, and went abroad to seek farther and fare worse. In one sense of the word, we found ourselves as much adrift in Dunkirk as we had been in midocean. I think it was Darius Green who once lamented:

*Never go to France unless you know the lingo;*
*For if you do, like me, I trow, you'll rue it sure, by jingo.*

And he was right. Those that talked French confused us, and those that talked English tried to rob us.

In order to get out of our dilemma, we decided to go Board o' Trade to Cardiff. Upon arriving in Wales, we found clean and comfortable lodgings at Mrs. Orth's, a kindhearted Norwegian woman who kept a respectable sailors' boarding house in Butte Terrace. After sojourning in Cardiff a week or two to recuperate and nurse our frostbites, Old Summertime and I slung our hooks on board an English topsail schooner or jackass bark, as they are sometimes called, and made a midwinter trip to the Mediterranean and back to escape further encounters with cold weather. After a pleasant and uneventful voyage, we returned to Cardiff in June and resumed our old quarters with Mrs. Orth.

But we soon became restive again. At Old Summertime's suggestion, we decided on a long deepwater voyage as our next venture. This course decided upon, we set about improving our outfits and replenishing our sea stock with part of our recent pay. When we had our bags snugly stowed with good substantial clothing, sea gear, and other necessary accessories, we considered ourselves pretty well found in regard to outfits and strolled off in search of a ship.

One day, while following our quest for a likely looking windjammer, we chanced upon a superbly built four-masted steel bark which was being loaded with railroad iron. She was bound for Newcastle, Australia, and her name was the *Walleroo* of Glasgow. A large canvas sign swinging from her headstays announced in big black letters this welcome legend: "Seamen wanted." Attracted as much, perhaps, by her stately and shipshape appearance as by the pendant advertisement, Old Summertime and I ranged alongside and proceeded to inspect the towering ship and her majestic rig.

While we were thus engrossed in our admiring survey, the first mate, an elderly, grizzled old sea-dog, whose name we afterward learned was Mister Toggle, happened to observe us. With brusque politeness, he invited us to "come aboard and look 'er over." We responded to the bluff invitation with becoming alacrity and scrambled over the rail with the eager agility of two schoolboys out for a holiday. We remained on board over an hour surveying and admiring the noble ship, noting her graceful rig, commodious quarters, and modern equipment as only sailors can, and we mutually pronounced her a beauty beyond compare.

She was certainly a large and powerful ship with immense carrying capacity. Her trim and beautiful lines, her graceful sheer, the spreading shrouds, and the broad ranging sweep of her towering lofty rake of her splendid steel masts, the symmetrical set of her yards, all betokened enormous sailing power and undoubted speed.

She had two plain but substantially furnished forecastles which, according to the inscription cut into the iron frames over the respective entrances, were each "Certified to accommodate fifteen seamen." Her afterhouse, or half deck, was designed to accommodate eight apprentices, two bos'ns, a cook, a cabin boy, and four quartermasters. The poop fittings, including the wheel, binnacle standard, wheelbox, skylights, charthouse, railings, etc., were all constructed of imperishable teak timber and fastened throughout with copper throughbolts in the strongest and most approved manner. Throughout, the ship was fitted with the most modern equipment and labor-saving devices then extant. She was a magnificent spectacle, lying quietly in her sheltered loading berth. Clothed in all the superlative majesty of her beauty, power, strength, and grace, she was the most advanced and finished product of centuries of scientific development in naval architecture.

Having finished our keenly expert, though unobtrusive inspection, Summertime and I turned reluctantly toward the gangway to take our departure. But Mister Toggle intercepted us.

"Well, whatcher think of 'er, lads?" he inquired in his bluff manner. "Ye don't see no 'Irish pennants,' nor 'dog's ears,' nor 'flyin' tossles' aloft, do ye?"

ABOVE: The U.S.S. *Alliance*, which Williams saw at Hiogo. A six-gun, 615-ton, screw-propelled steamer, the *Alliance* was built at Norfolk, Virginia, in 1875. (*Official U.S. Navy Photo from Naval Historical Division*) BELOW: The ship *Elbe*, of London, on which Williams served from April 22, 1891, to March 12, 1892, on his last voyage to Calcutta. (*Mariners Museum*)

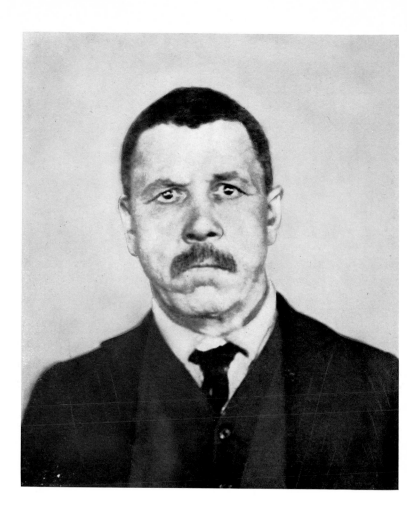

JAMES H. WILLIAMS in 1919. (*National Archives and Records Service*)

"No, sir," we answered with sincere admiration. "No, sir. She's as trim an' taut an' tidy as the Prince o' Wales's yacht."

"Right y'are, me hearties," exclaimed the honest old mate, elated by our undisguised appreciation of his craft, "an' a blame sight faster an' stronger an' more useful 'n th' whole damned R'yal Yacht Club fleet. How'd you fellers like a berth in 'er?'" he asked a little cautiously, regarding our appearance with evident approval. "We need men, but we wants men as is sailors. No dock rats nor turnpike sailors 'll do aboard 'ere. This 'ere craft was built ter sail, an' we wants men as kin git records out of 'er.

"No, lads," he confided emphatically, "this ship is well built, well stored, well insured, an' well found; an' now we're goin' ter see she's well manned. Now if you two chaps want ter ship 'ere," he continued, much to our mutual delight, "yez kin come aboard wi' yer dunnage whenever ye like, an' I'll turn yez to at five bob a day an' yer rations 'til we're ready ter sign on. Then yer gits whatever yez 'ave earned an' a day off ter spend it in the day we signs. Them's my horders direc' from th' skipper to every likely lookin' sailor what comes lookin' fer a berth 'til our crew list is full. What d'ye say?"

Early next morning, Old Summertime and I vaulted over the ship's rail, dun and dunnage, prepared for duty. We worked by the *Walleroo* nine days before she was ready to sign. Of course, there was not a great deal to do. The ship was in well-nigh perfect condition aloft, and the decks were constantly cluttered with cargo gear. Meanwhile, our friendly old first mate had selected half a score of congenial shipmates for us, and everything was pleasant and prosperous.

One morning, the captain came aboard quite unexpectedly and informed all hands that his articles were open at the shipping office. We were to sign on that day. The captain was quite a young man, with firmly set, unflinching features and a wide-awake, business-like look in his searching blue eyes. Our first impression of his character did not belie the mate's previously expressed personal estimate: a fearless driver, obviously proud of his splendid command, but a just and considerate man toward his crew.

We all signed articles that day for the voyage and enjoyed our promised day of liberty in which many and diverse interesting incidents occurred which propriety forbids me to relate. But we started on our voyage the following day. Our passage south was rapid and uneventful. Captain Duncan always exacted implicit and uncomplaining obedience from all on board and gave in return humane treatment, wholesome food, and regular watches.

We doubled the Cape of Good Hope in September and began to circle away to the south and eastward along the run of the great arc that was to bring us down to the higher parallel on which we were to begin to run our easting down. We kept on circling away to the southeast until we had reached forty-five degrees south latitude, whereupon we squared away for our great run toward the coast of Australia.

Everything went well for the first few days and the ship was making record time. We had circled around to our chosen latitude on Mercator's projection and were rapidly driving away toward the western coast of the Lone Continent. Early one morning, however, the wind, which hitherto had blown steadily from about due west, began to veer rapidly toward the southwest and came in powerful, intermittent gusts accompanied by heavy squalls of cold, drenching rain. The sea birds hovered low in slow, sweeping circles, and the sun rose a somber, forbidding, blood-red disk behind a veil of drizzling mist. Soon it was enveloped and completely obscured in a heavy bank of lowering storm clouds.

Our prudent old mate was a Manxman by birth and a thoroughgoing, well-seasoned old sailor from clew to earring. He saw the signs of the rapidly developing tempest and respectfully urged the skipper to shorten down to topsails and prepare to heave to while there was yet time and opportunity. But Captain Duncan was a diligent commercial student more concerned and better versed in countinghouse returns than in the knowledge of practical seamanship. So he turned a deaf and scornful ear to Mister Toggle's entreaties and obstinately determined to carry on.

But the clouds continued to lower and the wind and sea to rise until by noon we were in the vortex of a great circular storm of incredible fury and destructive power. Then the skipper relented sufficiently to allow us to take in the lighter sails and to single reef the topgallant sails, but otherwise he still held on before the wind and sea. Before nightfall of that fateful day, our three topgallant sails had been blown from the reefs and the rags tied up. We were still driving under three lower topsails with all our courses closely furled and doubly secured with extra lashings to prevent them from bursting the gaskets. Now, more than ever, our faithful old mate pleaded earnestly with the captain to heave to before it became too late.

The sea, which had been rising constantly before the cumulative power of the mighty wind, had now assumed mountainous proportions; and the ship, with her enormous cargo of iron rails, was wrenching and straining at every joint to the limit of her superb resistance. But the skipper still remained obdurate and immovable; no amount of persuasion could alter his mind.

Early in the night, the wind appeared to have reached the height of its velocity and power, but the sea still continued to rise and assail us on all sides with relentless energy and destructive power. About midnight, a lowering cloud of appalling blackness fell over the ship like a sable robe over a coffin; then, at last, when it was too late, our young, cocksure skipper lost heart and finally gave the desperate order to make all fast, goosewing the main topsail, and prepare to heave to.

After two mortal hours of the hardest and most hazardous labor ever performed by a desperate crew, we got her snugged down as ordered. Then we laid our main topsail yards against the lee backstays, pointed all our other yards end to windward, and then both watches mustered aft for "safety" on the poop. The wheel was rolled slowly alee, and gradually the noble ship, responding to the pressure of her goosewinged topsail and the released influence of her helm, obediently raised her graceful bows high in air to meet the shock of howling wind and raging sea.

But just as the ship came broadside to, she tumbled helplessly to windward and slid sidelong down the steep slope of a receding sea. Her trucks pointed to windward at an acute angle and her decks presented themselves to the battering energy of a rapid series of mountainous waves that overwhelmed us in an instant and seemed destined to crush and destroy our devoted ship.

At that terrible moment, we were startled by a loud, metallic rumble below decks followed by a muffled crash of the mighty impact of steel on steel, the terrible import of which we all recognized at once—our treacherous cargo of steel rails had shifted, fetched away from its fastenings by the unusually heavy careening of the ship. She was helplessly hove down on her beam ends with all the weight in one wing. The cargo had burst her bilges and the seas had burst her inclined deck. The ship was rapidly foundering and all was lost.

For one brief, terrifying instant, as I stood clinging blindly to the pinrail, I realized the awful lostness and utter loneliness of our fearful extremity. But then the innate pride and courage engendered within me by a lifetime of constant experience with the hazards of the sea came to my rescue. I looked the situation squarely in the face. "A sailor must live like a dog, but he can die like a man," I muttered. Then I bowed my head devoutly over the rail and in a few hastily spoken words of prayer I committed my soul to my Maker and my body to the deep.

Then I gazed about at the wild, bewildering scene and in a transport of mental fascination thought: "We all must die!" For a brief interval, I observed the towering, angry crest of an onrushing sea driving relentlessly upon us and gleaming in a jagged, fiery glow of luminous phosphorescent flame which lit up the pale faces of my doomed shipmates in its unearthly glare "like spirits in a dream."

Then came a terrific rending crash, the snarling twang of sundered steel shrouds, and the mingled din of falling wreckage and splintering spars. I caught fitful glimpses of our severed backstays writhing and twirling and twisting like anacondas on the pitch-black darkness. Then I felt a sudden intense pain in my head and felt myself wafted away, away, through ethereal lightness and illimitable space. One great thought seemed to possess my subconscious mind—"This is death!"

# 14 · CASTAWAY

After a period of oblivion which seemed a millennium, I at length heard a throbbing ringing sound in my ears, such as I had once experienced before at a hospital when I was about to succumb to the effects of an anaesthetic. I felt someone tugging persistently at my body, and I heard a sonorous voice urging me in strident tones to "Hang on, Jim*may*. Hang on, Jim*may*." "And this," I thought subconsciously, "must be the resurrection."

Then my eyes opened, not in heaven, but on a wild, breaking, bewildering sea, a lowering sky, and myself adrift with Old Summertime on a floating spar to which he was endeavoring to lash me fast with the end of a gasket to prevent me from slipping off.

"Where am I? Who are you?" I inquired as my senses slowly returned.

"This is me, Jim*may*! Don't yer know me, Ol' Summertime? The ship's gone an' we're adrift on a spar. But bear up, Sonny," he went on, evidently encouraged by my return to consciousness, "ther wind's goin' down an' ther sea's a-smoothin' out. Soon it'll be daylight an' someone may see us an' pick us up. I guess you got a thump on ther nut when th' riggin' come down, but yer seem ter be comin' round all right, thank God. So hang on, boy!" And hang on I did, with instinctive desperation.

At last the morning did come. The sun arose over a wild chaos of endless smother and a dreary vista of watery wastes and tumbling seas. We surveyed the horizon, but there was not an object in sight. We kicked off our heavy sea boots and discarded our oilskins and outside clothing during the day to "lighten ship," so to speak, and drifted along in scant array. We talked little but thought much. Toward night, Old Summertime began to weaken and show evident signs of physical distress. But by the same token, I began to strengthen and take command of the situation. The difference in our ages asserted itself under the strain of long exposure and constant immersion. Old Summertime was more than twice my age, and the weight of years bore heavily upon him. The pain in my head and the ringing in my ears had ceased by now, and I had recovered my normal senses. My hair was thickly matted with mingled blood and sea water, but my youth bore me up and I felt, even then, the pride of command.

The spar to which we were clinging was the mizzen-topgallant yard, a weighty pitch-pine stick over fifty feet in length which had evidently broken clear of the slings in the catastrophe. It was now floating clear, its tattered sail bent and furled, and all its sundered attachments dragging in the water. All day long we drifted helplessly about without sight or sign of passing sail.

The storm had subsided, leaving only a lumpy troublous cross sea to mark its wake. In fact, I think it must have blown out in that terrific climax which destroyed our ship. What occurred after the devastating seas breached our decks, I do not know for certain. But according to the testimony of Old Summertime, I was knocked overboard by some of the wreckage falling from aloft. In spite of my dazed condition, I managed to clutch the floating spar and cling tenaciously to it until he leaped into the sea and joined me. The ship did not founder immediately after broaching. Her fabric was too strong and durable for that. She remained afloat for a time and continued to forge ahead before the combined stress of wind and wave, leaving her wreckage some distance astern before taking her final plunge; otherwise we must have gone down with her in the mighty whirlpool of her loss. Old Summertime said he saw her disappear. I did not.

As the day wore on, the pangs of hunger and thirst began to assert themselves. We had eaten nothing for fully twenty-four hours prior to the disaster because the heavy weather prevented us from breaking out stores or lighting the galley fire. The sea fowl hovered and circled inquisitively above us in tantalizing array, and oh, how I longed to grasp one so that I might gorge on its warm flesh and blood!

At length, darkness closed in over the troubled and merciless waters. During the night, Old Summertime constantly grew weaker. Finally, his head fell limply across the spar, and I had to support his face with my hands to keep it out of the brine. Then he talked in a rambling, senseless way about fields and orchards and meadows and "Betsy." He called down such frightful imprecations on the head of his erstwhile frostbite skipper, Blow 'Em Down Baker, that I realized his reason was adrift, and I tried to take measures accordingly. First, I lashed him securely to the spar with one of the inner gaskets. Then, loosing a portion of the slack sail cloth, I wrapped it around his face to prevent him from drowning. Then I hung on beside my raving shipmate through that long night and wished for the day.

After a seemingly interminable period of blank darkness, the gray morning broke again, and a blood-red sun arose slowly from the horizon and glowed feebly through a murky mist bank in the east. I gazed in every direction for a hoped-for sail. But to the north and south and west naught could I discern except tumbling sea, lowering sky, and pinioned sea fowl. But when I trained my gaze to the eastward, I noticed a dark, jagged, irregular object strongly silhouetted against the sun's disk, which was slowly rising from the water's edge.

I gazed long and intently at the dusky object looming opaquely against the sun's wake. What could it be? Was it a tangible solid object, or a mere figment of a feverish overwrought imagination? Was it real, or an optical illusion? As the sun rose slowly and silently above the sullen sea, the dark object still remained outlined against the horizon. Yes, there could no longer be any doubt about it! It was *land! Land, solid, firm,* and *stable land!* Barren and inhospitable, perhaps, but LAND! If we could only reach it, we might yet be saved.

Once satisfied that the evidence of my eyes was a tangible object, I gave vent to my exuberation in ringing, joyous shouts. "Land! Land! Land! Land!" My abrupt yells startled the sea birds feeding among the waves and aroused Old Summertime from his deep lethargy. Raising his head slowly from the protecting folds of canvas in which I had enveloped it, he inquired excitedly, "Land? Land? Who said land? What away, Jim*may*? An' how does she b'ar?"

I pointed out the dark object to my shipmate, and he fixed his trained blue eyes upon it intently for some moments before he spoke. Then he reached out his hand and said quietly but earnestly: "Yes, Jim*may*, it's a spur o' some kind. There must be lots o' 'em hereabouts, but how're we goin' ter git to it? How d'ye know we ain't driftin' away from it now?"

"I know," I replied, "because it wasn't there last night, and it was there at sunrise this morning. Besides, it's a good deal higher now than when I first sighted it. The wind here is steadily from the west'ard, and I believe the current sets the same way—to the east-'ard."

I tried hard to be convinced by the soundness of my reasoning, though God knows that, except as to the direction of the wind, I had but little foundation for my faith. But I wanted to encourage my comrade and keep from being discouraged myself. So in spite of inward misgivings, I sought to maintain an outward show of dauntless optimism.

"We'll drift there by noon," I told my shipmate cheerfully. "Let's watch how fast we gain." I had, of course, heard of the great divergent currents in the Southern Ocean, but I knew little of either their general trend, rate of motion, or range and extent. We could only trust to guesswork at best, and to luck. One thing we could do—watch the island and so estimate the velocity and direction of our drift. The wind, at least, was fair, and with the help of the sea it could be depended upon to heave us eastward.

To our infinite joy, we easily perceived that it gradually loomed higher and higher above the water. It grew steadily larger and its rugged features grew constantly more distinct and clearly defined. We reckoned that we must be drifting at the rate of about three knots per hour. We should, we thought, pass the rock in about three or four hours. But how near? That was what troubled us now. Would we pass close enough to make a landing by swimming? Then a horrible thought flashed across my mind. "Could Old Summertime swim?" To the uninitiated, the thought may seem a strange one, but it is not when we reflect that the proportion of deepwater sailors who can swim is scarcely greater than the same proportion among haymakers.

Old Summertime and I had somehow never touched upon the subject of personal aquatics in any of our conversations, so I was ignorant of his ability in that line. Once or twice I caught myself on the point of blurting out the brutal inquiry, *"Can you swim?"* but managed to check the unspoken thought in time.

As we gradually approached nearer the island, we could see that we were drifting obliquely to the southward. Then it occurred to me that by clinging to the end of the spar and swimming deeply it might be possible to keep it headed across the current and allow the wind and sea to do the rest.

I had often towed a heavy yawl boat in the same manner, just for sport, and knew by experience that it required but little propulsion applied steadily in a given direction to move a very heavy object floating in the water. Anyway, I decided to try the experiment. I slipped out to one end of the yard and, grasping the slack of the brace pennant, began to swim as strongly as possible to the northward. Soon, I felt the spar coming with me in spite of the tideway. My limbs were so stiff and cramped from long exposure that my first exertions caused me intense pain. But gradually I limbered up and began to apply more vigorous strokes to my self-imposed task.

At length, encouraged by my success, I loosed the yardarm gasket and made a towline by turning a running bowline in its end and throwing the loop over my shoulders like a harness. This arrangement not only made my work much easier and more effective, but it also enabled me to rest and exert my power to better advantage by simply changing my position in the water whenever I chose.

A heavy shower passed over us during the forenoon, which was a veritable godsend. We tore the flannel linings from inside our sou'westers, which, besides our belts and underclothes, were the only articles of clothing we had retained, and we caught the domes of our big black helmets nearly full of fresh water. The lifegiving fluid revived us wonderfully, for by this time the pangs of consuming thirst had become well-nigh maddening. Our lips and tongues had become parched and swollen and thickly encrusted with accumulated particles of salt.

After the shower had passed, we saw to our intense delight that our island loomed gaunt, rugged, and spectral not more than a mile and a half away. During the last hour or so of our lucky drift, Old Summertime, revived by the shower, also slipped off the spar and, harnessing himself to another gasket, put his own shoulder to the wheel and helped me tow. His action belayed all my previous misgivings as to his ability as a swimmer.

Having at length effected a comfortable margin of leeway to the northward of the towering rock, we could afford to rest on our oars, so to speak, and allow the general trend of combined natural forces to drift us ashore. As we approached the gaunt peak, we observed on its northwesterly border a small beach of dark-colored shingle about an eighth of a mile in extent and extending inward for perhaps one hundred fifty feet. This scant depression, sloping down to the water's edge, was buttressed on either end and all around by great black boulders and towering cliffs that appeared to be practically inaccessible. Therefore, the cove seemed to be the only available landing place. Since we were not very well equipped for surveying operations, we proceeded to make for it instead of carrying our explorations any further.

At length, one end of our unwieldy but faithful raft bumped sulenly against the western spur of the rock. It then caught in a tide rift which seemed to run very strongly to the southward along the edge of the cliff and went crashing and banging along the jagged crags on its eternal way to the South Pole, the last abandoned relic of the wreck of the *Walleroo*. As soon as the first contact occurred, Old Summertime and I slipped our lashings and swam for the little cove scarcely a hundred feet distant.

With the final energy of exhausted men, we dragged our aching bodies to a safe distance above high-water mark. Throwing ourselves down, we immediately fell into a heavy slumber. We could not have slept more than a few hours, however, for it was still daylight when we awoke, aroused, no doubt, by the intolerable gnawing at our inwards. We both arose feeling faint and weak, and our one mutual, ravenous desire was for food. But what can be found to eat on a barren rock; a rock that is really bald and barren?

I have never been fastidious in the matter of diet. Anything digestible, whether clean or unclean, has always served me for food; and I have never yet had any quarrel with my innards. In the Bering Sea, I gorged on raw whale blubber until the train oil fairly oozed from the pores of my skin. At Desolation, in the Antarctic, I waxed so fat and impudent on a protracted diet of blubber seal and penguin pork that all the officers in the ship detested me. In the Sandwich Islands, I once reveled for six weeks in the delicious aroma of esculent dog steaks, baked *à la Kanaka* in a hole in the ground. I must also confess to the casual assimilation of various repulsive-looking but sweet-tasting reptiles, not to mention insects. I also know that under straitened circumstances tallow candles are very palatable.

Old Summertime told me that he once sailed in a Spanish ship where on Christmas day the steward killed and skinned three cats to make "rabbit pie" for the cabin dinner. I see no reason to doubt my veracious old shipmate's yarn, for I, too, have sailed in some of those tall-water ships

> *Where pussy cats and long-tail rats*
> *Were never to be seen;*
> *We ground 'em into sausage meat*
> *In Dunderberg's masheen.*

Old Summertime and I were nearly famished. The clamor of our stomachs was too painful to be endured, so we started in an aimless, feeble way in search of food. Crawling down to the water's edge, we were delighted to observe that the whole beach below low-water mark was thickly strewn with large, white conch shells. It was about half tide, but we waded out to the conch bed and easily secured a fine mess of the big, fat mollusks.

We first smashed the big, flinty shells on a rock. Then, after dragging forth fat, slimy creatures, we proceeded to pound them between two stones, thus reducing them into a tough, gristly pulp which we greedily bolted. But our weakened stomachs revolted at this unusual diet. In ten minutes, we had rejected all we had eaten. We must have derived some nourishment from the substance, however, for immediately afterward we felt stronger and went off together in search of a water supply.

After a short search among the bluffs, we came upon a circular, dish-shaped basin nearly ten feet across, bored in the living rock. It had evidently been churned out in remote ages by the action of the sea, and it was full to the brim with clear water, which, glory to God, was fresh. I should mention in passing that in the course of our subsequent explorations we discovered many other similar water holes in various parts of the island, all of them brim full of rain water. Old Summertime and I plunged into the well-filled cistern like frogs into a pond, and we scrubbed and laved and drank until surfeited, nor did we even pause to reflect that this might be the only water hole on the island.

Feeling wonderfully refreshed, we gathered a quantity of dry seaweed from the beach, made a bed under the sheltering edge of a great rock, and lay down to sleep. We slept soundly the whole night through and when we awoke the sun was more than an hour high. After a drink and a morning dip in our "well," we returned again to the shore to try another session with the conches. This time we took more pains to pound the pulp up fine and to eat it more deliberately. We soon found that we could not only enjoy this primitive diet, but that we could also retain it in our systems without internal distress. We each consumed the entire contents of a full-grown conch shell and afterward felt quite hearty again.

Then we started on a general tour of exploration. Our island home was about a mile and a half in circumference, a spur of native rock, evidently of volcanic formation. To the northeast and southeast, and in plain sight, lay two kindred peaks, similar in all physical aspects to the one we now inhabited, and obviously of the same origin. The three isolated peaks are probably the protruding pinnacles of a great submarine mountain. As we afterwards learned, they are known to geographers and navigators as the Crozet Rocks, and are claimed by France. They lie near the forty-sixth parallel of south latitude, and a little to the eastward of the fiftieth meridian of east longitude.

Being barren and unproductive, except for bird guano, they are never visited for commercial purposes. They lie in the track of vessels running their easting down along the higher parallels in the summer season, and are sometimes sighted by an occasional skipper wishing to make a landfall for the correction of his chronometers. But they are never sighted by ships passing north of the forty-fifth limit. Hence the majority of sailors have never even heard of their existence.

The south side of our island rose almost abruptly from the water to an altitude of over two hundred feet. The top sloped gradually northward in great rugged terraces of frowning crags and massive boulders of storm-blackened rock. Except for the cove, the whole island was an upright pinnacle of somber, frowning rock, heavily buttressed on all sides and practically inaccessible from the sea.

On the summit, multitudes of sea fowl assembled and filled the surrounding air with the incessant din of their discordant cries. After a pretty stiff climb, we managed to reach their roosting place. What a graveyard of animal ancestry it was! The top of the cliff was covered with a crowning fringe of bird deposit fifty feet in thickness. Everywhere lay the skeletons, feathers, and beaks of departed patriarchs. On top of all this putrid mass were hundreds of nests, strewn helter-skelter all over the cliffs. These nests were loosely stuck together in the most reckless and shiftless manner imaginable.

There were thousands of fledglings waddling awkwardly about over the bones of their ancestors, waiting to acquire the strength of wing and lung to tumble off and fly away to seaward. There were also scores of superannuated old patriarchs, waddling helplessly about with drooping wings and gasping beaks, waiting to die. Some of these we dispatched for mercy's sake, but we soon found our applicants for mercy too many to be accommodated and so gave up the task. Many of the nests we found were filled with nice, fresh eggs, and we promptly cracked and gobbled a number of them, to the great distress of their rightful owners who hovered, fluttering and screaming, angrily above us.

After a day spent in rambling over the rocks, we returned to our retreat at the cove, ate our frugal supper of sea conches, now supplemented with uncooked omelets, and turned in feeling confident that if we ever died on that rock it would not be from starvation or thirst.

Throughout our enforced sojourn on Crozet Rock, we were compelled to eat our food raw because we had no means of kindling a fire. Besides our staple diet of conches and eggs, we discovered a very acceptable substitute for vegetable food in a species of rock weed which hung in clusters from the ledges around the water's edge. It was really a seaweed which naturally attached itself to the rock for support. It grew in small spreading branches from a parent stem, and the tips of the branches put forth little globular berries. These, we found, contained a pasty gelatinous substance which was far from unpalatable and, I have no doubt, fairly nutritious. As a matter of fact, I believe it was our liberal consumption of this marine growth that saved us from scurvy during the long period of nearly three months we were marooned at Crozet.

One of our first and most natural thoughts was to set a signal for passing ships to see. This we accomplished by attaching the leg of an old pair of underdrawers to a stray stick, which we providentially found among the jetsam strewn on the beach, and planting it on the very highest pinnacle of the island. No signal was ever more diligently attended, and no war banner was ever more faithfully guarded. Every morning at daybreak, one of us climbed that steep cliff and set our modest pennant; every evening at dusk, the other went up and took it down. It was as carefully folded and stowed away at night as a man-o'-war's most treasured ensign.

> *He set a cross upon the beach,*
> *Lest time should go astray;*
> *And with his knife he cut a notch*
> *To mark each passing day.*

We were unable to follow Robinson Crusoe's ingenious device in this regard, because we had absolutely nothing with which to make a cross. But we were still minded to keep track of the passing days. At the eastern end of the cove, about ten feet above the gravel, there jutted an oblong shelf of rock with a level top. This we called "Almanac Rock," and every morning, while one of us went up to "Lookout Peak" to set the "colors," the other went and placed a small stone on top of "Almanac Rock."

> *And there to shield him from the storm,*
> *And keep him safe and sound;*
> *He built a hut, and thatched it o'er,*
> *And fenced it round and round.*

Here again, Defoe's redoubtable hero had much the best of us, for our bare rock afforded none of the romantic materials for hut building. Could we have saved the big three-ton spar on which we landed, it would have been a source of almost endless wealth as well as constant usefulness and comfort to us. The resinous pitch pine would have provided both fuel and the means of striking fire. From the wires in the brace pennants and the remnants of sailcloth, we could have made fishhooks and spun fishing lines and woven small weirs. The blocks and sheaves and bands and bolts—in fact all the ironwork and roping would have been invaluable to us in countless ways. But why regret it? We landed almost too exhausted to save ourselves, much less to drag a three-ton spar ashore with all its multitude of weighty attachments.

But as the season advanced and the rains increased constantly in frequency, duration, and volume, it became apparent to us that if we were to survive a shelter of some kind was imperative. The climate was bleak and mainly sunless at this season, and, although the temperature was not too severe to be endured by seasoned men like us, the continual drenchings were intolerable.

So we set about to build a house with such materials as we had. Rocks and seaweed were both abundant, but difficult to amalgamate into a concrete and abiding whole. But where there's a will there's a way. We selected a sheltered spot in the lee of the western cliff, high enough up to shed the rain quickly. Then we spent a whole week gathering dry seaweed, spreading wet seaweed to dry, and dragging heavy stones, such as we thought best suited to our purpose, to our building site.

I think we spent fully three weeks erecting that primitive little dome. We built the walls in circular form after the model of an Eskimo igloo, filling in the interstices between the irregular surfaces of the stones with closely packed seaweed pounded down as hard as possible. It was the roof which taxed our amateur architectural skill. We wanted, of course, to draw it together so that it would be perfectly tight and at the same time safely self-supporting. But owing to the uneven shapes and sizes of the stones procurable, we found this an impossible feat. So we built a pillar of stones straight upward through the center of the enclosure and let the peak of the roof rest upon it. Then we packed it as tightly and securely as possible on top. On the lee side, we left a small opening, just large enough to crawl through, and selected a suitable slab to close it with in case of an occasional shift of wind.

Finally, we surveyed our habitation with honest pride. We crawled in and took absolute possession, lying down on the thick couch of dried seaweed which we had provided, and called it "home." And, by the way, that was the only house on earth in which I was ever even a part owner. Never was mighty monarch or imperial potentate seated on his gilded throne half so happy as we poor forsaken castaways in our primitive shack on that bleak October day.

Throughout our stay on the island, we kept ourselves, when awake, perpetually occupied with something. Whether useful or useless mattered not. We were always busybodying with this or that to pass away the time and divert our thoughts from our lonely and desolate condition; otherwise we would have gone mad. Above all, never did we relax our vigilant lookout. A hundred times a day, we eagerly scanned every degree of the visible horizon in the vagrant hope of sighting a sail. On several occasions, we did observe passing ships at an extreme distance, but none of them ever saw us or our signal. Who ever expected to find anybody on the Crozets?

In the course of time, we tore away and ate all the "millet weed" around the shores of our cove. So, having acquired a fondness for this marine plant, I often made frequent excursions to gather it by swimming around the edge of the rock. One day, while so employed, Old Summertime, who was watching me from the beach, suddenly uttered a wild, exultant yell.

"Come in, Jim*may!* Drop ther darned seaweed an' come in quicker'n lightnin'! Here's a ship right abreast ther rock hove to ter take us off!"

I dropped my armful of weed, and with a few rapid, eager strokes regained the beach. There Old Summertime met me. Grasping me excitedly by both shoulders, he dragged me rudely from the water's edge. Then he pointed solemnly over my shoulder with one hand, turning me around meanwhile with the other. "Look thar! Jim*may*," he shouted. "Look thar!" And there, almost at my feet, was a big, shovelnose shark about twenty feet long, with his nose and gleaming jaws protruding nearly a third of his monstrous length ashore.

As I picked up a stone to throw at him, he slid off the beach into his own element. Fully ten minutes, the disappointed brute swam eagerly about my course through the water, just as accurately as a hound will retrace the track of a lost quarry.

"Jim*may*," said Old Summertime gravely, as the shark glided stealthily away, "Jim*may*, we've on'y got two lives ter lose an' can't spare nuther uv 'em."

Finally, our long sojourn on the barren rock came to a glad and unexpected end. One morning, we went as usual about our duties. It was Old Summertime's turn to scale the cliffs, set the colors, and bring down the fresh eggs. It was my turn to remain below, set the "Almanac," and cull the beach for fresh mollusks for our breakfast. The morning was thick and misty, and I recall that when my comrade returned from aloft he reported that there was nothing in sight. Indeed, it was so thick he could not see our neighboring islands.

While we were busy with our bath and breakfast, the mist suddenly lifted, but we did not notice it at the time. Meanwhile, the observant skipper of a large four-masted bark passing to the southward of the rock noticed our signal. Growing suspicious, he braced his yards and skirted along the eastern side of the island on the port tack where the towering cliffs still obscured the great ship's mast from our view. Still uneasy in his mind, the noble skipper braced sharp up and stood back against his course along the north side of the island until he had "opened" the little cove. There, through his glass, he saw us both standing on the beach.

When we suddenly saw that great ship standing hove to in the offing, we went into a delirious transport of unrestrained joy. When we saw a large boat shoot from beneath her counter and make with long sweeping strokes direct for our haven, we went completely insane and cut up the most ridiculous didoes imaginable. We danced and yelled and clawed each other like a pair of wild men. The moment the boat's keel touched the gravel, we rushed into the water breast deep and dragged her bows high and dry ashore. The boat was in charge of the second officer of the ship, a Mister Hawes, and was manned by four able seamen.

Mister Hawes and his crew jumped out on the beach and proceeded to fire all manner of questions at us. Then we learned that the boat and crew belonged to the bark *Constant,* of Glasgow, Scotland, and that by a lucky coincidence she had been a sister ship of the ill-fated *Walleroo.* She, too, was bound to Melbourne, Australia.

"How long have you been here, lads?" asked Mister Hawes sympathetically when we had answered all his other inquiries.

"Dunno sir, eggsactly," answered Old Summertime. "I guess we'll have ter read our almanac fust an' find out."

"Almanac!" exclaimed the mystified mate. "Did you save an almanac?"

"Come on, sir, and we'll show you," I said.

Then we led the party to "Almanac Rock," and Old Summertime and I sat down and counted our tallies as gravely as two old priests performing a most sacred religious rite. Eighty-five stones, besides the day just begun but never to end on that rock for us. After the party had inspected our little shelter, they took us to the boat and pulled off to the ship. The boat was immediately hoisted in and we squared away, and long before night the Crozet Islands were out of sight astern.

There is little more of importance to relate. A month later, we arrived in Melbourne where our arrival was the sensation of the hour and furnished a colorful story of shipwreck, hardship, privation, and heroic rescue that was widely published and fully commented on by every newspaper and "marine" editor in Australia.

But I must not neglect to pay a tribute, however humble and insignificant, to the brave-hearted captain and crew of the *Constant.* Summertime and I, when discovered, were absolutely destitute of all material belongings. We had tacked and tucked our last shreds of raiment about us as well as we could, but when they found us our personal appearance was dangerously near the truth.

In half an hour after we had boarded the *Constant,* however, we possessed more clothing, pipes, tobacco, knives, and notions than any two men in the ship. The crew fairly fought each other for the privilege of giving us their things. Captain Trump, the master of the ship, also took us aft and presented both of us with complete new outfits of clothing and sea gear, which, I should add, were never charged to us.

Our joint statement concerning the foundering of the *Walleroo* was carefully written down and attested, and we were duly entered in the logbook as part of the *Constant's* crew. Moreover, through Captain Trump's intervention at Melbourne, the owners allowed us full wages from the day we sailed from Cardiff at the rate of three pounds, ten shillings per month. They further compensated us for the loss of our clothes and gear to the value of ten pounds sterling. This was done because our arrival set aside all controversy concerning the loss of the *Walleroo* and enabled them to demand the immense sum for which she was insured without delay or further payment of premiums for reinsurance.

Never in this world have there been two hardier or healthier or harder-looking men than Old Summertime and I when rescued. We were as bronzed as South Sea islanders. The soles of our feet, from constantly climbing over the rocks, were heavily calloused, and we were as surefooted and agile as mountain goats. We were both naturally hairy men, and under the influence of the climate and unhampered by any unnecessary chafing gear, the hair on our bodies and limbs had grown to abnormal lengths, in places completely covering the epidermis. My hair stood upright like the tassels on a fodder shock, and Old Summertime's hung down over his shoulders like that of the "Wild Man of Borneo." Our beards clustered over our cheekbones, concealing everything except our eyes and noses. In fact, as one of our rescuers jokingly remarked, we "looked like a pa'r o' dummed ol' gorillas."

## 15 · THE AUTOBIOGRAPHY OF A LABOR LEADER

I drifted into the labor movement as naturally as a ship goes with the tide or before a leading wind. I was originally endowed with a fair share of common sense, strong democratic tendencies, and a sympathetic nature. I knew the tricks of my trade and sympathized with my associates in misfortune. I first became identified with the labor movement at Calcutta in the summer of 1889. All I knew of trade-union tactics at that time was what I had gleaned from time to time from newspaper reports of strikes, lockouts, boycotts, labor riots, etc., and I must confess that I was not prejudiced in their favor.

I had not yet had an opportunity to investigate the causes which led to such unpleasant methods. I was only a sailor and, like most others of my class, had a sublime and abiding reverence for law and order and always bowed supinely to the rules promulgated by my masters. But there is a point at which patience ceases to be a virtue, and where oppression becomes the parent of rebellion. So it was in my case. I had already endured the onerous exactions and cruel conditions of the unjust American shipping system more than half of my life and always noticed that the more I yielded the more I had to yield and the less thanks I got. I wanted to make a stand for what I considered my rights, but did not know exactly how to proceed.

I could hand, reef, and steer, box the compass or send down a royal yard, but I knew nothing of trade-union principles. The conditions existing in Calcutta at that time were certainly not calculated to redound to the sailors' best interests. As individuals, we were powerless against the crimps who infested the port and who, owing to the indifference of the officials, continued to deprive us of our rights and our earnings from voyage to voyage.

I had often observed in hoisting a topsail that we all pulled, not only in the same direction, but in unison and with the same purpose—to raise the yard. This idea set me to thinking. If by concerted effort we could raise a topsail yard, why could we not raise our wages by the same method?

I consulted with some of my shipmates and we decided to write to England for permission to establish a branch of the Amalgamated Sailors' and Firemen's Union in Calcutta. We also asked the president of the Board of Trade in London to have the rules of the board enforced in Calcutta. Both requests were granted.

After a short but rather exciting period of agitation, we succeeded in inducing a majority of the seamen in port to enroll in the union. The sailors' chaplain at Calcutta then was the Reverend Father Hopkins\*, a Church of England minister, and since none of our members could or would accept the position we elected him secretary.

Father Hopkins had manifested much interest in our cause and entered heartily into all our plans. He always counseled us to confine our arguments among the "black legs" to moral suasion, and we always did, though sometimes with the assistance of a hardwood club. Father Hopkins had two assistant missionaries to assist him in his work among the seamen and he permitted them to act as walking delegates for the union. But sailors as a rule are prejudiced against sky pilots and Devil-dodgers. So it was that shortly after the leading spirits of the movement had left the port, the organization began to decline. When I returned to Calcutta two years afterward on the ship *Elbe* (†), it had degenerated into a guild. A sky

\* See also page 117.

pilot is all right in a pulpit, but it takes a laborer to run a trade union.

Although, indirectly, I have devoted some of my attention to all seamen's unions, my direct labors among seafaring men were confined to the Atlantic Coast Seamen's Union, which was organized in 1888. I first heard of the movement at Demerara, British Guiana, when I was homeward bound from a deepwater voyage in 1889. On reaching the coast, I made inquiries concerning the condition, purposes, and policies of the union, and after consideration I decided to become a member.

I first came into prominence in 1893. In the early part of that year, the sailors had succeeded, through the power of organization, in raising their wages from sixteen to thirty dollars per month, but they had made the mistake of utilizing the crimps as their principal organizers.

In December, I reached Boston, fully recovered from my enforced vacation on Crozet Rock, and found there was a strike on. The shipowners and crimps had decided that eighteen dollars per month was enough for a man before the mast and that two dollars to the crimps for the chance was about the right figure. Later on, the wages were further reduced to sixteen dollars per month, and the shipping fee accordingly raised to three dollars.

I shall never forget that terrible winter siege. At the beginning, our finances were low, but as the shipowners laid up about 50 per cent of their tonnage so that they would not have to hire union men and managed to sail the remainder with scabs, we were soon in sore straits. Then it was we perceived the folly of temporizing with our enemies.

We had a large meeting room at 152 Commercial Street. In addition, we had an office and two large upper floors. From the middle of December until March 10, 1894, there were from two hundred to three hundred sailors sleeping on the hard bare floors and benches every night. So many hungry men were hard to control, and somehow, although our secretary was a good man, I gradually and unconsciously assumed actual charge of the situation.

The winter was unusually severe even for New England, and many others besides sailors were suffering from want. Soup kitchens and bean foundries were opened at various points in the poorer quarters of the city, and I often walked for miles through banks of snow in the piercing wind to find the place where I could get the largest plate of beans or the largest bowl of soup for a nickel.

I took a leading part in all the many meetings we held that winter, and as a rule my advice was adopted. Mass meetings were held almost daily to keep up the enthusiasm of the men. The crowd was divided into squads of four. Every morning, each squad would separate, each man going in a different direction to see what he could bum. In the evening when the squads assembled, each man was to share with the other members of his squad whatever he had found, borrowed, or stolen. Persuasion committees were organized to watch, report, and intimidate scabs. A committee was appointed to preserve order in the hall at night, and no one could gain admission after 10 P.M. Each member was required to assist in keeping the hall clean.

Thus we struggled along. Before spring, we had succeeded in practically tying up the shipping of the port. The crimps tried in every way to continue their business and we tried in every way to circumvent them. There was one crimp who was particularly obnoxious. He was the most persistent and unprincipled scoundrel of them all. He kept a boardinghouse and was also a shipping agent— a double-headed jackal. He owned a horse and wagon and was in the habit of putting crews on board vessels at night. I decided to put a stop to his night work and I did.

I induced a chum of mine to go to this man's house and board a few days, get the bearings of the house, and report to me from time to time what was going on. One bitter cold evening, my chum reported that a crew of scabs was to be sent away after midnight to join a vessel lying at South Boston. I told him to get the key to the barn. While he was gone, I went to the office, took a slingshot from the desk, and then returned to my chum, who had in the meantime obtained the key. Then I went after a hammer and cold chisel. We unlocked the stable door and went in. After some difficulty, we got the horse's shoes off. These we took, with the harness, and threw over the dock. Next, I took a wrench and slacked up the nuts on the wagon wheels, leaving them just on a thread. Then we locked the door. My chum returned the key to its place and went to bed.

The cold was intense but I waited patiently outside the stable until about half past one before our crimp came out to harness his horse. When he missed the harness his rage was pathetic and his profanity so extreme that I almost fancied I could smell brimstone. While he was invoking all the blessings of perdition on the sailors' union, I was nearly exploding with merriment.

He did not notice his horse's hoofs nor his wagon wheel until he left the stable and found himself, six scabs, and two big policemen sitting shipwrecked on an ice patch at a spot where I had accidentally thrown several buckets of water. This was only one of the many tricks we played on the crimps that winter, but it is illustrative of our methods.

On March 1, 1894, the sailors of Boston made a demand for an increase of ten dollars per month in wages and the abolition of shipping fees. The struggle was short but bitter, and there were many broken heads before we were through. In ten days, however, we won. Mr. A. C. Walker was secretary of our union at that time, and he often urged me to accept an official position in the organization, but I declined.

In April, 1894, however, I went to Providence, Rhode Island, where we had a branch in charge of Mr. Horace Atkinson (†). On the day of my arrival, Mr. Atkinson showed me a telegram from our New York agent advising him that a crew had been sent by train to his port from New York at seven dollars per month below the regular wages. Next morning, a committee sent to the depot to intercept them failed. The men and their baggage were taken on board, and the vessel, being light, was hauled out into the stream. About midnight that night, Mr. Atkinson and I went out in a small boat to "pull" the scabs. It was an ideal night for such a venture.

There was not a breath of wind, the water was smooth, and drizzling rain was falling. There was no moon.

We pulled quietly alongside the schooner and after much difficulty I climbed over her rail at the port fore rigging and dropped on deck right abreast the forecastle door. Mr. Atkinson remained in the boat. It was a very hazardous undertaking, as I knew the captain and mate were keeping watch on the poop and would not hesitate to shoot me if I were discovered. Besides, I knew that when I entered the forecastle I would have six men to deal with single-handed.

Darkness favored me and I gained the forecastle unobserved. When I got inside, the six seamen were all asleep in their bunks. I awoke them and began to stow their clothing into their canvas bags. They wanted to know what I was doing. I told them that there was a fleet of boats alongside loaded with union men and that I had been sent on board as a committee to notify them that unless they went quietly with me a committe of twenty would be sent on board to drag them out. They took the bluff and proceeded to pack up. As fast as the bags were ready, I lowered them over the side one by one into the boat. The men followed. As we had a gun in the boat, they made no disturbance while we rowed toward the shore. The next day the vessel shipped a crew of union men.

On July 2, 1894, I was elected delegate at Philadelphia, while Mr. Atkinson was elected business agent at the same port. We had a strike while I was there and won it in a week. During the strike, I organized a persuasion committee, consisting of six of the best fighting men I could find—the worst cards in the pack. Whenever we learned that a nonunion crew was to be signed, we would waylay them. They were seldom eager to ship after our committee was through arguing with them.

Shortly after the strike was over, I was sent to New York as business agent with instructions to close up the branch. New York had been a drain upon our resources for a long time and had never paid running expenses. On my way to New York, I determined not to close the branch as directed, but to organize the sailors instead.

I could not bear to haul down the union's colors and become the leader of an unconditional surrender.

I have always been proud of that decision, for by 1900 shipping there was practically in the hands of the union and at least 95 per cent of the coasting sailors were members of it. Besides this, we formed a Marine Firemen's Union, for time and experience convinced us that we had to broaden our membership to include more than sailors. To become effective the union would have to cover all the men of our craft, regardless of grade or rating on shipboard, and also truly international in scope and influence. Therefore, we eventually formed the International Seamen's Union, admitting to membership all classes below the grade of master. It embraced a number of separate unions, including sailors, firemen, engineers, cooks and stewards, mates, fishermen, and others who "do business either in great waters" or on rivers and lakes.

I must also note with pride that I did a large share of the work which preceded the enactment of the shipping law, the White Act, by Congress on December 21, 1898, which revised the entire maritime code of the United States. This measure, although incomplete in itself, worked great benefit to both seamen and commerce. To understand why, one need only review conditions and maritime laws prior to the passage of this act.

Until 1898, nearly all our laws relating to seamen were those of the eighteenth century. The sailor was almost universally subjected to the grossest extortion while ashore and the most extreme brutality while afloat, for all of which abuses he had no legal redress. He was the slave of the monger, the property of the vessel, and the chattel of the crimp. He could neither choose nor reject his employment, fix his own wages, nor pay his own board bills while on shore.

The crimping system, especially, was a nefarious practice which had long defied effective legislation. Crimping has been defined as the act of a person who by misrepresentations decoys or induces others into his power or into some state of servitude. This definition, however suggestive it may appear, conveys to the mind of the average landsman but very little conception of the unfair methods used by the crimps to entrap sailors into service. It is utterly impossible to present properly the various phases and ramifications of a system which has defied both investigation and genuine exposure. Minor details must, therefore, of necessity be sacrificed in order that the chief features may be properly emphasized and the legislation of 1898 appreciated.

The practice of obtaining recruits for maritime service by means of fraud, impressment, or misrepresentation is as old as the history of oversea ventures. The crimping system is a relic of a bygone age when human rights and personal liberties were less sacred and the press gang was regarded as a necessary, if not legitimate institution for the procuring of seamen. The onward march of civilization long ago abolished the press gang; but in the United States its progeny, the crimping system, survived and flourished throughout the nineteenth century, cultured by avarice, nurtured in the pool of vice and human degradation, a curse to our merchant marine and a libel on our boast of equal rights. All other nations, by means of stringent legislation, practically wiped crimping out of existence; but the general laxity and ambiguity of our laws relating to seamen tended to foster rather than suppress this evil.

The crimp may be classed under two heads: the shipping master and the boarding master, each of whom has one or more understudies whose honorable appellation of "runners" suggests their exalted calling in life; while the term "jackal" applied to them by sailors is perhaps still more suggestive of their real characteristics.

The duties of a runner, usually a third-rate mixed-ale pug and all-around tough, consist in inducing seamen, especially the unsophisticated class arriving in foreign vessels, by hook or by crook to desert; to pilot them into the clutches of the boarding master, to convoy them on board some outward-bound ship when their time on shore expired, and to do sundry other things which may be lumped under the head of what sailors term "dirty work"; for all of which important services Jack himself would pay with compound interest out of his advance note.

The keepers of sailors' boardinghouses in New York long ago formed an association to control the shipping by monopolizing the available supply of seamen at all times. It was a chartered organization under the laws of the State of New York, and, by virtue of a secret alliance with the shipping masters, was able to secure such supreme control over the shipping of the port that for over thirty years it was practically impossible either for a seaman to secure employment or a master to secure a crew without the consent of the crimps. No seaman, particularly if engaged in the foreign trade, could possibly secure a berth without first paying tribute in the form of "blood money" to these sharks. As an instance of their extensive business methods, it may be mentioned that even the Sailors' Homes, institutions built and established by philanthropic citizens for the special benefit and better protection of seamen, were actually forced to join the crimps' association and adopt substantially the same methods.

Prior to 1884, it was lawful for a seaman to stipulate in his shipping agreement for an advance of any portion of the wages he might subsequently earn to his wife, mother, other relative, or to "an original creditor" to liquidate any just debt for board or clothing which he might have contracted prior to engagement. This law proved a veritable bonanza to crimps who, of course, were the "original creditors."

Although the average wage of an able seaman prior to the 1890's was only fifteen dollars per month, he was compelled by the crimps, before embarking on a voyage of three or four months' duration only, to sign away to an "original creditor," and before they had been earned, forty dollars' advance wages in liquidation of what was, in the majority of instances, an unjust debt for a little board and clothing and a good deal of chain-lightning whisky. It was a mere waste of time for a seaman to endeavor to secure employment for himself. No shipping master dared ship him unless he boarded in an Association boardinghouse; and no master of a vessel dared engage him for fear of being boycotted by the crimps who, before allowing the seaman to work, had to be appeased with "blood money." It can be seen that the result of such a system was to compel improvidence among seamen and, by stifling self-respect, to crush all ambition and desire to succeed in life.

"Blood money," as it was called by sailors, was that part of the advance wages over and above the amount justly due for board and clothing which the crimps appropriated for their pretended services in procuring employment for a seaman. Very often, it amounted to the whole of the advance; for, whether he owed the crimps anything or not, not one cent of his advance wages was ever returned to poor Jack. As may be supposed, the direct result of these pernicious practices was to drive, first, all native-born seamen, and, second, the better class of foreign seamen from our merchant marine, leaving our ships to be manned by the offscourings of the world.

Unchecked by law and undeterred by public sentiment from pursuing their nefarious business, the crimps finally became so bold and unscrupulous in their dealings with seamen that, in order to protect the latter, Congress in 1884 enacted a law prohibiting the payment of advance wages except to a near and dependent relative. This act was made to apply as well to foreign vessels sailing from our ports as to those of the United States. It was hoped by these means to deal the crimping system its deathblow by depriving it of that on which it subsisted, the advance wages of seamen; but the crimp was equal to the emergency.

A meeting of the members of the Sailors' Boarding House Keepers' Association was called. It was unanimously agreed not to allow a seaman to ship from the port of New York on any foreign voyage until the master of the ship paid to the crimp, in the shape of a "bonus," the equivalent of the advance wages, the payment of which to an "original creditor" had been prohibited by Congress. This scheme worked to perfection, for the crimps had a legal lien on a seaman's clothing and other effects while he boarded in any of their dens and could thus easily prevent him from going to sea.

The masters of vessels, moreover, were loath to ship stragglers who might offer themselves for service for fear that the crimps would prevent them from obtaining a full crew when ready to sail. Under the circumstances, there was no alternative for owners of vessels but to accede to the terms of the crimps or tie up their ships and allow them to rot. The majority of shipowners chose the former as the lesser of two evils, and the shipment of seamen was conducted somewhat as follows: if the going wage out of the port for able seamen was, say, fifteen dollars per month and the probable duration of the voyage about four months, then the seaman was forced to sign for five dollars per month. The crimp would receive in advance a rake-off of ten dollars for each month of the prospective voyage, amounting in all to forty dollars. This constituted the "bonus." In the case of seamen bound on long voyages of fourteen or fifteen months' duration, the seaman would be shipped for twelve dollars per month, the amount of "bonus" remaining approximately the same—forty dollars.

Of course, it is easy to see that the practices described worked great hardship on both owners and seamen. The state of affairs became so intolerable at last that shipowners, goaded on by the action of the crimps, actually petitioned Congress to have the law relating to advance wages of seamen, as it existed prior to 1884, re-enacted. After long and careful deliberation by the proper committees, Congress, in June of 1886, amended the act of 1884, permitting the seaman

to stipulate in his shipping agreement for an allotment of all or any portion of the wages which he may earn to his wife, mother, or other relative, or to an original creditor in liquidation of any just debt for board or clothing which he may have contracted prior to engagement, not exceeding ten dollars per month for each month of the time usually required for the voyage for which the seaman has shipped.

This law, too, proved itself a complete failure. The dominant idea of the bill was that the allotment of "not exceeding ten dollars per month" should not be paid until the money had actually been earned by the seaman, thus safeguarding the owner's interests in case of accident or desertion. This arrangement did not suit the crimps, however, who, still intent on having their pound of flesh, soon found means of compelling the shipowners to pay them the whole amount of the sailors' allotments within three days after the departure of the vessel, thus violating the law and practically re-establishing the advance system as it had existed prior to 1884.

Finally, in 1898, Congress sought to correct the situation. Sections twenty-four and twenty-five of the White Act repealed the law of 1886 and attempted to protect seamen against the crimps by first outlawing the payment of "wages in advance of the time" earned. It then limited the amount that could be allotted to an "original creditor" for any just debt to one month's pay. Crimping was declared a misdemeanor, punishable by heavy fines, and in certain cases imprisonment.

Even so, the crimps continued to circumvent the intentions of the legislators. The provisions of the law, especially those applicable to foreign vessels, were very generally ignored by crimps, brokers, and owners. Illegal advances were persistently given and shipping fees regularly extorted from seamen, all statutes to the contrary.

The plan most frequently adopted by the crimps to ensure their nefarious business was the bonus system. Seamen were compelled to sign articles for one shilling (24 cents) per month for the first month, or for a longer or shorter period as the length of the intended voyage might warrant. These fraudulent agreements were invariably sanctioned by the foreign consuls resident in the United States. What happened to the higher salary the sailor should have received? The master of the ship, acting in collusion with the crimps, either paid the first month's wages of his crew over to them *in toto,* or else divided it with them. Throughout all these dishonest and illegal transactions, the crimps covered their tracks with the most consummate adroitness, and for many months it was impossible to secure tangible evidence against them. But the organized seamen, although greatly in the minority, never grew weary.

Appeals to the foreign consuls urging them to stop the abuses being perpetrated upon innocent seamen in their presence proved unavailing. The consuls refused to act without specific instructions from their respective governments, and since those governments remained in blissful ignorance of the whole subject, no such instructions were forthcoming.

It was this state of affairs which determined the Seamen's Union in Baltimore to take the matter into its own hands and, if possible, put an end to the outrages. I had gone to Baltimore in January, 1899, with nineteen cents in my pocket, and I had succeeded, after a hard struggle, in organizing the sailors of that port. We found three seamen who volunteered to ship through the crimps and thereby furnish the evidence upon which to prosecute them in the courts. In due course these three reformers were shipped in the British steamship *Ethelred* (†) through the firm of Goodhues, Garland & Nicholson.

At the British consul's office, they were instructed to sign for one shilling for the first twelve days and were told that they would receive the full rate of wages thereafter. The men obeyed these instructions and went to sea. Upon their return to Baltimore, they were proffered the munificent sum of $3.17 as compensation for their services during a period of sixteen long days and an equal number of nights.

This liberal offer was rejected and the case was taken into the Federal court for adjudication. Goodhues, Garland & Nicholson were promptly arrested and on November 23, 1899, were tried and convicted of extorting "blood money" from seamen and sentenced to pay a fine of three hundred dollars, the maximum penalty.

It is a matter of significance in connection with this famous case that in returning their verdict the jury recommended the prosecution of the master and broker of the ship also for conniving with the crimps to defraud seamen. The judge, in passing sentence, expressed regret that the statutes did not provide more adequate punishment.*

This conviction astounded the crimps. The association which had

* Williams expressed his long-felt obligation to the United States Attorney for the District of Maryland, John Carter Rose, when, in a letter of April 1, 1927 to Hamilton Holt, he called Holt's attention to Rose's death on March 26. (Ed.)

long existed among them was disbanded, most of the foreign ships dispensed with their services, and thus the sailor was left free to dispose of his own labor on the best terms obtainable.

But the great *dénouement* was yet to come. The *Ethelred* case became the subject of an extended correspondence between the governments of the United States and Great Britain which resulted in the issuance by the British Foreign Office of a circular addressed to Her Majesty's consuls throughout the United States instructing them to refuse to sign men for nominal wages and to do all in their power to discourage the designs of crimps. The *Ethelred* case was cited in the circular and the consuls were advised, in case their rulings were impugned, to invoke the aid of the United States courts.*

This was a great and decisive victory for the sailors of Baltimore. In striving to protect themselves from injustice, they had unconsciously succeeded in securing protection for their fellows in all parts of the country. Congratulations showered in upon us from all sides and seamen rejoiced the world over.

A second major reform, also embodied in the legislation of 1898, related to the rules and regulations for the protection of life, limb, and health of American seamen. In 1890, the organized seamen of the United States had petitioned Congress for certain reforms along these lines. Two of the most important features of their bills, which were seven in number, requested a scale of provisions in kind, quantity, and quality as good as our convicts received in state and federal penitentiaries.

The seamen set forth in their memorial that thousands of seamen were rotting and dying in all parts of the world annually from the ravages of scurvy and other scorbutic diseases which were easily preventable; that their constitutions were so weakened by malnutrition that they were peculiarly liable to the epidemic diseases infect-

* Evidence substantiating Williams' account concerning the *Ethelred* can be found in the Annual *Report* of the Commissioner of Navigation for the fiscal year ended June 30, 1900. 56th Congress, 2d Session, *House Documents,* Volume 54, No. 14, pp. 354-55.

ing tropical ports; that the then existing food scale had been in vogue for at least 150 years, was in general use in the British navy in Lord Nelson's time, and had been copied verbatim from the British statutes long before the Revolutionary War and preserved intact to disgrace our own maritime code.

Furthermore, the seamen submitted food schedules obtained from various prisons throughout the country as showing the comparatively sumptuous and eminently wholesome fare served out to public malefactors. Verily, "no man would go to sea who had brains enough to get into jail."

Congress ignored the petition of 1890, and only after a shocking episode which occurred in 1897 did our legislators consider the abuses involved under existing laws. On March 21 of that year, the American sailing ship *T. F. Oakes* (†) hobbled feebly into New York harbor. Immediately on reaching quarantine, twelve members of her crew were taken to the United States Marine Hospital at Staten Island, all in the most advanced stages of that loathsome disease, scurvy. Six other members of the crew had died and been buried at sea long before her arrival.

The crew of the *T. F. Oakes* had originally been engaged at Shanghai nearly a year before. Thence the ship proceeded to Hong Kong to load for New York. While crossing the China Sea, the men realized that the ship was already short of provisions and not properly supplied to proceed on her long voyage to New York. While lying at Hong Kong, therefore, they appealed to the United States consul to be discharged. Their complaints were ignored and they were ordered to return to duty or go to prison.

The passage was an unusually long one, occupying 259 days. While crossing the Pacific, scurvy broke out and two men died. The crew appealed to the master, Captain E. W. Reed (†), to put into Honolulu for supplies. The appeal was ignored. They pleaded again later to make for Valparaiso, to be again denied. Two men died off the Horn. The master was appealed to again to call at Montevideo, but this was met with the same refusal. Again, he refused off Brazil and the West Indies. Meantime, two more men died.

The last united appeal was made off the Bermudas, with the answer: "Sandy Hook or Hell!" The result was as before stated.

On March 23, two days after the arrival of the ship, I presented the matter to the Social Reform Club of New York City. The next day, the Honorable Ernest H. Crosby and I visited the victims at the hospital. On March 26, all the resources of the club were voted for the relief of the sufferers and every possible comfort and protection was given to the sufferers.

Legal proceedings were instituted in the United States District Court, but a jury returned a verdict of "not guilty." Subsequently, the seamen libeled the *Oakes* for $91,000 damages. The case was heard in the fall of 1897 and damages awarded of $2,019 to be apportioned among eight of the libellants.

Why such a failure of justice? The United States statute then in force provided that "any master or other officer of any American ship who, from motives of hatred, malice or revenge, and without justifiable cause, beats or wounds a seaman, or inflicts upon him any cruel or unusual punishments, or withholds from him suitable food and nourishment, shall for every such offense" be punished. Malice was not proved. Dr. Henry Anthony Baker, called as an expert witness, testified that one case, two dozen bottles of fortified limejuice served during the voyage, would have prevented the disease.

At last, however, Congress had been aroused, and I am proud and honored to be able to state that when it voted upon the White Act in December, 1898, through the powerful influence and intensive activities of the Social Reform Club, the entire delegation from New York in both houses voted solidly for the radical seamen's act. This measure not only revised the whole maritime code concerning allotments, but it also established new requirements concerning food and health which made a future *T. F. Oakes* case absolutely impossible.

The new law was a step in the right direction. It did much to improve the personnel of our mercantile marine; it made our sailors better and more independent men; it made possible the punishment by law of brutal officers and unscrupulous land pirates; it gave the sailor more food and better quarters; it secured the sailor in his right to wages and enabled him to find his own employment; it abolished the theory that one man's liberty could be weighed against another man's money; and the sailor was no longer compelled to choose between life in a prison cell and death in an unseaworthy vessel.

Still, as the following account illustrates, there were many defects in the law and many other improvements needed before the status of sailors approached that of men in shoreside professions. Efforts at correcting abuses by union activity proved unavailing. Many bills were introduced into Congress, some to be passed by the House, some to be approved by the Senate, but none sanctioned by both bodies. Not until 1915, with the passage of the notable La Follette Seamen's Act, were very important and far-reaching amendments to the federal statutes protecting seamen and regulating commerce adopted by Congress.* The old-time crimping system was, thereby, practically abolished, and its former activities absolutely prohibited. Had the act of 1898 succeeded in this purpose, the tale which follows would never have been written.

* Some of the very provisions of the La Follette Seamen's Act reveal the adverse conditions which existed previously. Each seaman was to be allotted 120 cubic feet of air space in his living quarters, penalties for desertion were abolished, a sailor could demand half of his wages due to date at any port, and the assignment of wages was absolutely forbidden. (Ed.)

## 16 · SHANGHAIED

After seven years ashore devoted to improving the lot of the seaman, I decided to regain my sea legs. A few short voyages did the trick, and I found myself in Norfolk, Virginia, in March, 1903, with the sum of fifty dollars, a clear conscience, and a roving commission. Soon after my arrival, I met my old shipmate and crony, Spike Riley, similarly equipped, and together we proceeded to enjoy ourselves and celebrate our chance meeting. For three days, we lived off the fat of the land. On the fourth day, we lived on free lunch and promises. The fifth day was Sunday, and my lordly bank roll had dwindled from a plethoric total of fifty dollars to a beggarly relic of fifty cents.

About nine o'clock that evening, we went up to the sailor's mission where, according to the local beachcombers, we could get a clean night's lodging for twenty cents with coffee and sinkers thrown in in the morning. When we reached the mission, a gospel meeting was in progress, so Spike and I decided to wait outside until the end of the service before applying for shelter and a bed.

While loitering outside the mission, listening to the psalm-singing chorus within, we were suddenly approached by a well-dressed, affable young man who at once engaged us in conversation. He was very polite, apparently well informed, and profuse in his profound expressions of heartfelt sympathy for the poor, despised, and downtrodden sailor. By the cut of his jib and the glibness of his gab, I mistook him at first for a nimble-witted con man, but we soon made him out to be a full-fledged jackal in search of hard-up sailors to sign for advance notes.

He suggested, in a friendly disinterested way, that we go down to the house with him and secure an introduction to the boss. And since needs must when Diablo drives, down to the house we went. Spike and I had been around long enough to know the risks involved. The tales of the forecastle are replete with the names of iniquitous parasites who achieved international reputations as masters of the shanghaing business. What sailor never heard of "Scar Face" Johnson, Paddy West, or "Shanghai" Brown?

The shanghaied victim is always either enticed on board under some mental delusion not to be realized, or else driven on board by some physical force not to be resisted. A dead body was once carried on board an outward-bound ship at the port of New York and deposited in a bunk in the forecastle under the pretense that it was a drunken sailor, and three months' advance was collected for the "stiff." The master of a Norwegian ship was once shanghaied at New York for a common sailor and found himself on the way to sea in a Yankee ship when he awoke from the stupefying effects of the drinks and drugs which had been administered to him by the local crimps in "Hell's Half Acre." On another occasion, a minister was enticed out to a ship in a small boat and shanghaied on the pretext that a dying man on board wanted the consolation of religion. As the unsuspecting dominie was clambering precariously up the rope ladder to the rail, the ship was already under way in the stream, and the crimp shouted to the skipper from the stern sheets of the wherry, already dropping astern: "That's a good man goin' up now, Cap'n. Take good care o' 'im." I never heard how the sky pilot enjoyed his cruise, but I should like to have heard his first sermon after he returned. I'll wager he did not have to look for a text.

So, alive to the dangers, Spike and I followed our Norfolk jackal as he led the way through a maze of dark streets in the direction of the house. On the way thither, thirsty Spike warily suggested that it was a long while between drinks, whereupon our friendly jackal promptly offered to show us where to get the best whisky in America for five cents a drink and set 'em up himself. He said the place was kept by a friend of his and that we would have to be very quiet to gain admission as it was Sunday night.

Debouching from the main street into a dark and dangerous alley, our pilot led us to a gate in a high board fence. Opening this, we passed into a disreputable back yard in the rear of a weather-beaten frame house. The kitchen was closely shrouded by means of a blanket suspended from the top of the frame on the inside, but feeble streaks of light filtered through the ragged edges of the improvised shroud. The hum of muffled voices was plainly audible from within.

Our pilot gave three mysterious knocks and then we waited. Presently, a small slide in the panel was pushed back, a bleary eye peered out, and a thick voice inquired, "Who dat?" The jackal gave the password, the big wooden bar across the inside of the door was let down, and we walked in. The bar was at once replaced and we were told to "go right into de back." There we found assembled a motley crowd of both races and both sexes—mostly mixed-ale tanks of the genus *bum,* all eagerly awaiting a drink, a racket, or an easy graft.

The bar, a slapped-up affair of pine boards, was reeking with the overplus of stale beer, and was presided over by a sinister looking Cracker with a freckled face.

"Step right up, gents, 'n' paternize th' bar," he piped reassuringly as we pushed our way cautiously through the mob of thirsty star customers to reach the improvised dispensary. The jackal politely invited us to "order 'em up." Spike demanded a "big noggin o' 'kill-me-quick,'" while I modestly sang out for mixed ale.

The slinger averred apologetically that the crowd had drunk him all out of both beer and whisky that day, but proudly asserted that he still had an excellent quality of gin left. After consultation, Spike and I agreed to compromise on the gin and ordered it up, forthwith.

When the slinger drew the cork from that bottle, the fumes that ascended were almost audible. I rather incautiously remarked that that brand of gin needed no advertiser. The diabolical scowl bestowed upon me by the slinger in resentment of this impolite crack should have been sufficient to have reminded me of my manners. It wasn't, however, and when I innocently inquired if the stuff was made at the city gasworks I clean forgot that I was within the barbarous region of lynch law.

The next thing I noticed was a big black bottle hurtling along in my direction with all the poise and dignity of a three-inch shell on a war errand. Long and intensive training as a sailor had made me an expert in the skillful art of dodging in times of danger, so I stooped just a fraction of a second before the well-aimed bottle whizzed past my head and shattered on the wall behind me.

Spike and I had been in many a tight place together by then and understood each other's moves perfectly. The bums who habitually frequented the disreputable place began to manifest a united and sinister interest in the proceedings at this juncture, and we both realized at once that prompt, decisive, and effective action on our part was now necessary if we were to escape with whole skins.

After dodging the war-like bottle, I instantly bounded upon the big doorkeeper, who was preparing for action, and landed like a round shot on his solar plexus. He doubled up with an agonized grunt and smashed stern first through a flimsy wall. The partition collapsed with a crash, and at the same instant loyal old Spike reached up and quickly extinguished the lone gas jet, leaving the place in total darkness.

Then Spike and I got together—we could tell each other by the feel—and while the slinger was loudly cursing and wildly groping for the fugitive matchbox we stumbled over the ruins of the fallen partition into the main part of the shrouded speak-easy and made for the door. Near our goal, we got into a promiscuous mix-up with several of the bums, but we finally managed to break clear and get the door open. Then we ran pell-mell into God's night and took leg bail, followed by a volley of obscene curses and general hardware.

At the street corner, the welcome glare of a friendly arc lamp protected us from further pursuit, and we paused to investigate our personal casualties. Spike had a long, ragged scratch along one side of his face that must have been executed by one of the ladies present at the exciting melée. He also had in his hand the property matchbox, which he had been crafty enough to grab from the bar during the excitement to prevent the bloodthirsty slinger from relighting the gas. Foxy Spike! I exhibited a promising contusion over the right cheekbone which next day blossomed into a lustrous black eye.

In a few minutes, we were rejoined by our whilom friend, the jackal. He apologized for his friend's erratic behavior, saying in extenuation of his vicious actions that he was too drunk to appreciate a joke. He begged us not to blame him for our misadventures, however, as we could get all the drinks we wanted down to the house. So down to the house we went, fit and proper candidates for a trip to Shanghai.

The house was a weatherbeaten, ramshackle old structure that stood somewhat back from the public street as though conscious of its own deformities and striving to avert condemnation proceedings. It was fronted by the decayed and decrepit remains of an aged picket fence enclosing a long-forsaken refuse heap.

We found the distinguished boss seated comfortably in the large untidy kitchen. Surrounded by a motley group of unsophisticated turnpike sailors, he was carefully instructing them in the manifold advantages of a seafaring life and the undisputed merits of a high advance system. His red, rusty face was further emblazoned by the lurid effects of a tawny moustache, a booze-blossom nose, and an ingratiating leer. A well-worn derby hat was poised precariously on the knob of his bullet-shaped head with as much independence of movement as it might have exhibited if dangling from a peg.

The jackal promptly introduced Spike and me as "two old-time friends of his in search of a berth." The boss thereupon extended his glad hand in affectionate greetings and treated each of us to a welcome home shake that mildly suggested the tempestuous velocity of a main jib sheet slatting wildly in stays in a stiff sou'wester. After this formal and forceful introduction, the boss promptly proceeded to sustain the ancient and honorable good name of the crimping fraternity. Producing a big black bottle and a cracked teacup from a nearby mess locker, he slammed them ostentatiously on the rough deal table and invited us with a flourish to "set in an' make ourselves to home!" Spike, disdainfully ignoring the cracked teacup, applied himself thirstily to the bottle without further ceremony. I used them both. When the boss asked my opinion of the excoriating liquid, I just gasped in frantic accents and groped blindly for a convenient water jug. I fear he took me for a nautical tenderfoot.

In answer to our eager inquiries on the subject, the boss informed us that shipping was great, never better: a big fleet of good ships in port all loaded and outward bound and no crews available. He strongly advised us, therefore, to become his personal guests for the night, partake in the morning of a good breakfast, which of course would cost us nothing, after which we could see the shipping master and pick and choose as we pleased in regard to berths.

The night being far spent, we decided to accept this generous invitation and asked to be shown to bed forthwith. Whereupon the boss lighted a tallow dip and proceeded to lead the way. Across the wide, old-fashioned hall and up the bare, rickety, dust-laden old staircase we went, our footfalls resounding through the house with that lonesome distinctness and hollow reverberation that awakens the echoes of the past and tells in weird and voiceless monotones of long abandonment and complete and lonely emptiness.

Opening a door near the head of the stairs, our pilot ushered us into our prospective sleeping quarters. The dilapidated room looked dingy and neglected; the stagnant atmosphere smelled musty and dank. The neglected walls, which had originally been painted pea-green, were now streaked by dripping moisture and covered with successive layers of clinging dust. The ceiling was liberally festooned with aged cobwebs. The broken window panes had been thoughtfully replaced with bundles of old rags and newspapers. The floor was bare and unswept, and the bulging ceiling threatened to descend and join it at any moment.

The furniture in the room consisted of four battered iron bedsteads evidently stolen from a junk shop, some remnants of dirty bedding, and a forsaken old mantelpiece liberally adorned with congealed candle grease and dirt. Three of the beds were already occupied by a trio of unfortunate sleepers who looked to us like down-and-out lumberjacks recovering from a debauch.

The boss apologized for his scanty sleeping accommodations, saying that he had just started in business and had not as yet found time to get in his new furniture. The well-advertised fact that his disreputable joint had been a menacing nuisance among the waterfront slums of the port for years, he seemed to consider a closely guarded secret known only to himself and his criminal associates and accomplices. Every fool who fell into his trap was naturally assumed to be ignorant of the game, and where ignorance is bliss why cultivate wisdom? Victims arriving after midnight, decorated with a fresh crop of blooming black eyes, were fair game and could be easily bunkoed.

Three of the beds being already occupied, the boss amiably suggested that Spike and I should "double up" in the fourth. This proposal having been tentatively agreed upon, he set the candle on the mantelpiece and with a cordial good night left us to make the most of a dubious situation.

While making a cursory survey of our unattractive surroundings, Spike requested me *(sotto voce)* to inspect the bed sheets and ascertain which side was the safer. After a brief but intensive inspection of the suspected articles, I presently and emphatically reported that both sides were positively and indisputably dangerous. In confirmation of my decision, I exhibited animate evidence.

In this dilemma, the only alternative left was to take to the road again until morning. This we decided to do. We experienced no difficulty in escaping from the rambling old house—you could get out of it almost anywhere—so emerging into the purer atmosphere of the night we bore each other company until morning.

On returning to the dump about seven o'clock, we found all hands up and busily astir. A loud sizzling from the smoky kitchen and the greasy aroma of burning fat proclaimed that breakfast preparations were in progress. The boss greeted us with his usual cheerfulness and hoped we had enjoyed a good night's rest and our morning constitutional. An early stroll was a fine thing for the health, he opined, as he showed us the city water tap and community towel (?) in the back yard. After indulging in a lazy man's splash under the refreshing influence of the tap, I wiped on my handkerchief. Spike, being minus such a luxury, used the lining of his vest.

At eight o'clock, breakfast was announced, and we all sat down to a substantial meal of fried beef, slightly overdone and certainly overtough, plain spuds, rye bread, and bootleg coffee.

There were a number of unfortunate send-offs in the house, but none of them except ourselves appeared to be seamen or sea-minded. But any man who can walk is worth a month's advance to Crimp & Co., so what matters it what becomes of him after he has been safely shanghaied and his note is cashed?

Nothing occurred during the forenoon, although Spike and I hung tenaciously around the shack in hopes that something would turn up to save us from another sleepless night. At one o'clock, a dinner of rye bread and stew was served. About two o'clock, our host arrived in hot haste and ordered all hands to line up and look their best, as the shipping master was waiting outside to inspect the crowd. We found the high and mighty one standing carelessly outside the broken-down fence waiting to survey us. The boss introduced him to the crowd in general as Mister Cassidy, the leading and most influential shipping agent of the port, and advised us to listen attentively to his instructions.

Mr. Cassidy was a large, florid-faced, prosperous-looking man, gorgeously arrayed in a checkerboard suit, a loud necktie, and a dazzling smile. After a critical inspection of the unkempt stragglers before him, he proceeded to unfold in terse, official, and decisive accents the woeful tale of our prospects for the immediate future.

A number of ships were about to clear, he announced, but only one, the *Besant*, a British tramp bound to the Orient, was so far listed to sign on a crew. She was ready to engage a number of substitutes, he explained, to fill out her complement which had been somewhat decimated by desertions. Any of us who desired to ship, he concluded, would receive four pounds, five shillings per month wages, one month's advance, a select outfit, and a square deal.

An hour later, eight of us, including Spike and me, were lined up at the British consulate to "sign on." The consul's clerk read over the terms of the shipping articles in a dreary monotonous tone that was scarcely audible. The only part I heard distinctly was the final clause, when the scribe suddenly raised his eyes from the text and, looking us over severely to let the dire proviso sink in, announced emphatically: "No liberty or money to be granted abroad except at the master's option; and no grog allowed!"

Having now finished our business for that day, we returned with our boss to his disreputable barracks and awaited supper, which when served consisted of bloater, bread, and tea. By this time, in deference to our united and vehement protests, special arrangements had been completed for Spike's comfort and mine. We were given clean single beds in a spare room by ourselves and enjoyed a decent night's rest.

Next morning, all hands were called early and ordered to prepare for sea. For sustenance and rejuvenation, each man was treated to a stiff noggin of red rum in lieu of breakfast. We were then presented with a promiscuous lot of bundles supposed to contain our "good sea outfits" promised by Mr. Cassidy in his presigning address. We then shouldered our bags and tramped down to the wharf under close convoy of a select gang of jackals. At the dock, we found a tugboat lying alongside with steam up ready to transport us and our belongings down to Lambert's Point where the ship awaited us. Within an hour we were on the huge tramp and faithfully delivered over for the next six months to our new bondmaster, the skipper.

Mr. Cassidy had faithfully promised to settle up with us for the balances of our advance wages on board the ship in accordance with the square-deal clause in his antesigning declaration. While we were busily occupied in getting ourselves properly stowed in our quarters, Mr. Cassidy had gone up to the captain's chart room to sign on the new cook, who had been engaged too late to appear at the consulate and was, therefore, to take a "pier head jump"—that is, to sign articles after arriving on board. The cook signed for twenty-five dollars advance, and Mr. Cassidy obligingly went ashore to cash the note, promising to return at once and settle up all around. He must have been unavoidably detained, for up to the time of sailing, four hours afterward, he had neither returned nor been heard from! Sad to relate, we never received the balances of our hard-earned advances.

When I came to examine my "good outfit," I made an inventory of account between Mr. Cassidy and myself. My bundle contained the following itemized articles, to each of which I have appended the full market values based on the retail prices prevailing ashore at Norfolk at the time. Since certain of the listed articles were intentionally spurious and unfit for service, their practical valuation was nil at any price.

| | |
|---|---|
| One "donkey's breakfast" or straw mattress ....... | .50 |
| One small shoddy quilt ........................ | .35 |
| One dungaree suit (boy's size and worthless to me) | .75 |
| One pair bluchers (boy's size and useless to me) .. | 1.00 |
| One "cheap jack" razor and ditto strap .......... | .75 |
| One sheath knife and belt ..................... | .50 |
| One pound of tobacco and one dozen matches .... | .50 |
| One day's board ............................. | 1.00 |
| One pint of rotgut whisky ..................... | .25 |

|  | |
|---|---|
| Total outfit | $ 5.60 |
| By cash | 3.50 |
| Received | $ 9.10 |
| One month's advance | $20.56 |
| Value received | 9.10 |
| Balance due | $11.46 |

We all realized that we had been bunkoed and that we would have to work a month for Mr. Cassidy before we could claim anything for ourselves. The bunch of raniks who had never been to sea before were shipped as able seamen and charged ten dollars for the chance. One of them claimed to be an expelled college student and another had been a counter jumper in a dry-goods emporium. Fine material for sailormen! The cook also shipped on a ten dollar fee basis but was actually swindled out of twenty-five dollars. Yet the navigation laws of our nation strictly prohibited the exaction of all "blood money" charges or other illicit deductions from seamen's wages.

All the raniks were speedily reduced to the grade of ordinary seamen with wages of two pounds five per month. But what mattered that to the wily crimp? Or what concern was it to him that we had to stand their wheels and do double duty in general on their account? Did he not get just as much for a ranik as for an able seaman?

When Spike Riley relieved me on the lookout at eight bells that night, he laid his hand on my shoulder and said in his old jocular way, "Well, Sonny, I guess we got shanghaied this time. But never mind, our turn will come yet."

"That's right, Spike," I assented. "Vice will bring its own vengeance. We work hard and give far more than we get, but we can go down the world singing chanteys at our work because we are honest. The crimp may live in laziness and vice on the proceeds of his crimes, but he can never realize the true happiness we sailormen enjoy at sea sharing each other's labors, confidences, trials, and pleasures."

Walking aft to the bridge, I reported to the officer on watch. "Riley's on the lookout, sir. Lights are bright and all's well."

Ten minutes later, I was stowed away snugly in my bunk, where the moaning of the wind in our vibrant shrouds and the constant swash of the friendly old Atlantic, lapping and roaring against our bows, soon lulled me to sleep. What cared I for crimes and crimps? The prince of crimps was never so happy as I!

## POSTLUDE

And now, after many voyages too numerous to mention, I go down the world alone, the last of the "Yankee Squad," a vagrant man without home or habitation, kith or kindred, fireside or friends. Like old Barney Dent of lamented memory, I seem only to be knocking around to save funeral expenses. A sailor of sixty is a man old before his time and useless to the world.

It is now many years since I crawled through the hawsepipes and glanced up hopefully at the tapering yards and lofty spars of a latter-day windjammer. In those days there were but two classes of seamen—officers and sailors. The use of steamers had not yet become general in ocean traffic and the marine fireman or stoker was not much of a factor in maritime affairs.

The average time of the liners between Europe and America was twelve to fifteen days, and their average tonnage per ship was less than one-quarter what it is now. Tramp steamers were still in the experimental stage, and many were the jokes inspired in the humorous minds of lounging sailors by their grotesque and clumsy appearance.

But the glory of the seas is passing away in the opening glamour of a new era. Garry Owen, "Splitnose" Sweeney, and all the rest of the old packet rats have passed away, and the stately Black Ball liners and the magnificent tea clippers of which they were so justifiably proud have all either gone to Davy Jones's locker or been relegated to Rotten Row.

The liner and the tramp now set the pace and rule the sea; even the modern sailing ship is divided against herself, and the legal term "Seaman" is rapidly becoming more and more involved and comprehensive in meaning and scope. In the olden days it was an axiom that a sailor should know everything and do everything and say nothing. Today the motto of the sea is, "Every man in his corner!" In the sailing ship, the same man worked everywhere, from truck to keelson, and from taffrail to martingale.

The art and method of receiving, stowing, and discharging all kinds of cargo were important parts of nautical education, and the A.B. or forecastle graduate possessed a deal of practical and technical knowledge which could be acquired in the fullest degree only by long and arduous practice, as well as close application and special aptitude. The old-fashioned A.B. *was* somebody. He was educated in the highest degree—a thorough master of his profession —intelligent, cool, resourceful, strong, and courageous; a paragon of patience, a wonder of endurance, with every sense and every faculty, mental or physical, trained and attuned to the highest tension; alert, obedient, and ever ready to act; a man who not only knew what he did but why he did it; the highest development of a strenuous, man-making epoch in the most arduous and dangerous of human avocations; a peer among the noblest of God's noblemen; a factor and a fighter in war, and in peace the herald of the world's progress. Such and much more was the merchant Jack of yore. *Pax vobis.*

The distinguishing trait of the twentieth-century substitute sailor is selfishness, a habit never acquired by the genuine old-timers. "Damn you, Jack, I'm all right," is being gradually adopted by the lords of the forecastle and quarter-deck alike in place of the old-time motto of generous consideration that was world famous: *"Remember your shipmates!"* The old Cape Horner knew all things, hoped all things, accomplished all things. The new era mercenary who has displaced him learns one thing and does one thing until he becomes fascinated with it and regards it as the *only thing*.

But enough of these garrulous complaints. The past cannot be recaptured, no matter how great its virtues, except in the recesses of our minds. And often in the still watches of a soft and tranquil night as I lean idly over the rail of some ship in port and gaze dreamily across the brilliant expanse of rippling, starlit waters, bright memories of the past rise in disordered procession and crowd my wondering mind like phantoms in a dream. And many a stalwart form seems to arise and beckon to me from out the surging solitudes, many a lingering vision of bygone days, of storm and tempest, of abysmal darkness and sunlit seas, and many a riotous orgy of fun and frolic, of unrestrained debauch and bachannalian excess in the roistering turgid slums of a hundred seaports.

Such visions reappear to harrow and reproach me as I gaze; but last and always longest my vivid recollection dwells with fondest retrospection and cherished repose, and seems to reproduce again, as on a phantom screen, the ineffaceable picture of one wild night in the raging midst of the stormy Southern Ocean. Again I seem to see the storm-panoplied forms of the stalwart seamen grouped negligently around the mighty windlass, and the lithe and graceful form of the ruddy-faced Pengelley stretching easily along the length of the rude bunkboard, his open lammie revealing in fullest measure the shapely convolutions of his faultless throat, rising, throbbing, undulating, and pulsing in rhythmical precision to the measured notes and passionate appeal, and to the melodious pathos of what was to be his farewell song.

And suddenly awakes that far-off chorus of sonorous manly voices, rising clear, sibilant, fearless, resolute, and resounding; reverberating high, insistent, eternally triumphant above the thousand deck noises, the screaming mastheads, and the mighty storm; and whether it be the musical chime of the silver-toned watch bell, the lazy rustle of a baffling sail, the weary complaint of a straining spar, the playful splash of a side wash, or the harsh inflection of some human voice that arouses me from the enchanted scenes of my far-off reverie, I find my heart still throbbing and my soul still surging to the slow and sweet cadences of that sad and sacred old refrain, the sailor's love song, "Anchor's Weighed."

> *Anchor's weighed;*
> *Anchor's weighed;*
> *Farewell, farewell;*
> *Re-mem-ber me-e.*

# Published Writings by JAMES H. WILLIAMS

Unless specifically noted otherwise, all of the following references are to *The Independent* magazine. The chapter numbers in brackets refer generally to the corresponding chapters in this book. (*See also* pages 12-14.) (Ed.)

"The 'Crimping' System," XLIX (February 11, 1897), 171-72.

"The Sailor and the Law," LII (November 15, 1900), 2733-37.

"The Autobiography of a Labor Leader," LIV (November 6, 1902), 2634-38. [Chapter 15]

"The Story of a Modern Voyage, or 'Across Lots' to China," LV (November 26, 1903), 2790-96.

"Shanghaied," LV (December 31, 1903), 3102-07. [Chapter 16]

"How We Live to Make Her Go," LVI (January 7, 1904), 18-22.

"How We Live to Keep Her Going," LVI (March 24, 1904), 653-61.

"Spike Riley's Revenge," LVI (June 23, 1904), 1427-32. [Chapter 11]

"From the Crosstrees to the Stokehold," LVIII (March 2, 1905), 486-95.

"The Prodigal's Return," LIX (November 2, 1905), 1021-27.

"Billy: A True Yarn," LX (January 4, 1906), 27-32. [Chapter 9]

"Miss Chapter," LX (April 19, 1906), 908-15.

"A Son of Ishmael," LXI (November 29, 1906), 1267-71. [Chapter 1]

"Good Old Summertime" [poem], LXII (January 31, 1907), 269.

"An Indian Hurricane," LXII (May 23, 1907), 1184-89. [Chapter 12]

"Joseph O'Brien, Irishman," LXIV (February 20, 1908), 395-404. [Chapter 10]

"Castaway" (Part I), LXIV (April 23, 1908), 904-10. [Chapter 13]

"Castaway" (Part II), LXIV (April 30, 1908), 952-61. [Chapter 14]

"Conditions on the Coast," *Coast Seamen's Journal*, XXI (June 17, 1908), 3.

"Wages and Conditions," *ibid.*, (July 1, 1908), 3.

"The Dip of the Sentinel," *ibid.*, (July 22, 1908), 3.

"Comparison of Methods," *ibid.*, (August 5, 1908), 10.

"Betrayed" (Part I), LXV (August 20, 1908), 407-13. [Chapter 3]

"Betrayed" (Part II), LXV (August 27, 1908), 470-75. [Chapter 4]

"The Sailor's 'Chanties,'" LXVII (July 8, 1909), 76-86.

"For the Want of a Becket," LXXII (April 18, 1912), 818-26. [Chapter 5]

"Man the Life Boat," LXXII (May 2, 1912), 941-44.

"Jack in the Doghole," LXXII (May 23, 1912), 1104-06.

"Manning Our Merchant Marine," XCI (September 22, 1917), 469.

"Better Berth for Jack Tar," XCI (September 29, 1917), 502-03.

"Thar' She Blows," CV (April 2, 1921), 331-32. [Chapter 2]

"Save Himself Who Can!" CV (April 30, 1921), 445-46. [Chapter 8]

"Nail the Flag to the Mast," CV (June 25, 1921), 665-66.

"Stranded," CVI (August 6, 1921), 45.

"Can the Lame Ducks Swim?" CVI (September 24, 1921), 145-46.

"The Passing of Pengelley" (Part I), *Seafarer and Marine Pictorial*, II (February 1922), 3-14. [Chapter 6]

"The Passing of Pengelley" (Part II), *ibid.*, (March 1922), 43-53. [Chapter 7]

# GLOSSARY

ARTICLES — The papers signed by seamen in which their term of service, duties, etc., are stipulated. A contract.

BACKSTAY — A supporting rope or stay leading from a masthead backward to the ship's side.

BARK — A sailing vessel of three or more masts, fore-and-aft rigged on the after mast and square-rigged on the other masts.

BEAT — To proceed forward into the wind by sailing first on one tack and then on the other in a zigzagging fashion.

BECKET — Generally any bight or loop of rope that may be readily grasped by the hand, as the bail of a draw bucket. Specifically, a short loop of hemp or wire rope permanently attached to the iron jackstay on a yardarm to which sailors may cling in time of danger.

BELAYING PIN — A tapered wooden or iron pin, usually inserted through a rail, to which a rope can be secured.

BEND — To fasten (two ropes together, a sail to a yard, etc.)

BENDS — The thick longitudinal outside planking on the sides of a wooden ship.

249

BINNACLE — A stand or pedestal of nonmagnetic material, firmly attached to a ship, which houses the compass and a lamp.

BLOCK SCORES — The grooves in the sides or end of a block to admit the straps.

BLUE PETER — A blue flag with a white square center used as a signal to recall boats, indicate immediate sailing, etc.

BOAT LEG — The distance and course covered by a ship on one of its tacks to windward.

BOBSTAY — A rope or rod from the outer end of the bowsprit to the ship's prow or stem to steady the former.

BOLLARD — A post used to secure hawsers.

BOW — The forward end of a ship.

BOWSPRIT — The heavy spar which extends forward from the stem of a ship.

BRAIL — A rope attached to the leech or corner of a sail, running through a block, and used to take in a sail. Used as a verb, it means to haul the sails up or in by means of the brails.

BULWARKS — The solid, often fence-like, side of a ship projecting above the deck level.

BUMBOAT — A small boat used to peddle provisions to vessels while in port.

BUNT — The central part of the foot of a square sail. Also the part of a furled sail bunched at the center of the yard.

BUNTLINE — A rope used to haul up a square sail to the yard for furling.

CACHALOT — The sperm whale.

CAPSTAN — The vertical, revolving cylinder or drum upon which a cable chain, or rope is wound to raise the anchor or other heavy weights.

CAPSTAN BAR — A bar inserted into the head of a capstan, and used to turn the capstan.

CHOCK — A wooden or metal fitting attached to the deck through which a line can be passed for mooring or towing.

| | |
|---|---|
| CLEW | — The after lower corner of a fore-and-aft sail or the lower corner of a square sail. |
| CLEW GARNET | — One particular rope used to haul up a square sail to the yard. |
| CLEW IRON | — The metal ring in the corner of a sail to which the clew lines are tied. |
| CLEW LINE | — A rope used to haul the clew of a square sail to the yard. |
| CLEW UP | — To raise the lower corners of a sail to the yard with the clew lines. |
| COIR | — The fiber of the husk of coconuts twisted into a rope. |
| COURSES | — The lowest square sails on the masts of a square-rigged ship, identified as fore course, main course, etc. |
| CRIMP | — An agent who procures seamen by inducing, swindling, or coercing them. |
| CROSSJACK | — A square sail attached to the lowest yard of the mizzenmast. (Usually pronounced "cro'-jack.") |
| CUTWATER | — The part of the stem below water. |
| DEADEYES | — Round blocks pierced by three holes for ropes. |
| DOGWATCHES | — The two short watches, from 4 to 6 P.M. and 6 to 8 P.M. |
| DOUBLE PURCHASE | — A type of pulley tackle or any similar apparatus used to raise heavy bodies. |
| DOWNHAUL | — Usually a rope used to haul down a sail. Sailors came to use the term "pay oneself off with the jib downhaul" to describe desertion. |
| EASTING | — The distance eastward of a ship on any course taking it in that general direction. |
| FIDDLEHEAD | — An ornamental scroll on the bow of a ship. |
| FIFE RAIL | — A rail built around the lower section of a mast in which belaying pins are secured. Also a rail around the bulwarks of the quarter deck. |
| FLEMISH HORSE | — A short footrope attached to the outer end of a yard. |

FLUKE — The tail of the whale, each triangular half being a fluke.

FORECASTLE — The area of a merchant vessel in the forward part of the ship used for seamen's quarters.

FOREPEAK — The area in the hold of a ship formed by the angle of the bow.

FROM CLEW TO EARRING — Thoroughly or completely.

FURL — To roll up a sail tightly against a spar, yard, stay, or mast by winding gaskets around it.

FUTTOCK PLATES — The metal plates attached to the top of a lower mast which hold the upper ends of the futtock shrouds.

FUTTOCK SHROUDS — Short metal rods connecting the futtock plates to an iron band around the mast.

GAFF — The spar carrying the upper edge of a fore-and-aft sail.

GARNET — A tackle to hoist sail or cargo.

GIN — An iron or steel tackle block containing one or more pulleys.

GOOSEWING — To haul up a square sail in the middle and at the lee clew, leaving the weather part extended.

HALYARDS — Tackle or rope used to raise or lower yards, sails, etc.

HAWSEPIPES — The pipes placed in a ship's bows through which cables, chains, or ropes pass.

HOLYSTONE — A soft sandstone used as an abrasive to scrub decks.

JACKSTAY — Generally a vertical rope or rod on a mast on which yards can be raised or lowered, or a similar rod along a yard to which sails are secured.

JIB — Triangular sail set on a stay stretching between the bowsprit or jib boom and the forward mast. Large vessels carry several, named according to location.

JIB BOOM — A lighter spar extending outward from the bowsprit.

JOSS — Pidgin-English for a Chinese idol or god.

| | |
|---|---|
| **KNIGHTHEADS** | — The two timbers in the forward part of a ship extending from keel or stem to support the end of the bowsprit. |
| **LANYARDS** | — Ropes to secure and tighten rigging or to fasten anything on a ship. |
| **LARBOARD** | — The left side of a ship to a person standing on deck and looking forward; same as "port." |
| **LAZARETTE** | — A general storage place on merchant ships, located near the stern. |
| **LEE QUARTER** | — The direction in which the wind is blowing. |
| **LEECH LINES** | — The ropes attached to the leeches or edges of a square sail or to the after edge of a fore-and-aft sail and used to raise the edges of the sail. |
| **LIZARD** | — A rope with a thimble or block, to serve as a leader, on one or both ends. |
| **LOBSCOUSE** | — A ship's stew. |
| **MANAVLINS** | — Odds and ends of food. |
| **MARTINGALE** | — A short perpendicular spar projecting downward from the outer end of the bowsprit, and used to guy down the jib boom; also, the stay stretching from this spar to the end of the jib boom or flying jib boom. |
| **MIZZEN** | — A fore-and-aft sail set on the mizzenmast. |
| **MIZZENMAST** | — The third mast on a four- or five-masted vessel; the aftermost mast on a three-masted vessel. |
| **MONKEY BRIDGE** | — Any bridge located in a peculiar place or used in an unusual fashion. |
| **PANTILES** | — Seabiscuits. |
| **PARREL** | — A sliding rope or metal ring around a mast which holds a yard but permits vertical movement. |
| **PAWL** | — A ratchet device which engages with notches so as to permit a drum or wheel to turn in one direction, but to lock it from turning in the other. |
| **PEMMICAN** | — A cake made from dried meat pounded into a paste and mixed with dried fruits and fat. |
| **PLIMSOLL LINE** | — A mark on the hull of all British merchantmen which is required by law to show above |

the water line to prevent overloading. Since 1930, by international agreement, nearly all nations abide by this rule.

PORT — The left side of a ship to a person standing on deck and looking forward. Also called the "larboard" side.

RAKE — The overhanging part of a vessel, fore or aft, or the angle of a vessel's masts or overhang of stem or stern.

REEF — To decrease the expanse of sail by tying up the reef points to a gaff or yard.

ROYALS — The square sails next above the topgallant sails.

RUN — The very bottom and afterpart of a ship from where it begins to slope inward and upward toward the stern.

SAMSON POST — A post used in securing a cable.

SCUPPERS — Channels and openings along the side of a ship to permit water to run off the deck.

SHEER — The upward curve of a deck, bulwarks, or lines of a ship.

SHROUDS — The long ropes or wires running from the mastheads to the sides of a ship to steady and support the masts.

SKYSAIL — A square sail above the royal in a square-rigged ship.

SOUJI-MOUJEING — Cleaning operation.

SPANKER — On a ship or bark, a fore-and-aft sail rigged on the after mast; on a schooner-rigged vessel of more than three masts, the fourth or the last mast or sail.

SPAR — Generally any wooden or metal pole used as a mast, yard, gaff, etc.

STARBOARD — The right side of a ship to a person standing on deck and looking forward.

STAY — A rope or wire extending from the upper part of a mast downward and attached to a lower mast or part of the vessel to steady the mast.

STAYSAIL — Any sail rigged on a stay, usually triangular and set between masts.

| | |
|---|---|
| STERN | — The after part of a ship. |
| TACK | — To sail a ship into the wind by alternately changing its course from one bow to the other. |
| TAFFRAIL | — The rail across the stern or after part of a ship. |
| TOPGALLANT | — A square-rigged sail next above a topsail or upper topsail. |
| TOPSAIL | — Generally, on a square-rigged vessel, the square sail above the lowest sail on the mast. In later years, most square-riggers carried double topsails, the upper and lower topsails. |
| TRUCK | — Wooden or metal piece attached to the head of a mast, usually rigged with small holes for signal-flag halyards. |
| TRYWORKS | — A brick furnace on a whaling ship where the blubber is melted down into oil. |
| TUCK | — The part of a ship at the stern where the planking or plating meets the sternpost. |
| VANG | — A rope or wire, running from the outer end of a gaff, which is secured on deck to steady the gaff. |
| WEST, PADDY | — Liverpool boarding-master of traditional forecastle yarns which related how West schooled ignorant landlubbers in a smattering of sea lore and palmed them off on ships' captains as veteran sailormen. |
| WINDLASS | — A horizontal barrel-like cylinder which when turned winds a cable or line, thus raising a weight like an anchor. |
| YARD | — A long, round, tapering spar attached crosswise to a mast and suspending a sail. |